TROPICAL TIME MACHINES

Reframing Media, Technology, and Culture in Latin/o America

Tropical Time Machines

Science Fiction in the Contemporary Hispanic Caribbean

Emily A. Maguire

UNIVERSITY OF FLORIDA PRESS

Gainesville

Publication of this work made possible by a Sustaining the Humanities through the American Rescue Plan grant from the National Endowment for the Humanities.

This book will be made open access within three years of publication thanks to Path to Open, a program developed in partnership between JSTOR, the American Council of Learned Societies (ACLS), University of Michigan Press, and The University of North Carolina Press to bring about equitable access and impact for the entire scholarly community, including authors, researchers, libraries, and university presses around the world. Learn more at https://about.jstor.org/path-to-open/

Copyright 2024 by Emily A. Maguire
All rights reserved
Published in the United States of America

29 28 27 26 25 24   6 5 4 3 2 1

Library of Congress Cataloging-in-Publication Data
Names: Maguire, Emily, 1972– author.
Title: Tropical time machines : science fiction in the contemporary Hispanic Caribbean / Emily A. Maguire.
Other titles: Reframing Media, Technology, and Culture in Latin/o America.
Description: 1. | Gainesville : University of Florida Press, 2024. | Series: Reframing media, technology, and culture in Latin/o America | Includes bibliographical references and index.
| Summary: "Exploring works of science fiction originating from Spanish-speaking parts of the Caribbean and their diasporas, this book shows how writers, filmmakers, musicians, and artists are using the language of the genre to comment on the region's history and present-day realities"—Provided by publisher.
Identifiers: LCCN 2023050680 (print) | LCCN 2023050681 (ebook) | ISBN 9781683404583 (hardback) | ISBN 9781683404828 (paperback) | ISBN 9781683404644 (pdf) | ISBN 9781683404712 (ebook)
Subjects: LCSH: Science fiction, Caribbean (Spanish)—History and criticism. | Caribbean fiction—21st century—History and criticism. | Science fiction—History and criticism. | Caribbean Area—History. | BISAC: PERFORMING ARTS / Film / Genres / Science Fiction & Fantasy | LITERARY CRITICISM / Caribbean & Latin American
Classification: LCC PN3433.5 .M34 2024 (print) | LCC PN3433.5 (ebook) | DDC 810.99729—dc23/eng/20231124
LC record available at https://lccn.loc.gov/2023050680
LC ebook record available at https://lccn.loc.gov/2023050681

University of Florida Press
2046 NE Waldo Road
Suite 2100
Gainesville, FL 32609
http://upress.ufl.edu

CONTENTS

List of Figures vii
Acknowledgments ix

Introduction: A Time for Science Fiction in the Hispanic Caribbean 1
 1. Shades of *Destiempo:* Caribbean Time and the Rise of Science Fiction 16
 2. The View from the Future Possible 37
 3. The Countertimes of Caribbean Cyberpunk 72
 4. In the Time of the Zombie: Remaking a Caribbean Icon 108
 5. After World's End: Caribbean Postapocalyptic Narratives 147
Epilogue: Future Possibilities 182

Notes 193
Bibliography 209
Index 231

FIGURES

1. ADÁL (Adál Maldonado), still from "Coconauta Interrogation" (2016)   31
2. Robot dancers in the video for Harold López Nussa's "El buey cansao" (2020)   39
3. Frank Achon, "Havana Cyberpunk 2059" (2021)   73
4. Erick Mota, "De la serie Habana Cyberpunk. 5ta avenida, Miramar" (2021)   75
5. "Surviving" in *Juan de los muertos* (2011)   121
6. Rita Indiana as "La Montra" in the video for "Como un dragón" (2020)   185

ACKNOWLEDGMENTS

This book's long journey into being began in May 2001, in Havana. It was there, in the bookstore in the Palacio del Libro, that my friend Alexander Pérez Heredia thrust a small volume into my hands, saying, "Este libro es muy bueno." The "really good book" turned out to be the first edition of Raúl Aguiar's *La estrella bocarriba*. Although not strictly science fiction, the novel led me to Yoss's 1999 anthology *Reino eterno*, which in turn opened my eyes to the creative ways in which science fiction was being written in Cuba.

This book would be nothing without the friendship and collaboration of science fiction writers themselves. Yoss, Raúl (Aguiar), and Erick Mota were my first guides into the world of Cuban science fiction, and I could not have had better Striders to show me the way. Their encyclopedic knowledge of the genre, their personal experience of some key moments of its history, and their absolute generosity in sharing their time, knowledge, friendship, and work made my own tentative steps into this world possible. It is thanks to their generosity that I was able to sit in on sessions of the Taller Espacio Abierto during nearly annual visits to Cuba between 2008 and 2017. It was through the Taller that I met other writers: Leonardo Galas, Maelis González Fernández, Carlos Duarte Cano, Elaine Vilar Madruga, Erick Flores Taylor, Bruno Henríquez, Alejandro Rojas Medina, and too many others to list here. In Santo Domingo, Odilius Vlak engaged me in a wide-ranging conversation over various days of a visit in 2017. Rafael Acevedo and Melanie Pérez Ortiz were kind enough to invite me to participate in the 2019 Congreso de Ciencia Ficción in San Juan where I was able to learn more about the Associación Dominicana de Ficción Especulativa from Aníbal Hernández Medina, Rodolfo Báez, and Liberato Tavárez.

As this book has taken shape—and changed form—over the past decade and a half, I have benefited from a wonderful network of mentors, friends, and colleagues who have read drafts, asked questions, debated points, invited me to share my work, shared their work, listened to me babble, and directed me to important bibliography. A million thanks to Gerard Aching, Natalie Belisle, Kathryn Belle, Nathalie Bouzaglo, María del Pilar Blanco, César Braga-Pinto, Alexandra Brown, J. Andrew Brown, Lena Burgos-Lafuente, Corey Byrnes, Miguel Caballero, Francisco Cabanillas, Zaida Capote Cruz, Odette Casamayor-Cisneros, Jeffrey Coleman, Deborah Cohn, Antonio Córdoba, Jorge Coronado, John Alba Cutler, David Dalton, Vero Dávila, Guillermina De Ferrari, Ezekiel Del Rosso, Walfrido Dorta, Paloma Duong, Caroline Egan, Harris Feinsod, Jorge Fornet, Víctor Fowler, Christina García, Maia Gil'Adi, Sam Ginsburg, Libby Ginway, Aníbal González, Johan Gotera, Erin Graff Zivin, Javier Guerrero, Lucille Kerr, Edward King, Stephanie Kirk, Silvia Kurlat Ares, Adrián López Denis, Teresa López Pellisa, Jacqueline Loss, Lilianne Lugo Herrera, Justin Mann, Jorge Marturano, Gabriela Nouzeilles, Joanna Page, Pedro Porbén, Yasmín Portales Machado, Gabriel Restrepo, Zorimar Rivera Montes, Elizabeth Schwall, Mónica Simal, Elzbieta Sklodowska, Kip Tobin, Vicky Unruh, Alejandra Uslenghi, Sarah Ann Wells, and Kelly Wisecup. All of you have made this project infinitely better.

A particular thanks to Lessie Jo Frazier and Eden Medina, who have read nearly every chapter of this book at multiple stages, and to the two anonymous readers who offered helpful suggestions for revision.

Dara Goldman (1971–2022), who often came up to Chicago from her home in Champaign-Urbana, was a key interlocutor at various stages of this project and a good friend. I miss her terribly.

A Faculty Fellowship from Northwestern University's Alice Kaplan Institute for the Humanities in 2017–18 made some of the key work on this project possible. My thanks go to Jessica Winegar, director of the Kaplan Institute that year, as well as to the other Kaplan faculty and graduate fellows, for their comments and insightful questions about the project. I also thank the graduate students in my classes on "Utopia and Dystopia in Caribbean Cultural Production" (Winter 2017 and Fall 2022) and "Science Fiction in Latin America" (Fall 2020). Our wide-ranging conversations on some of the texts covered in this book helped me reframe my own readings of them.

Stephanye Hunter, editor extraordinaire at the University of Florida Press, supported this project almost from the beginning. Thank you for the encouragement and feedback at various stages of the process, and for your patience when unexpected administrative duties forced me to postpone deadlines. Thanks also go to the series editors, Héctor Fernández L'Hoeste and Juan Carlos Rodríguez, for their astute suggestions, to Zubin Meer for his careful copyediting, and to Carl Good for his invaluable proofreading and indexing of the manuscript.

Although they have been heavily revised and altered, this book includes pieces of the following articles and book chapter: "Walking Dead in Havana: *Juan de los muertos* and the Zombie Film Genre," in *Simultaneous Worlds: Global Science Fiction Cinema,* edited by Jennifer Feeley and Sarah Ann Wells (University of Minnesota Press, 2015); "The Heart of a Zombie: Dominican Literature's Sentient Undead," *Alambique: Revista Académica de Ciencia Ficción y Fantasía,* vol. 6, no. 1, 2018, 1–20; "Deformaciones literarias: Embriología, genealogía y ciencia ficción en *El Informe Cabrera* de José 'Pepe' Liboy," *Revista Iberoamericana,* vol. 83, April–September 2017, pp. 259–60; and "Temporal Palimpsests: Critical Irrealism in Generation Zero's *Cuba in Splinters*," *Revista de Estudios Hispánicos,* vol. 51, no. 3, June 2017, pp. 325–48. I thank *Alambique, Revista Iberoamericana, Revista de Estudios Hispánicos,* and the University of Minnesota Press for generously allowing me to publish parts of those essays here.

This book is dedicated, with all my love, to Rafael Limongi Marques and to Miguel César Maguire Marques. After spending so much time away from you thinking about possible futures, I am so happy to return to be with you in the present.

Introduction

A Time for Science Fiction in the Hispanic Caribbean

Cuban writer Maielis González Fernández's short story "Lánguido epitafio para los viajeros del tiempo" ("Languid Epitaph for Time Travelers," in *Sobre los nerds y otras criaturas mitológicas,* 2016) begins with the classic trope of the immigrant returning home. A transplanted Cuban now living in "New-New Jersey," the story's protagonist packs his bag for a visit to his birthplace. He leaves behind not only "la comida transgénica, los portafolios, las interfaces neuronales" (7) [the genetically modified food, the portfolios, the neuronal interfaces], but also "los implantes y servomecanismos" (8) [the implants and servomechanisms], body-altering technologies that connect him to the highly developed world in which he now lives.[1] For to return to his native land is also to travel back in time, to a place that is not (yet) connected to this technology; his trip home will not be by airplane, but rather, by time machine.

Yet the traveler's return does not go as planned. When he arrives at his destination after three hours of time travel, he decides to postpone any family encounters in order to indulge his tourist fantasies. From his comfortable seat on a terrace, cool drink in hand, he gazes out at the colonial urban landscape of "aquella antiquísima villa que una vez llamaron Havana [*sic*]" (10) [that ancient city once called Havana], when his eyes come to rest on a lone figure crouched in a doorway. The figure wears battered glasses and a heavy backpack; more significantly, they are staring fixedly at a tiny screen, immersed in cybernetic adventures. The protagonist immediately recognizes this person as a "nerd," a kindred spirit to the protagonist's own technologically inclined tastes and desires. But the presence of this nerd is also a sign of how much has changed:

> Comprende resignado que si aquellas funestas criaturas—a cuya mitología él también pertenece—han logrado llegar hasta allí, si con-

viven de manera armónica con el resto del escenario de mulatas bamboleantes con flores apoyadas en la cadera, el espacio-tiempo, para el resto de los lacónicos y embotados viajeros, como él pretende ser, ha dejado de resultar, ya para siempre, un terreno seguro. (11)

[He understands resignedly that if those ill-fated creatures—to whose mythology he also belongs—have been able to get all the way here, if they can coexist peacefully with the rest of the scene of sashaying mulattas with flowers on their hips, then for the rest of the laconic and befuddled travelers (as he claims to be), space-time has stopped being—and will never again be—steady ground.]

The futuristic science fiction framework of González Fernández's story takes the figurative positioning of the Caribbean as "stuck in time" and makes it literal fact. Geographic divisions in this future reality are not only spatial but also temporal; different access to and use of technology places the island on a different temporal plane from "New-New Jersey." Taking the idea of "unplugging" literally, the protagonist tries to escape the pace of his own technology-driven life by visiting a place that is stuck in another time and by adopting the special, "suspended" time of the tourist.[2] His escapist fantasy is shattered, however, when he realizes that the very elements that make up his daily reality in New-New Jersey have reached the Cuban capital. The figure of the nerd leaning against the arch of a colonial building not only ruins the picturesque illusion of his fantasy; it also introduces an element of complexity into the simplified image of "old Havana." If cybersurfing nerds can coexist with "mulatas bamboleantes," Cuban stereotypes connected to a colonial past, then the island's temporal separateness from the rest of the technologically advanced, digitally inclined world is an illusion. In truth, as González Fernández's story slyly suggests, this distance was always an illusion. Although use of the adjective "languid" in the story's title introduces an intentional slowness, suggesting that it may take time for (time-)travelers to realize that this kind of journey is impossible and unnecessary, the identification of the text as an "epigraph" declares that the simplified, clichéd experience the protagonist thought he was seeking is no longer possible.

Even as González Fernández's narrative offers a critique of non-Caribbean perceptions of Caribbean temporality, it also serves as an allegory for the changing place of science fiction in Hispanic Caribbean cultural production, the subject of this book. Like the nerd in González Fernández's story, science fiction crept into Caribbean cultural production initially unseen and unannounced, but its presence across cultural media is now significant. The last two decades have seen a remarkable rise in the presence and visibility of science fiction in the cultural production of the Spanish-speaking Caribbean and its diasporas. The publication of science fiction novels and short stories—both in print and online—has proliferated, alongside the increasingly frequent appearance of science fiction in films, music videos, theater, and visual and digital art. In Cuba, which has produced science fiction literature since the early 1960s, this has meant the (re)legitimation of the genre through literary prizes and dedicated book series, the appearance of new online journals and writers' workshops, and the release of independent film and video productions. In Puerto Rico and the Dominican Republic, which did not previously have a robust tradition of science fiction writing, the last two decades have witnessed the emergence of cultural conferences, workshops for writers and artists, anthologies devoted to the genre, and the incorporation of science fiction elements in film, video, and musical production.[3] Although science fiction may have been initially viewed as an isolated literary phenomenon (like the lone nerd hunched in the doorway), it is now clearly part of a much broader mediascape that is altering mainstream cultural discourse both on the islands and in their diasporic communities.[4]

This surge in the production and circulation of science fiction makes it clear that for Caribbean creators, the genre speaks to the region's experience of our current moment. Despite their divergent political histories, the three places—two countries and one US colony—whose cultural production I examine in this study share certain characteristics in the world of globalized capital. In the last decades, all three have struggled with economic restructuring and with the significant, sometimes tragic, impact of climate change on island environments. Each place has increasingly relied on tourism as a primary source of capital. Each has impelled the growth of diaspora populations that both identify with and contest previous narratives of national identity. And each has seen the emergence of a community of writers, artists, and media creators who are engaging in "their own critical dialogue with narratives of crisis, media exceptionality, and subjectivization" (Arroyo, *Caribes 2.0* 10). Science fiction increasingly has become a tool for engaging with this contemporary Caribbean landscape. I agree with Samuel Ginsburg when he asserts, "Science fiction narratives are not merely a method of escaping current realities, but a tool for articulating their lasting social, political, and rhetorical effects" (*Cyborg Caribbean* 8). An examination of the genre's presence within recent cultural production reveals not only how science fiction engages with contemporary Caribbean conditions, analyzing and critiquing the ways in which international processes of globalization and national systems of leadership have reinforced the islands' marginalization, but also how it uses the future possible to alter the approach of readers and viewers to the region's stories, offering them an escape route from what might seem the predictability of the present.

This study argues that science fiction in the Hispanic Caribbean is particularly significant for the ways in which the genre engages with temporality. By foregrounding science fictional elements, including stock tropes such as the zombie and the postapocalyptic scenario, the hybrid texts that embody what I call a *science fictional turn* in recent Caribbean cultural production articulate a definitive shift in their narrative worlds, a move away from a world engaged with the past to a world that articulates a critique of the problems and concerns of the present from the point of view of futurity. Centering their future imaginings on the Caribbean, these recent science fictions work against the impulse of neoliberal globalization that seeks to delink time and place. The texts themselves function as time machines, projecting future Caribbean imaginings in which time and place are intimately connected.

What Has Not Yet Happened: The Science Fictional Mode

To understand the significance of science fiction's appearance in recent Caribbean cultural production, we need to first consider what constitutes science fiction and how the genre operates. Both critics and writers have consistently argued that science fiction is fundamentally different from mainstream realist literary and cinematic narrative, but elucidating just what constitutes that difference has proved more challenging. Indeed, as Paul Kincaid has observed, the challenge of defining what constitutes science fiction has, in a certain perverse way, become one of the hallmarks of the genre (14). John Rieder asserts that science fiction (in the Anglophone context) emerges not from "high" literary culture at all but from "the mass cultural genre system," and as such it was developed and is shaped by "the set of artistic and commercial opportunities and constraints afforded by the emergence of mass culture" (*Science Fiction and the Mass Cultural Genre System* 10). While mentions of science fiction often conjure images of spaceships, distant planets, and extraterrestrials, scholars of the genre have shown that science fiction's narrative and descriptive possibilities far exceed these elements, what film scholar Rick Altman identifies as the "semantic characteristics" of a genre (8).[5] Darko Suvin, one of the first critics to attempt a definition of science fiction, separates science fiction writing from both naturalistic literature and from genres such as myth, fantasy, and the fairy tale by identifying it as "literature of *cognitive estrangement*" ("On the Poetics" 372).[6] The premise of a science fiction narrative may be completely unknown or strange, but it is developed in a way that is coherent with the "extrapolating and totalizing rigor" of scientific systems (374). Seen this way, science fiction is thus a branch of realism, as Ursula K. Le Guin and numerous scholars subsequently assert, in that its logic relies on the author's own context (what Suvin refers to as the "zero world"), which serves as a starting reference point.[7] Only the imaginative—estranging—framework sets it apart from realist fiction's mimesis.

Yet some critics have questioned what science fiction is doing with its supposedly estranging referents. In *Do Metaphors Dream of Literal Sleep? A Science Fictional Theory of Representation* (2010), Seo-Young Chu builds on Suvin's initial characterization but turns it inside out. Chu identifies science fiction as what she terms "high-intensity realism," a realism that requires more "energy," because so many elements "defy straightforward representation" (7), proposing a different reality that requires a more complete explanation. For Chu, science fiction does not necessarily argue for the existence of things beyond our worldview; rather, its "intensity" (to use Chu's description) is a function of needing to explain things within our worldview that *do not yet* exist. Chu points out that "the science fictional status of a text . . . may vary with circumstance" (8). George Jetson's videophone seemed creatively science fictional to the first viewers of *The Jetsons*, yet it now can seem like a realist element in the era of Zoom, Facetime, and other videochat technologies.

Whether one follows Suvin's or Chu's version of science fiction's relationship to realism, both definitions understand science fictional texts as creating and inhabiting closed fictional universes. In this sense, their conceptualizations of the genre fail to account for much recent cultural production in the Caribbean, where, in contradistinction to earlier examples of science fiction that identified themselves explicitly as "genre fiction," recent literary and cinematic fictions notably employ science fictional elements *alongside* or *in addition to* other narrative modes, such as magical realism or the fantastic, sometimes in the same text. Furthermore, while some of the production and consumption of science fiction in Cuba, Puerto Rico, and the Dominican Republic still takes place in clearly defined communities of writers or fans, many of the recent examples of science fiction in Caribbean cultural production have emerged from within mainstream literary or cinematic markets. In the texts I analyze, science fiction is a dominant mode, but it can be one of several in a text's hybrid narrative landscape.

To understand how science fiction might be used in a text that does not adhere to a uniformly science fictional environment, I make use of theories of science fiction that locate its difference in language and narrative construction, such as those of novelist and critic Samuel L. Delany, who argues that science fiction constitutes not so much a genre as a different mode of expression. If realism can be said to describe "what has happened" or "what could have happened," and fantasy describes "what could not happen," science fiction's difference, according to Delany, operates through the way in which it describes—with verisimilitude—"events that have not [yet] happened" ("About 5,750 Words" 11), thereby expanding the relational capacities of descriptive language. Seen this way, science fiction might still be said to be a language that seeks to describe an experience or an existence beyond our day-to-day reality, but in the subjunctive plane of the future possible rather than the dreamed, imagined, or fantastic.

Science fiction's narrative positioning of itself within the future possible distinguishes it from genres such as magical realism, which has enjoyed a particular foothold in Caribbean literature. Magical realism, as it appeared in the so-called Latin American Boom of the 1960s and after, also employs realism's logic in constructing its narrative world.[8] As Wendy Faris notes in her definition of the genre, magical realism also revolves around questions of time, as it "disturbs received ideas of time, space, and identity" (*Ordinary Enchantments* 7). Yet it operates via a perceptual split, what Faris identifies as "two contradictory understandings of events" (7) and what Brenda Cooper terms "the paradox of the unity of opposites" (5). The magical realist narrative presents as real events that in the reader's world could only have occurred through magic, what Delany would identify as something that "cannot have happened." Yet the magical realist text requires the reader to perceive these events as simultaneously real *and* magical. The text thus exists simultaneously in the mimetic space of realism and in the estranging space of magic. What further separates magical realism from science fiction's construction of temporality is its connection to the past. Cooper argues that the magical realist novel "arises out of particular societies—postcolonial, unevenly developed places where old and new, modern and ancient, the scientific and the magical views of the world co-exist" (216). The instability that the dual perception or unity of temporal opposites forces upon the magical realist narrative is temporally connected to the past through the characterization of magic as "prescientific." The awesome yet possible environment that science fiction posits thus contrasts with magical realism, which splices elements that "could not happen" into a realist framework of "what has happened."

Magical realism's relationship to time may be something akin to the temporal relationship that film critic Bliss Cua Lim identifies in Filipino films that contain supernatural aspects. Lim posits that the fantastic elements in this cinema indicate what she terms "immiscible times," specifically: "multiple times that never quite dissolve into the code of modern time consciousness, discrete temporalities incapable of attaining homogeneity with or full incorporation into a uniform chronological present" (11–12). This kind of temporal mistranslation, Lim argues, underwrites colonial declarations about the "primitiveness" of subordinate cultures.[9] For her, the presence of the fantastic thus reveals the fracture between a dominant (Western, colonial) worldview and another, autochthonous one that continues to exist as the trace of a previous way of being.

Unlike the supernatural elements that Lim analyzes, Caribbean science fiction is not necessarily concerned with excavating or making visible subordinated worldviews. Yet through its introduction of new, alternate realities and altered temporalities, it, too, is engaged in breaking with the temporal status quo, in interjecting an immiscible temporal dimension into what is often assumed to be an established and uniform way of seeing the procession of time and thus of reality. Against narratives that want to consign the region and its inhabitants to the sidelines of the contemporary conversation, a mere insistence on coevalness can be the assertion of a kind of immiscibility, an insistence on visibility.

Although I have just tried to distinguish between science fiction and magical realism through the former's use of "cognitive logic," in truth, as Carl Freedman and China Miéville have shown, these two modes of writing are distinguished more by the construction of their narrative conventions than by the actual scientific nature of science fiction's material elements. Freedman argues that science fiction is less about cognition than about what he terms the "cognition effect." As he explains, "The crucial issue for generic discrimination is not any epistemological judgement external to the text itself on the rationality or irrationality of the latter's imaginings, but rather . . . the attitude of the text itself to the kind of estrangements being performed" (18). Miéville, taking Freedman's observations still further, argues that "cognition is a *persuasion*" (238, italics original), and that "the reader surrenders to the cognition effect to the extent that he or she surrenders to the authority of the text and its author function" (ibid.). Indeed, in the tension Caribbean fictions establish between cognitive "persuasions" and more fantastic elements, they not only explore the border of science fiction and fantasy but also propose expanded ideas of what might count as "science" within a Caribbean context.

If other genres and previous characterizations of Caribbean cultural production have positioned the region as exceptional, outside Western temporal structures, occupying a repeating or static time, or even anchored to the past, science fiction as a mode of narration breaks this cycle, establishing a different relationship not only with or to the future but to global understandings of history, temporality, and interconnectedness. This shift moves the narrative from a fictional world in which "what cannot happen" is made possible to an environment that depicts "what has not yet happened (but might)." The alternative temporalities that Caribbean science fiction texts employ gesture toward future possibilities; they can *also* include elements of what might have been viewed as "magic," but these elements are often used to push for a more expansive understanding of what science can be. While Caribbean writers, artists, and filmmakers who have recently begun to utilize science fiction play with the genre's narrative tropes of discovery and conquest, these creators are engaging with their world—not just the fictional world, but also the sociopolitical context that surrounds them—from a position of futurity that allows for a more critical engagement with Caribbean realities.

José Esteban Muñoz's work on the utopian dimension of queerness has strongly influenced my thinking about science fiction's potential within the Hispanophone Caribbean context. In *Cruising Utopia: The Then and There of Queer Futurity*, Muñoz argues for seeing queerness as an "ideality," a future possibility: "Queerness is essentially about the rejection of a here and now and an insistence on potentiality or concrete possibility for another world" (1). I do not mean to appropriate Muñoz's concept, developed within the specific critical and material conditions of queer theory, for use in examining science fiction. Nor do I mean to suggest that science fiction as a genre is inherently queer (though several of the texts this study examines do trouble heteronormative social structures). Yet Muñoz's observation of the ways in which some of the queer performances he analyzes disrupt the "rigid binary" between present and future (49) finds an echo in the temporal disruptions posed or enacted by the science fiction texts I examine. Many of the cultural artifacts I analyze here also insist in various ways on potentiality, allowing us to glimpse other possible worlds. This does not mean that these possibilities are positive or utopian in an ideal sense; much of Caribbean science fiction is, in fact, quite dark, if not dystopian. Yet I understand it to be utopian in the sense that it opens spaces of possibility.[10] Like Muñoz, I also draw—though less directly—on the work of Ernst Bloch, the philosopher most known for his work on utopia. For Bloch, hope is what allows the possibility of utopia to come into being. More than an emotion to be experienced, it is *"more essentially . . . a directing act of a cognitive kind"* (*Principle of Hope* 12).[11] Bloch saw utopia in broad terms, as an active imagining reaching toward the future. As Muñoz states, "Utopia is not prescriptive; it renders potential blueprints of a world not quite here, a horizon of possibility, not a fixed schema" (97). Despite the dark tone of some of the works examined here, I see science fiction in Caribbean cultural production as active imagining working to expand and make visible the "horizon of possibility."

Reading, Viewing, Listening "Science-Fictionally"

Tropical Time Machines explores the multiple ways in which science fiction both plays with and problematizes ideas of time in Caribbean cultural production. In the hybrid cultural artifacts I examine, science fiction, rather than operating as a set genre, functions as a modal emphasis on the future possible. This future possible intervenes in these texts to highlight temporal stagnation, to make visible outmoded systems that continue to operate in the present, to offer alternative visions of Caribbean reality (both utopian and dystopian), and to argue for radically new ways of envisioning both sociopolitical futures and the literary canons on which national identities and histories are built. I argue that science fiction provides a new language through which Caribbean writers protest and critique political and social inequalities, as well as a means for reframing and reimagining national identities.

Of course, the global science fiction tradition already contains several long-established narrative tropes that play explicitly with time. From H. G. Wells's *The Time Machine* (1895) to *Bill and Ted's Excellent Adventure* (1989), to the inimitable TV series *Doctor Who* (1963–89; 2005–present), machines or other devices, whether mechanical or chemical, have made it possible for characters to make radical jumps in time, allowing creators to juxtapose different time periods and craft meditations on historical causality. Another popular time-related science fiction subgenre is the "uchronia," or alternate history, which imagines what a present or future time would look like if past events had turned out differently, thus "foregrounding the notion of cause and effect" (Hellekson 22) as well as the question of how the dominant historical narrative is itself shaped. Although time machines and alternate histories are features of several of the texts analyzed here (including, of course, González's "Languid Epitaph"), it is not my intention to provide an accounting of the presence of these temporal conceits within Hispanic Caribbean science fiction. Rather, I argue that in the Caribbean context, science fiction *itself* operates as a time device in the region's cultural production through the ways in which it upsets expectations of Caribbean temporality and historical narrative.

Tropical Time Machines begins by examining how the development of science fiction in the Caribbean is entwined with the region's relationship to modern temporalities. In "Shades of *Destiempo:* Caribbean Time and the Rise of Science Fiction," the study's first chapter, I consider the ways in which the Caribbean has been viewed as temporally out of sync in relationship to homogenizing narratives of Western temporal progress, both in the intellectual and political discourse of Caribbean and Caribbean diasporic subjects themselves and through the way in which these island nations have been viewed by outsiders. Alongside this exploration, I provide a cultural history of science fiction in each of the three countries of study. The future possible mode of science fiction that recent Caribbean fictions have increasingly taken up provides texts with new tools with which to comment on present Caribbean experience, engage with the region's place in a global economy, and critique the particularities of local race, gender, and class hierarchies.

This study insists on an examination of science fiction in Caribbean cultural production, rather than the broader term "speculative fiction," because I believe that science fiction, both as a temporal future possible and a "mega-text" of familiar semantic iconography, is making a particular intervention into Caribbean cultural discourse. At the same time, in their deployment of science fiction, Puerto Rican, Cuban, and Dominican writers and artists are creating new grammars for the genre, pushing readers and viewers to expand and reframe their understanding of what constitutes the "future," what counts as science, what can be imagined, and what is possible. Ultimately, these fictions attempt to break the reader out of their own ossified ideas of Caribbean time and space.

Despite the diverse trajectories of science fiction in the cultural production of Cuba, Puerto Rico, and the Dominican Republic, which I discuss in detail in chapter 1, each national context is marked by an explosion of science fiction production since 2010. Given its newness, much of that production understandably has yet to receive significant critical attention. Until recently, writing about Caribbean science fiction tended to be limited to national arenas. Much of the scholarship on science fiction has come from writers and creators themselves; in Cuba, for example, Yoss (né José Miguel Sánchez Gómez), Rinaldo Acosta, and Néstor Román, among others, have both produced science fiction texts and provided excellent historical accounts of the genre's development. Critics writing from within US academia such as Samuel Ginsburg, Juan Carlos Toledano Redondo, Pedro Pablo Porbén, and Antonio Córdoba have also contributed excellent analyses in articles and book chapters, but Ángel Rivera's *Ciencia ficción in Puerto Rico: Heraldos de la catástrofe, el apocalipsis y el cambio* (Puerto Rican science fiction: Heralds of catastrophe, apocalypsis, and change, 2019) is so far the only book-length study that combines an overview of the genre in Puerto Rico with an in-depth analysis of major works (but it is limited to literature in Puerto Rico). The two-volume *Historia de la ciencia ficción latinoamericana* (A history of Latin American science fiction, 2021), edited by Teresa López-Pellisa and Silvia Kurlat Ares, provides invaluably detailed histories of science fiction literature for every country in the region, but it is not explicitly comparative. Ginsburg's *The Cyborg Caribbean: Techno-Dominance in Twenty-First Century Cuban, Puerto Rican, and Dominican Science Fiction* (2023) is the first monograph to approach regional science fiction from a comparative perspective. Like Ginsburg's book, this study argues for the relevance of analyzing works from all three countries together to understand the ways in which science fiction is changing cultural production in the region more broadly. Indeed, given the increasing communication and collaboration between creators from the various islands and those in the diaspora, as well as the levels of contact between writers, directors, artists, critics, and fans in person and across various media platforms, I see much of this recent work as emerging from within complex and fertile networks of Caribbean sociability.[12]

"The View from the Future Possible," the book's second chapter, zeroes in on the ability of science fiction's future possible to (re)shape our way of reading and seeing, performing a reshaping of canons and histories. I argue that science fictional elements in hybrid Caribbean texts operate as "ab-realism," a term coined by critic Sherryl Vint to describe narratives whose science fiction and fantasy elements are deployed to simultaneously reveal "the absurdities of real life" and "activate the utopian traces of another world" ("Ab-realism" 41). By exposing the constructed nature of past and present experience, Caribbean science fiction turns the tables on the hierarchical understanding of these temporal states as both fixed and superior to the future possible. The chapter examines three texts that use abrealism as a technique to question the reader's view of familiar Caribbean histories or tropes. Dominican writer Odilius Vlak's *Crónicas historiológicas* (Historiological chronicles, 2017) inserts science fiction elements into some of the most significant or iconic moments of Dominican history, a gesture that forces the reader to examine the construction of historical narrative as well as their understandings of possibility and causality. Identifying itself as "historical science fiction," *El Informe Cabrera* (The Cabrera report, 2008) by Puerto Rican writer José "Pepe" Liboy incorporates science fiction as both dystopian backdrop and a means of canonical restructuring to paint a complex and critical portrait of a future Puerto Rico, interweaving a futuristic scientific narrative about the embryological creation of a future child with a meditation on literary creation and literary inheritance. Finally, Cuban director Arturo Infante's film *El viaje extraordinario de Celeste García* (Celeste García's extraordinary journey, 2018), takes one of the most common narrative tropes of Cuban and Cuban diasporic fiction—the decision to leave Cuba and the emigrant's journey—and gives it a science fictional twist, revealing the artifice and imagination apparent in the journey itself. By identifying their texts as science fictional, Vlak, Liboy, and Infante offer the genre's future possible to Caribbean cultural production as a kind of "escape route," a new way of reading and seeing that decenters present reality and opens new space for what could be.

To reveal the diversity of ways in which science fiction in recent cultural production contests current temporalities and proposes alternative perspectives, *Tropical Time Machines*'s remaining three chapters provide three different "case studies" that explore how temporality is altered or reshaped in three different subgenres of science fiction: cyberpunk, zombie fictions, and postapocalyptic narratives. It is my contention that their tropes, which are not necessarily associated with questions of time, function as temporal devices in a Caribbean context, constructing temporally separate narrative spaces, signaling to the lingering presence of the past in the present, and troubling relations of narrative causality.

The study's third chapter, "The Countertimes of Caribbean Cyberpunk," explores the rise of cyberpunk, a technologically focused, antiauthoritarian subgenre of science fiction that was taken up by Caribbean authors in the late 1990s and early 2000s, a period corresponding to two distinct national crises: the Cuban Special Period of the 1990s (and its aftermath) and the

Puerto Rican financial crisis of the early 2000s. As a response to these environments of crisis, the world(s) of the texts themselves—both the virtual realities they explore and the flesh-and-blood future worlds they portray—become temporal heterotopias: spaces both logistically and temporally removed from readers' current realities. When these texts conjure globalized dystopia, they place Caribbean spaces in the center of these alternative futures. Rather than importing the aesthetic of global capitalism from North American examples of the subgenre, Cuban narratives such as those found in Michel Encinosa Fu's *Niños de neón* (Children of neon, 2001) are interested in the dystopia associated with this genre as a critical response to the failure of the Revolution's utopian discourse and its construction of fulfillment as forever postponed. Encinosa Fu's stories represent an attempt to craft not only other worlds but also other times beyond the Revolution's ongoing event. Although he would appear to be writing from a late capitalist moment more closely associated with the genre's rise, Puerto Rican author Rafael Acevedo's *Exquisito cadáver* (Exquisite corpse, 2004) offers a subversion of the genre's original tenets, as it employs a cyberpunk aesthetic only to reject the technological elements of his futurescape. His book uses the dystopian chronoscape of the cyberpunk detective story to stage an ethical intervention in Puerto Rican narrative.

Cyberpunk represented the adaptation of a foreign subgenre for Caribbean ends. "In the Time of the Zombie: The Remaking of a Caribbean Icon," the book's fourth chapter, shows how a more autochthonous figure, the Caribbean zombie, is deployed to represent certain kinds of temporal, ideological, or discursive stagnation. The temporally liminal nature of the zombie—suspended between life and death and between the future and the past—has made it a figure ripe for exposing the connections between the region's historical traumas, particularly the history of slavery and contemporary racialized practices of exploitation. The chapter examines four recent Caribbean zombie narratives that serve as examples of how zombies' temporal and biopolitical liminality makes them visible vehicles for highlighting ossified sociopolitical structures and continued systems of exclusion. Both director Alejandro Brugués's film *Juan de los muertos* (Juan of the dead, 2011) and Cuban writer Erick Mota's short story "That Zombie Belongs to Fidel!" (in *Cuba in Splinters: Eleven Stories from the New Cuba*, 2014) chronicle zombie epidemics or invasions in Cuba as a way of highlighting the friction between revolutionary narrative/state discourse and daily life on the island. Puerto Rican author Pedro Cabiya's novel *Malas hierbas* (2009; *Wicked Weeds*, 2016), which plays liberally and literally with making and remaking zombies, returns the zombie to its place of origin, where the figure provides a fertile vehicle for exploring Haiti's position with respect to the Dominican Republic. Finally, Puerto Rican author Pabsi Livmar's short story "Golpe de agua" ("Water Strike," in *Teoremas turbios,* 2018) returns the figure to the essence of the enslaved worker and strips away the borders separating human and zombie. As they reveal the repressive sociopolitical and ideological systems still in place in the region, all four texts also remake zombies themselves in ways that suggest radical alternatives—however potentially dystopian—to (neo)colonial, patriarchal systems.

The stock figure of the zombie provides a guide for readers and viewers of recent Caribbean zombie texts. "After World's End: Caribbean Postapocalyptic Narratives," the study's fifth and final chapter, explores the regional adaptation of another familiar form: the postapocalyptic narrative. Many postapocalyptic fictions dwell not on final endings but rather on the time "after the end," creating what critic James Berger refers to as a narrative "time loop" (6) between present and future. Through an analysis of three postapocalyptic texts, Cuban writer Erick J. Mota's novel *Habana Underguater* (2010), Dominican director José María Cabral's comedic film *Arrobá* (Enraptured, 2019), and Dominican writer Rita Indiana's novel *La mucama de Omicunlé* (2015; *Tentacle,* 2018), I argue that the intimate, ongoing, and unfinished nature of the Caribbean's relationship to catastrophe both complicates the binary nature of this time loop and disrupts the conditions for utopian hope. Set in a permanently flooded Havana, Mota's *Habana Underguater* is both a postapocalyptic narrative and an alternate history; it imagines what would have happened if the Soviet Union had "won" the Cold War and the United States had collapsed. Yet the militarized, politically fragmented city revealed in his novel palimpsestically recalls current social and political divisions as much as it explores future ones. Cabral likewise plays with the idea of alternate history in *Arrobá,* a comedy about three clownish bank robbers who use a time machine to return to the scene of a robbery gone bad. When the friends travel forward in time, the apocalyptic scenarios they view challenge the national possibilities of the postapocalyptic "time loop." Another complicated time-traveling fiction, *La mucama de Omicunlé,* takes place in a future Dominican Republic in which a biological-weapons accident has destroyed the island's ecosystem. The only hope for turning back this environmental damage rests on Acilde, a trans man whose gender-confirmation procedure serves as a spiritual initiation, allowing him to be present in multiple times simultaneously. Indiana disrupts the sense of a postapocalyptic ending entirely, first through her introduction of multiple kinds of time, then by frustrating the redemptive promise that these alternative times appear to offer.

Tropical Time Machines shows how Caribbean cultural production deploys science fiction for temporal ends, reshaping narrative tropes and figures—and with them ideas about the Caribbean itself. These works speak to one another across media and beyond individual national contexts. While it would be impossible in a study such as this to give a full accounting of all the dynamic cultural artifacts produced in the Caribbean since the new millennium that engage with science fiction, I have chosen to investigate patterns, repeated tropes, or uses of science fiction and its elements that appear across media and modes of production. Highlighting the recent contributions of women creators to the corpus of Caribbean science fiction, the book's epilogue examines two very different texts, the video for Rita Indiana's song "Como un dragón" (from *Mandinga Times*, 2020) and Puerto Rican writer Yolanda Arroyo Pizarro's short story "Mûlatress" (in *Prietopunk*, 2022) as examples of science fiction's potential within Caribbean cultural production. Indiana's song and video and Arroyo Pizarro's story reveal how Caribbean science fiction, while not negating the past, uses it as material from which to construct future-oriented fictions. I see both as offering space for reflection and hope, even in our currently dark time.

1

Shades of *Destiempo*

Caribbean Time and the Rise of Science Fiction

> He was a hardcore sci-fi and fantasy man, believed that was the kind of story we were all living in. He'd ask: What more sci-fi than the Santo Domingo? What more fantasy than the Antilles?
>
> Junot Díaz, *The Brief Wondrous Life of Oscar Wao*, p. 6

"What more sci-fi than Santo Domingo?" asks Oscar Wao, the protagonist of Dominican American writer Junot Díaz's 2007 novel *The Brief Wondrous Life of Oscar Wao*. The question is a clever play on Cuban writer Alejo Carpentier's now-classic essay "De lo real maravilloso americano" ("On the Marvelous Real in America" 1949), which ends by asking provocatively, "¿Pero qué es la historia de la América toda sino una crónica de lo real maravilloso?" [But what is the history of America but a chronicle of the marvelous real?]. Carpentier coins the term "lo real maravilloso" [the marvelous real] to describe a Latin American reality that he perceives as "beyond" what has been understood as possible according to the official Western historical narrative, or linear progressivist history. Due in part to the intersection of multiple spiritual and cultural worldviews, for Carpentier, Latin America and the Caribbean are regions of the world whose reality cannot fit into or be fully comprehended by the boundaries of a rational, Western consciousness. The marvelous real locates the Caribbean as a temporal, conceptual other, though Carpentier's narrative seeks to revalue this otherness as deriving from a "natural" excess.[1] Even as Oscar's question recasts the Dominican Republic's violent history in the tropes of the literature to which Oscar, a voracious reader of science fiction, most relates, Díaz's move from "the marvelous real" to "sci-fi" is clearly a conscious gesture, a wink to the readers of Latin American literature in his audience. It is also a commentary on how both narrative and temporal perspectives have shifted in the intervening decades. If Carpentier sought to consider Latin America's historical uniqueness (and, implicitly, literary autonomy) in contradistinction to Europe's, Díaz's use of science fiction "invites his reader to assimilate the experience of Antillean diaspora" (Blanco 52), acknowledging the ways in which Caribbean-imagined communities and histories have evolved. Díaz's shift to science fiction also suggests that the estranging qualities of this mode are particularly suited to this contemporary moment.

Taking Díaz's playful reference as a meaningful starting point, this chapter charts the recent history of the rise of science fiction in Hispanic Caribbean cultural production alongside recent shifts in the perception of the region's relationship to time. The increasing popularity of science fiction in the past two decades parallels a shift in how Caribbean space is positioned in relation to time. As Carpentier's concept reveals, the region has frequently been viewed as out of step with Western narratives of temporality (not unlike other parts of the Global South). However, in the past two decades, this *destiempo* [untimeliness] has come to be associated with conditions of ongoing crisis. Science fiction's construction of temporality, in its divergence from that of magical realism, offers an abrupt departure from the ways in which the Caribbean and its literature have been positioned with respect to both dominant historical narratives and the Western teleological conception of time as incessant progress.[2] Given science fiction's short Caribbean history, increased regional interest and activity in the genre marks a significant attempt to break with previous narratives of Caribbean temporality, offering alternative methods—and spaces—for viewing the relationship between the present and possible futures.

The Caribbean is not alone in having witnessed a rise in the popularity of science fiction and its subgenres. The genre is flourishing worldwide and has been particularly popular in Spanish-language cultural production. Expanded internet access and new digital publishing forms have facilitated communication among writers throughout Latin America and the Caribbean, and an increasingly deep field of science fiction literature has boomed in online journals and independent presses. New digital forms of film and video production have freed directors and producers from dependence on the subsidies of state cultural institutions, allowing film and video to be shared via numerous platforms.[3] As distribution of these different media has diversified, science fiction has moved beyond the popular constraints of "genre fiction" and narrow communities of fans to position itself within the cultural mainstream. The result has been an increased circulation of both science fiction literature and cinema among broader Spanish- (and Portuguese-) language audiences no longer limited by national borders.

Yet the significance of science fiction's increasing presence in mainstream media production varies across the region. In Argentina, Mexico, and Brazil, these new developments are but the latest chapters in longer national histories of science fiction.[4] In the Hispanophone Caribbean, in contrast, science fiction did not become an established genre in Cuba until the 1960s, and it has only gained a recognizable presence in Puerto Rico and the Dominican Republic in the last two decades. Undoubtedly, the Cuban, Dominican, and Puerto Rican writers who have recently chosen to employ science fiction are in dialogue with their predecessors in the Caribbean and elsewhere. But the genre's recent boom in Spanish-language Caribbean cultural production is more than just a variation on a theme or a progressive "next step" in a regional literature. Caribbean narratives of the last forty years have been frequently associated with magical realism, which dwells on the region's past or, more recently, with a hard-edged "dirty realism" that fetishizes the poverty of its inhabitants in the present. Science fiction's introduction into mainstream cultural production, clearly a conscious decision on the part of its creators, marks a new direction within this cultural production. In particular, the rise of ongoing trans-Caribbean collaborations and dialogues among creators reveals the ways in which they employ the genre to expand imaginative possibilities. As Díaz's creative use of science fiction implies, the genre has become a preferred Caribbean mode from which to engage our current moment.

A Place "Where Time Unfolds Irregularly"

Although both Caribbean raw materials and labor were fundamental to European and North American economic development since its "discovery" by European explorers, the Caribbean has never been situated as central to the dominant Western historical narrative. As Rudyard Alcocer observes, the region has long been described "as possessing a highly charged and sometimes peculiar relationship with temporality," one that sees Caribbean time as "flout[ing] the linear 'clock time' associated with modernity" (*Time Travel* 67–68). Lest a reader think that this characterization of Caribbean time ended with the post–World War II moment in which Carpentier was writing, Cuban critic Antonio Benítez Rojo, in the introduction to his seminal *La isla que se repite* (1989; *The Repeating Island*, 1996), describes the region's culture as "una cultura sinuosa donde el tiempo se despliega irregularmente y se resiste a ser capturado por el ciclo del reloj o del calendario" (xiv) [a sinuous culture where time unfolds irregularly and resists being captured by the cycles of clock and calendar (11)]. If, for Carpentier, it was Caribbean history that overflows ("desborda") the boundaries of Western conception, for Benítez Rojo Caribbean time itself refuses to be contained or governed by Western systems of order.

From a historical perspective, the Hispanic Caribbean's perceived untimeliness may have begun with its comparatively late independence from Spain; if much of Latin America achieved independence in the early decades of the nineteenth century, the Dominican Republic's complicated, multistage independence from first Spain and then from Haiti concluded in 1865, and Cuba's attenuated separation from Spain in 1898 rendered both countries late arrivals to modern nationhood.[5] Puerto Rico, which went directly from Spanish colony to US protectorate (also in 1898), continues to contend with its de facto colonial status. Yet shades of the *destiempo* with which Carpentier and Benítez Rojo characterize the Caribbean have persisted into the present day. Although the reasons given for their "untimeliness" vary, Cuba, Puerto Rico, and the Dominican Republic all have weathered the characterization of being somehow "out of time" or "out of sync" with Western models of temporality.

Cuba's "untimeliness" is intimately connected to its political development, most specifically to the 1959 Revolution, in which left-leaning revolutionaries overthrew the US-supported government of dictator Fulgencio Batista. Leader Fidel Castro's 1961 declaration that the Cuban Revolution was socialist and the government's subsequent alliance with the Soviet Union created a radical political break with the United States and its vision for the hemisphere, culminating in the US declaration of an embargo on nearly all exports to Cuba in February 1962. From 1961 onward, the language used by Cuban intellectuals and politicians to refer to the Revolution evinces a contradictory sense of time, in that the Revolution is never referred to as a finished event but rather as an ongoing present, a process or struggle leading to a utopian future that is always immanent but not imminent. Similarly, the Special Period in Peacetime, the Cuban economic crisis of the early to mid-1990s brought on by the collapse of the Soviet Union and the subsequent dissolution of Eastern Bloc trade agreements with Cuba, was a supposedly exceptional "moment" that has never officially ended. In contrast to the Cuban government's view of the Revolution's temporality, those outside the nation saw the Special Period as the beginning of the Revolution's end: "The Cuban Revolution of 1959 signaled a utopian moment that is squarely in the past" (145), observes Cuban American performance theorist José Esteban Muñoz in 2009. Cuban

American literary critic José Quiroga notes that as one of the last socialist nations, Cuba has often been characterized by writers, journalists, and politicians outside the country as being out of sync with a capitalist temporality: "Out of time, on a time of its own, stuck in time. For those of us with a strong personal investment in Cuba, these phrases kept reappearing after the Soviet Bloc collapsed and the United States engaged in diplomatic and commercial relationships with all its former allies but Cuba" (viii). Although the Soviet Union's collapse forced the Cuban government to form new economic partnerships and even to allow certain kinds of private enterprise, this expansion of a de facto capitalist economy has not resulted in a radical political restructuring. Despite Fidel Castro's transfer of power to his brother Raúl between 2006 and 2008, Raúl Castro's transfer of power to Miguel Díaz-Canel between 2018 and 2021, and the ratification and approval of a new constitution in 2018 and 2019, the single-party Cuban government has retained political control and continues to function as "the main capitalist actor as both owner and regulatory enforcer" in the island's economy (Duong 13).

But the vision of Cuba as "out of time" or frozen in time has also been projected onto the island by visitors. Media scholar Paloma Duong speaks of tourists wanting to "see Cuba before it changes" (35), as if Cuba existed in an exceptional state, in some kind of suspended animation. The musicologist Alexandra Vázquez finds something similar happening in the foreign marketing of Cuban music: "There is always a temporal abbreviation that guarantees quick, if not painless, consumption of Cuban music in these objects. They depend upon Cuba as time standing still—but its contents must nevertheless keep a syncopated beat" (11). Writing five years after Muñoz, Cuban writer Orlando Luis Pardo Lazo observes, "The local color still oversaturates everything, not only because of the island's institutional inertia, but perhaps because the foreign market only asks for more and more of this same Cuban bubble that grows and grows without ever bursting: typical topics, common characters, stereotypical settings and more than familiar forms" ("Preface," in *Cuba in Splinters* 12). For Pardo Lazo, the foreign gaze that finds something desirable in the island's (perceived) temporal disjunction only strengthens the temporal displacement created by the Revolution's own narrative and the country's technological challenges.[6]

While Cuba's exceptional position with respect to hemispheric geopolitics grounds statements regarding its temporal exceptionality, its unique political identity has also made it a hypervisible object from a foreign (specifically, US) perspective. The Dominican Republic, in contrast, has historically found itself "ghosted," as Dixa Ramírez puts it, overlooked and ignored by Western cultural and historical narratives, or conflated with neighboring Haiti (3). *Dominicanidad*, Lorgia García-Peña asserts, is in fact "a category that emerges out of the historical events that placed the Dominican Republic in a geographic and symbolic border between the United States and Haiti since its birth in 1844" (3). The anxiety produced by this border positioning resulted in Dominican lettered elites constructing narratives of Dominican identity as homogeneous and Hispanic (i.e., Spanish) in origin, a conceptualization that "ghosted" the country's own history as a colony with a large population of free people of color and, as Ramírez puts it, "erased, or at least whitewashed, Dominican forms of black subjectivity" (8). Maintained through what Néstor E. Rodríguez describes as a kind of discursive "colonización interna" (*Escrituras de desencuentro* 12) [internal colonization], this narrative was sustained and fortified during the dictatorship of Rafael Leónidas Trujillo (1930–61) and the subsequent presidencies of Joaquín Balaguer (1961–62, 1966–78, and 1986–96), who had served as Trujillo's vice president as well as an intellectual architect for the Trujillo regime. Although Rodríguez and Ramírez argue that recent cultural production can be seen as an attempt to, in the words of Ramírez, "counteract the territory's ghosting within larger Western discourses" (6), the persistence of this national narrative within lettered discourse has created a situation in which elite cultural production and discursive circuits can seem out of step with both popular culture and the country's sociopolitical reality. Furthermore, given the length of the Trujillo dictatorship, as well as Balaguer's continuation of many of Trujillo's practices during his three subsequent presidencies, it could be argued that the country has still not finished grappling with the imprint of the dictatorship and its aftermath.[7] The past is not yet past.

In the case of Puerto Rico, its intimate yet subordinate position with respect to the United States has elicited vivid statements of and experiences with temporal displacement. A US protectorate since 1898 and a "Free Associated State" since 1948, Puerto Rico functions as a de facto US colony; though the islands maintain a representative in the US Congress, residents of the islands cannot vote in US elections.[8] For decades, Puerto Ricans themselves have been divided over whether to seek US statehood or declare independence. In his recent book of essays, Puerto Rican critic Juan Carlos Quintero Herencia refers to the time in which Puerto Rico, especially in terms of its political discourse, finds itself as "la queda(era)" [the stuck(age)]: "La queda(era) es, cómo negarlo, otra manera de nombrar la parálisis politico-social que caracteriza al Puerto Rico de cambio de siglo, así como los discursos y las prácticas que contribuyen a ella misma" (12) [The stuck(age) is, why deny it, another way of naming the sociopolitical paralysis that characterizes this turn-of-the-century Puerto Rico as well as the discourses and practices that contribute to it]. For Quintero Herencia, as for others, the islands' status as a Free Associated State is perceived as a kind of limbo; the inability to move past it to another form of collective political identity has stalled national discourse at multiple levels.

In recent decades, the perceived stasis of Puerto Rican sociopolitical discourse has run parallel to—and been sharpened by—the islands' ongoing financial crisis, which is intimately connected to the colonial relationship between Puerto Rico and the United States. Puerto Rico's financial difficulties began in 1996, when Section 936 of the US tax code began a ten-year phaseout of the tax exemption granted to US companies for income originating from Puerto Rican subsidiaries. As a result, foreign investment fled the islands, coincident with both the 2006 global recession and the 2008 banking crisis. Debt, and the sale of government bonds, became a means for the government to address the resulting funding deficit.[9] In June 2015, then-governor Alejandro García Padilla announced that Puerto Rico could pay neither its debt, valued at US$ 72 billion, nor its US$ 49 billion in public pension obligations (Lloréns and Stanchich 86). The US government responded to this announcement by passing the Puerto Rico Oversight, Management, and Economic Stability Act (PROMESA) on 30 June 2016. Overseen by a seven-member Fiscal Control Board (known popularly as La Junta), PROMESA was tasked with creating a plan for the debt's repayment. Yet as Zorimar Rivera Montes observes, it "made clear that all government efforts to deal with the debt crisis would be put into helping debtors collect the debt, at the cost of economic development and social stability" (4). PROMESA's oversight also presented a clear challenge to Puerto Rican sovereignty.

The political response to Puerto Rico's debt has indelibly affected the islands' temporal narrative. As Jossianna Arroyo notes, "If, as in neoliberalism, time is measured in money, then those who don't have any, those who borrow and cannot pay ... exist under a temporality filled with shame and threats" (*Caribes 2.0* 16). Rocío Zambrana argues that the condition of indebtedness is a situation of relation both spatial and temporal: "To be in debt is to inhabit a space and time of capture, dispossession, expulsion, exploitation" (21). The Fiscal Control Board's decisions about Puerto Rico's debt have curtailed the ability of the islands' inhabitants to occupy a present and a future of their making. And, as Zambrana, Rivera Montes, and others have observed, the burden of austerity measures falls unequally on poor, nonwhite, and female or genderqueer inhabitants of the archipelago. One result of this situation has been a steady increase in out-migration; Mora, Dávila, and Rodríguez estimate that between 2006 and 2017, 597,000 Puerto Ricans left the island (209).

If Puerto Rico's, Cuba's, and the Dominican Republic's perceived contemporary "untimeliness" can be traced to their specific histories, as this brief overview indicates, they are united through historical and recent experiences of crisis. Although the word "crisis" may suggest a dramatic event or series of events, Rosalind Williams notes that the term has increasingly "[spread] out in time" (524), such that it now refers to "a drawn-out episode or series of episodes" (ibid.), or, more recently, "a chronic condition" (526). In the case of the Caribbean, the experience of these recent "states of crisis" often compounds a sense of stagnant temporality. Hurricane María's devastation of Puerto Rico in September 2017 provides just one example. The storm leveled the islands' fragile electrical grid, leaving many residents without power or secure housing for months. As Yarimar Bonilla details in her analysis of the hurricane and its aftermath, while Puerto Ricans waited for local and US governments to mount a substantive response, what had begun as an urgent state of emergency began to feel static rather than temporary: "The present did not expand in its eventfulness, but in its persistence. Time passed, and nothing changed. . . . The present no longer felt ephemeral, quickly dissolving into something new. Instead, the present lingered longer than it should. This created a frenzied state of repetition in which each day felt eerily like the last" (3). María's aftermath forced Puerto Ricans into an experience of "stuckness" as the accompaniment to an ongoing crisis, an experience of temporal sameness paradoxically both "unmoving" and "frenzied." While I delve more thoroughly into the narration of catastrophe in this study's last chapter, this stagnant temporality of disaster, not unlike the "slow violence" of environmental degradation that Rob Nixon documents, points to other kinds of temporal stagnation.

In describing the ways in which Cuba, Puerto Rico, and the Dominican Republic have each been viewed as "out of sync," or as operating "out of time," the assumption that is frequently reflected in these descriptions, whether externally or internally generated, is that to be "out of sync" is to be somehow "behind" in a teleologically constructed narrative of time as progress. This premise, certainly, underscored the attitude with which

Caribbean intellectuals in the early twentieth century approached their positions vis-à-vis modernity, and something of this idea can still be found in more contemporary descriptions. As Jossianna Arroyo notes, however, occupying an "out-of-sync" position can in fact be an act of resistance: "To be 'out of sync' in the neoliberal script traced by capitalism is to negotiate alternative paths in the present and the future" (*Caribes 2.0* 155). As this study shows, to actively construct alternative temporalities can be another way of forging alternative paths.

The specific characterization of temporality with respect to the Caribbean must be understood within the context of broader changes in our understanding of time, as scholars in the emerging field of time studies continue to document. As Joel Burges and Amy J. Elias observe in the introduction to their foundational collection, *Time: A Vocabulary of the Present*, since the modern (read: post–World War II) era, "the present has emerged as an experience of simultaneity in which temporalities multiply because they are synchronized as simultaneous on economic, cultural, technological, ecological, and planetary registers" (3). In other words, our collective understanding of "the present" has expanded, operating in a tension between "a singular time beholden to capital" (ibid.) and a sense of contemporaneity as culturally inflected and experienced through multiple registers.

If our global condition has made us increasingly conscious of the diverse ways in which we experience time, we also find ourselves in a particular moment with respect to historical narrative. It has now been nearly half a century since many of the revolutionary, postcolonial independence movements around the globe and three decades since the collapse of the Soviet Union and its large socialist political project initiated a radical shift in the horizon of political and social possibility. Media scholar Paloma Duong characterizes our current moment as "postsocialist," a term that for her does not so much refer to "what comes after socialism" as it describes "the moment(s) of irreversible rift between socialism as a critique of the capitalist present on the one hand, and the political projects that usurp its name on the other" (3). Like Duong, Jamaican theorist David Scott is interested in what he describes as "living *on* in the wake of past political time, amid the ruins, specifically, of postsocialist and post-colonial futures past" (2). Scott finds that what Duong would call our "postsocialist condition" has created "a more acute awareness of time, a more arresting *attunement* to the uneven *topos* of temporality" (2). Caribbean science fiction texts speak directly to this attunement, to this desire for temporal recalibration.

A Parallel Timeline: Hispanic Caribbean Science Fiction

The postsocialist condition and the amplification of Caribbean states of crisis has run parallel to the arrival of science fiction in Hispanic Caribbean cultural production. Although the appearance of science fiction in Cuba, Puerto Rico, and the Dominican Republic has followed a different trajectory in each case, these national histories of the genre converge in the last two or three decades, when science fiction entered mainstream cultural production in each context. In Cuba, science fiction literature first became a popular genre in the first years following the Cuban Revolution; though a few texts written before 1959 can be considered science fiction or precursors of science fiction, the 1960s saw the publication of a number of important science fiction novels and short story collections, notably Oscar Hurtado's *La ciudad muerta de Korad* (The dead city of Korad, 1964), Arturo Arango's *¿A dónde van los cefalomos?* (Whither the Cephalomos? 1964), and Miguel Collazo's *El libro fantástico de Oaj* (The fantastic book of Oaj, 1966) and *El viaje* (1968; *The Journey*, 2020).[10] Hurtado also edited two important anthologies, *Cuentos de ciencia ficción* (Science fiction stories, 1967) and *Introducción a la ciencia ficción* (An introduction to science fiction, 1971), which garnered a broader Cuban readership for the genre. However, though the revolutionary leaders guiding cultural policy might have initially viewed the popular nature of science fiction literature as a means to engage Cuban readers, Evangelina Soltero Sánchez notes that many of these early works of Cuban science fiction, "eran textos de una calidad literaria que exigían un receptor con cierto grado de cultura" (292) [were texts of a literary quality that demanded a reader with a certain cultural level]. With the onset of the "Quinquenio Gris," the "Five-year Gray Period" of intense censorship in the early 1970s, science fiction and other literatures of the fantastic, seen by some as too influenced by US cultural production, were officially discouraged in favor of socialist realism (Yoss, "Marcianos" 66).[11] As a result, nearly a decade passed in which no new Cuban science fiction was published.

Science fiction literature re-emerged in Cuba in the early 1980s, with the publication of Agustín de Rojas's socialist utopian epic *Espiral* (1982; *Spiral*, 2020); Gregorio Ortega's novel *Kappa 15* (1982); Daína Chaviano's *Los mundos que amo* (The worlds that I love, 1982) and *Fábulas de una abuela extraterrestre* (Fables from an extraterrestrial grandmother, 1987); the short story collection *Espacio abierto* (Open space, 1982) by Chely Lima and Alberto Serret, and the comedic science fiction works of F. Mond (Félix

Mondéjar), *Con perdón de los terrícolas* (Apologies to the earth-dwellers, 1983), *Dónde está mi Habana?* (Where is my Havana? 1985), and *Cecilia después, o ¿por qué la Tierra?* (Cecilia after, or why Earth? 1987). In tandem with the appearance of more publications, the genre began to receive institutional support through literary prizes, which funded the publication of winning novels and story collections, and through the creation of literary workshops that supported emerging writers.[12] Cuban writers formed two important workshops focused on science fiction during this period: the Taller Oscar Hurtado, founded by Daína Chaviano, and the Taller Julio Verne, founded by Raúl Aguiar in 1983.[13] Science fiction also branched out beyond adult literature into other domains; Alicia Alonso, founder of the prestigious Ballet Nacional, choreographed a ballet, *Misión Korad* (Mission: Korad, 1980), based on Hurtado's *La ciudad muerta de Korad*. Several children's comics publications, including *Cómicos* (1986–90) and *Zunzún* (1980), also published stories with science fiction themes (Soltero Sánchez 299).

Although science fiction literature by Cuban authors in the 1980s made up a small percentage of the island's publishing industry, more science fiction literature and film circulated in the 1970s and '80s in translation; Cuba's established relationship with the Soviet Union allowed for the publication of science fiction literature from countries of the Soviet Bloc, and this literature remained available even when censorship on the island discouraged production by Cuban writers. Spanish-language editions of works by Stanislaw Lem, Karel Capek, and the Strugatsky brothers circulated in Cuba long before they became known to a broader Anglo-American audience, and Cuban writers who were adolescents in the late 1970s and '80s recall avidly consuming Russian science fiction cartoons and movies such as *Amphibian Man* (Vladimir Chebotaryov and Gennadi Kazansky, 1962) alongside issues of *Sputnik*.[14] Chaviano briefly hosted a regular TV spot that featured both Soviet and American science fiction films (Yoss, "Marcianos" 69). As Cuban-generated science fiction began to re-emerge, the magazine *Juventud Técnica*, modeled after the Soviet magazine *Téjnika— Molodëzhi*, was instrumental in publishing short stories with science fiction elements. Cuban creators who came of age in this era thus drew on two distinct cultural canons of science fiction texts in their engagement with the genre.

The collapse of the Soviet Union and the economic crisis precipitated by its dissolution forced a slowdown in the production of science fiction in Cuba. The severe economic constraints of the Special Period in Peacetime, as Fidel christened the era, curtailed the production of both print and visual media, as materials and the energy to manufacture them were severely limited. Although *Timshel,* the first book by prolific writer Yoss (b. 1969) and winner of the 1988 Premio David, was published in 1990, the so-called crisis de papel [paper crisis] between 1991 and 1996 prevented many writers and artists from publishing the work they produced (Acosta, "La ciencia ficción cubana"). Cuban editor and critic Rinaldo Acosta observes that while literary histories usually attempt to account for the publication record, "para comprender los años noventa este enfoque no es suficiente y puede volverse incluso una limitación" ("La ciencia ficción cubana") [to understand the 1990s this focus is insufficient and indeed can become a limitation]. As Yoss notes, however, a lack of resources for local production did not reduce interest in the genre. Despite material scarcity and Cuba's restricted access to the nascent internet, the 1990s witnessed the production of a homegrown science fiction TV show, *Shiralad* (1993), written by Chely Lima, and Cuba's first digital science fiction journal, *Revista i+Real* (1994), edited by Bruno Henríquez and distributed via shared diskettes (Yoss, "Marcianos" 75). Henríquez also helped found a new writers' workshop, El hueco negro. The break represented by the political rearrangement of the Special Period created a space for new creative production to emerge, even if the literature from this decade would not be published until years later.

The group of writers who began to write in the 1990s was, as Soltero Sánchez observes, the first generation to be born after the Revolution (308). Supposedly the generation of "New Men" and "Women," they were educated under revolutionary ideals but came of age as artists and writers in a moment of national disillusion and rupture. Drawn to the Anglo American subgenre of science fiction known as cyberpunk, this group of writers included Yoss, Vladimir Hernández Pacín (b. 1966), Raúl Aguiar Álvarez (b. 1962), Fabricio González Neira (b. 1973), Michel Encinosa Fu (b. 1974), Juan Pablo Noroña (b. 1973), Ricardo Acevedo (b. 1969), and Alberto Mesa (1971–2015). Although they were not published until the end of the decade, in the early 1990s Hernández Pacín began drafting stories for his collection *Nova de cuarzo* (Quartz nova, 1999), as Raúl Aguiar began writing his multidimensional novel *La estrella bocarriba* (The upside-down star, 2001), and Yoss wrote most of the narratives that constitute *Se alquila un planeta* (2001; *Planet for Rent* 2014).

The Special Period in Cuba has never been declared officially over, but by the new millennium the island's economy edged closer to a recovery from the worst effects of the economic crisis, thanks in part to the 1995 Ley de Inversión Extranjera (Foreign Investment Law), which opened the island to foreign tourism and investment. Renewed governmental support for literary and cinematic production tracked the improvement in material conditions, as evidenced in the publication of anthologies such as *Reino eterno* (Eternal kingdom, 1999), edited by Yoss, and *Onda de choque* (Shockwave, 2005), edited by Hernández Pacín. The early 2000s also saw the publication of Encinosa Fu's *Niños de neón* (Children of neon, 2001) and *Dioses de neón* (Neon gods, 2006), as well as Anabel Enríquez Piñeiro's *Nada que declarar* (Nothing to declare, 2007).

In the early 2000s Cuba had one of the lowest rates of internet access in the hemisphere; nonetheless, the island experienced a boomlet of digital magazines focused on science fiction.[15] These included *Revista Digital miNatura* (1999–), *Disparo en red* (2004–8), *Qubit* (2005–), and *Korad* (2010–). This last is a publication of the writer's workshop Espacio Abierto, founded by Aguiar and Yoss in 2009 under the auspices of the Centro Onelio Jorge Cardoso, a cultural institution dedicated to educating and supporting young writers that is still active. Espiral and Espacio Abierto were two writers' workshops founded during this period. Many of the most recent generation of Cuban science fiction writers have come through Espacio Abierto or writing classes through the Centro Onelio, among them Erick Mota (b. 1975), Leonardo Gala (b. 1972), Carlos Duarte Cano (b. 1962), Yasmín Portales Machado (b. 1980), Erick Flores Taylor (b. 1982), Alejandro Rojas (b. 1984), Malena Salazar Maciá (b. 1988), Elaine Vilar Madruga (b. 1989), Maielis González Fernández (b. 1989), and Daniel Burguet (b. 1989).

Even as Espacio Abierto and the Centro Onelio continue to bring together science fiction fans and foster new science fiction writers, other Cuban writers have begun to employ science fiction in their work in less orthodox ways. The loosely associated group of writers known as the Generación Año Cero (Generation Zero), including Orlando Luis Pardo Lazo (b. 1971), Jorge Enrique Lage (b. 1979), Ahmel Echevarría (b. 1974), Lía Villares (b. 1984), Raúl Flores Iriarte (b. 1977), Erick Mota, and Michel Encinosa Fu, is named for the fact that many of its members began publishing—first in self-edited zines and blogs—around the year 2000. The group's identity coalesced around the publication of two US-published anthologies, the bilingual issue "Nuevarrativa cubana" ("Cuban Newrrative: An Anthology")—published first in the Pittsburgh journal *Sampsonia Way* (2013) and later in book form as *Generation Zero: An Anthology of New Cuban Fiction* (2014)—and the English-language collection *Cuba in Splinters: Eleven Stories from the New Cuba* (2014).[16] With the exception of Encinosa Fu, the Generación Año Cero writers do not identify their work as science fiction; Gilberto Padilla Cárdenas argues that the group's writers have cultivated "una suerte de orfandad literaria, de antigenealogía" (119) [a sort of literary orphanhood, an antigenealogy]. However, several members of the group have incorporated science fiction elements into their fiction, most notably Jorge Enrique Lage and Raúl Flores Iriarte. Lage's novel *Carbono 14* (*Carbon 14,* 2010) and short story collection *Vultureffect* (2011) are particularly notable for what Rachel Price has called "a total fusion of styles," which includes science fiction along with Japanese anime and noir ("Planet/Cuba. On Jorge Enrique Lage"). His more recent texts *Archivo* (Archive, 2015) and *Everglades* (2020) play explicitly with the relationship between science fiction and detective literature.

If the work of Generación Año Cero pushed science fiction elements into Cuba's literary mainstream, a similar process was at work in Cuban cinema. Except for animated films such as Juan Padrón's *Vampiros en la Habana* (Vampires in Havana, 1985), Cuban film since the early days of the Instituto Cubano de Arte e Industria Cinematográfica (ICAIC, founded in 1959), whether fictional or documentary, had been largely realist in nature. That changed in 2011 with the release of *Juan de los muertos* (Juan of the dead), Cuba's first zombie film and the second feature from director Alejandro Brugués. I examine *Juan* in in greater detail in chapter 4, but it is now far from the only example of Cuban science fiction film. Writer Eduardo del Llano had already made several short films in his humorous "Nicanor" series, some with science fiction premises, when he made *Omega* (2015), a feature-length film about warring factions in a postapocalyptic vegetarian society. Elena Palacios Ramé has directed several short films that provide Cuban reworkings of classic science fiction stories by Ray Bradbury and Isaac Asimov.[17] Arturo Infante's *El viaje extraordinario de Celeste García* (Celeste García's extraordinary journey, 2018), Miguel Coyula's *Corazón Azul* (Blue heart, 2021), and José Luis Aparicio's *Tundra* (2021) are the most recent examples of this new strain of Cuban cinema. Many of these films have been made thanks to the shifting conditions of cinematic production in Cuba. If cinema in the early decades of the Revolution was produced almost exclusively under the auspices of the ICAIC, films in the last two decades have increasingly been international coproductions funded by investors both within and outside Cuba, sometimes with the assistance of ICAIC, sometimes completely independently.[18] The growing use of digital technology has reduced costs, making it increasingly possible for directors to film even when the proposed project has not received official approval, as was the case for Coyula's dystopian *Corazón Azul*, an alternate history that imagines a genetically engineered race of Cuban "New Men."[19]

Although Puerto Rico, like Cuba, has a few texts that can be considered precursors of science fiction, namely Alejandro Tapia y Rivera's *Póstumo el transmigrado* (Póstumo the transmigrated, 1872), the first recognized examples of the genre are short stories from Washington Llorén's *El rebelión de los átomos* (The rebellion of the atoms, 1960) and Luis López Nieves's short story "Seva" (1984), which imagines an alternate history for the US invasion of the islands in 1898. For the rest of the twentieth century, however, Puerto Rican literature is dominated by what Ángel Rivera and María Teresa Vera-Rojas identify as identitarian realist literature, concerned largely with "los problemas que acarreaba la modernización de la sociedad puertorriqueña" (595) [the problems brought on by the modernization of Puerto Rican society].

While literature was preoccupied with more realist explorations, the visual art installations of ADÁL (Adál Maldonado, 1948–2020) anticipate the interest in science fiction in Puerto Rico that was to come. ADÁL's photographic series "Coconauts in Space" (1994–2017) uses doctored NASA photographs to craft an alternate history of a first moon landing by Puerto Rican astronauts in 1963. In ADÁL's narrative, the 1967 lunar expedition is shocked to find evidence of this earlier lunar landing. When "Coconauts in Space" was exhibited as part of the *Mundos Alternos: Art and Science Fiction in the Americas* exhibit, it was shown together with the video "Coconauta Interrogation/Intelligence Center."[20] The video purports to be the interrogation of a "humanoid alien" who has been found on the moon. In fact, he is a refugee from Puerto Rico, when "colonial conditions shifted [the] islands' vortex point" causing it to "disappear[r] from the physical dimension." While still focused on the challenges of Puerto Rico's colonial situation, ADÁL's video employs science fiction as a means of exploring the topic from a new perspective.

The new millennium marked the debut of a new generation of writers in Puerto Rico, one interested in thinking thematically beyond questions of national discourse. That was the year in which Pedro Cabiya (b. 1971) published his short story collection *Historias tremendas* under the nom de plume Diego Deni. Cabiya, now a longtime resident of the Dominican

Figure 1. ADÁL (Adál Maldonado), still from "Coconauta Interrogation" (2016).

Republic, has gone on to become a prolific writer of science fiction, with an oeuvre that includes the science fiction–inflected *Historias atroces* (2003), the novels *La cabeza* (2007; *The Head*, 2014), *Trance* (2008), *Malas hierbas* (2011; *Wicked Weeds*, 2016, analyzed in chapter 4), and, most recently, *Tercer Mundo* (2019). He has also experimented with science fiction in other genres, including the graphic novel *Ánima sola* (2012) and the poetry collection *Phantograms* (2013).

If Cabiya's *Historias tremendas* plays with science fiction, Rafael Acevedo's cyberpunk-inflected *Exquisito cadáver* (*Exquisite cadaver*, 2001), which draws on Philip K. Dick's *Do Androids Dream of Electric Sheep?* as well as Ridley Scott's 1984 film adaptation *Blade Runner*, announces its arrival. In addition to his own narrative contributions to the genre, Acevedo has been one of the genre's strongest promoters in Puerto Rico. Together with Melanie Pérez Ortiz, Acevedo has been one of the principal organizers of the Congreso de Ciencia Ficción Caribeña, an event celebrated in San Juan in 2014, 2015, 2016, 2017, 2019, and 2023 that has brought together Puerto Rican science fiction creators, critics, and fans along with writers and critics from Cuba, the Dominican Republic, and the United States. Cabiya's and Acevedo's books were followed by José Liboy Erba's *El Informe Cabrera* (2008).

This first trickle of science fiction production in Puerto Rico became a stream in the following decade. Among those writers whose narrative fiction can be considered science fiction are Gretchen López Ayala (b. 1974), Alejandra Reuhel (b. 1984), Alexandra Pagán Vélez (b. 1978), David Caleb Acevedo (b. 1980), and Pabsi Livmar (b. 1986). The corpus of recent Puerto Rican science fiction also includes several books of poetry, among them John Torres's *Undead* (2013) and Miguel Adrover Lausell's *Quantum Weaver Yocahú* (2015). Although Puerto Rican film has been slower to incorporate science fiction elements, Carla Cavina's *Extraterrestres* (2016) brings a science fictional dimension to what would otherwise be a delicate family drama through a subplot exploring intergenerational attempts to contact alien life on other planets.

In the Dominican Republic, almost no cultural production can be identified as science fiction until 1965. Although nineteenth-century narratives such as Francisco Javier Ángulo Guridi's *La fantasma de Higüey* (The ghost of Higüey, 1857) and *La ciguapa* (1866) explored the fantastic elements of Dominican folklore, realism was the favored mode for narrative fiction produced during the Trujillo dictatorship. Writer Juan Bosch, who briefly succeeded Trujillo as president following the latter's assassination in 1961, was well known for his realist narratives depicting rural Dominican life. Critics consider Efraim Castillo's (b. 1940) short novel *Inti huamán, o Eva again* (1968) to be the first science fiction novel published in the Dominican Republic. But while individual short stories with science fiction elements can be found in *Más allá del espejo* (Beyond the mirror, 1975) by Virgilio Díaz Grullón (1924–2001) and *Todo puede suceder en un día* (Anything can happen in a day, 1984) by Diógenes Valdez (1941–2014) (Leandro Hernández 360), the only full book that could be considered science fiction published in the Dominican Republic between 1968 and 2000 was Josefina de la Cruz's *Una casa en el espacio* (A house in space, 1986), a self-published novel with an edition of 1,500 copies.[21]

Despite this notable lack of literary precursors, interest in science fiction on the Hispanophone side of Hispaniola has boomed in the last two decades. One of the most visible and energetic promotors of the genre as it has emerged in the Dominican Republic has been Odilius Vlak (né Juan Julio Ovando Pujols, b. 1976), author of the short story collections *Exoplanetarium* (2015), *Crónicas historiológicas* (Historiological chronicles, 2017), and *Tintas de plasma* (Plasma inks, 2020) and editor of the first anthology of Dominican science fiction and fantasy literature, *Futuros en el mismo trayecto del sol* (Futures in the line of the sun, 2016). Vlak is also one of the organizers of *Mentes Extremófilas,* a collective of writers and artists that includes the visual artist Eddaviel (né Edison Montero, b. 1988), Morgan Vicconius Zariah (né Jimmy Díaz), Markus E. Goth (né Eddy Jiménez Calderón, b. 1978), and Peter Domínguez (b. 1992) (Rivera and Vera-Rojas 614). The group organized the country's first science fiction conference, which brought together literary and visual creators of the genre in Santo Domingo in 2016. Interest in science fiction in its literary form has also been generated by the Asociación Dominicana de Ficción Especulativa (Dominican Association for Speculative Fiction, ADFE). Founded in 2016 by Rodolfo Báez (b. 1983), Marcus E. Goth, Moisés Santana Castro (b. 1984), Yubany Alberto Checo Estévez (b. 1975), and Francis Santos (Rivera and Vera-Rojas 615), the group received initial support from the Cuban writer Eduardo Heras León, who assisted the group in establishing what was essentially a Cuban-styled writing workshop. In addition to publishing its own anthology of speculative fiction, *De galipotes y robots: Primera selección de la Asociación Dominicana de Ficción Especulativa* (Of werewolves and robots: First anthology of the Dominican Association for Speculative Fiction, 2019), the group launched a small press, Últimos Monstruos Editores, dedicated to publishing new science fiction and speculative fiction as well as new editions of older works.

Perhaps the most visible Dominican creator to incorporate science fiction in their work is Rita Indiana, who experimented with elements of science fiction in her short fiction collection *Ciencia succión* (2001) and her novel *Papi* (2005) before publishing *La mucama de Omicunlé* (2015; *Tentacle,* 2018), a wild postapocalyptic fable that combines a science fictional time-travel premise with elements of Afro-Caribbean spirituality. In addition to her literary production, Indiana is widely known as a musician whose work combines popular music and traditional Dominican rhythms, and she also incorporates science fiction elements in the videos of her songs, most notably "La hora de volver" (from *El juidero,* 2009) and "Como un dragon" (from *Mandinga Times,* 2020), both produced by Puerto Rican director Noelia Quintero Herencia. I examine Indiana's work in greater detail in chapter 5 and the epilogue. However, she is not the only Dominican musician to incorporate science fiction themes. In 2021, the electronic dance music trio MULA released their album *Mundos,* which includes the single "Ciborg." The album cover features a trio of female cyborgs, eyes covered with translucent bands and submerged in water up to their shoulders.

In the last decade, science fiction in the Dominican Republic has increasingly reached a wider viewing public through popular film. Historically, the country has not had a robust cinematic tradition; though a Cineteca Nacional (National Film Library) was founded in 1979, a lack of funding historically hampered the Dominican film industry. However, the 2010 Ley de Cine (Law Nos. 108-10, the "Film Law"), passed during the presidency of Leonel Fernández, legislated more sustained governmental support as well as the promise of increased visibility for national film production (Tolentino and Tomé 10). The recent trend in transnational cinematic coproduction, a practice that helps ensure funding for films, has allowed for a sharp uptick in the number of films—and the number of critically lauded films—to be produced in the country in the last few years. Despite the financial challenges of producing science fiction films, a number of recent Dominican films center on a science fiction–inflected premise, among them *Arrobá* (Enraptured, José María Cabral, 2013), analyzed in chapter 4, and *Melocotones* (Peaches, Héctor Váldez, 2017), both of which deal with time machines, and *OVNI* (UFO, Raúl Marchand Sánchez, 2017), about the arrival of an extraterrestrial.

A "Mestiza" Science Fiction

This narrative has treated the development of science fiction–inflected cultural production in Cuba, Puerto Rico, and the Dominican Republic as discrete histories, and, until recently, this has largely been the case. Although science fiction may be read and watched widely, science fiction production through the early 2000s was driven by local communities of creators and fans. This national specificity has been reified by the critical attention the genre has received in each context, which has also tended to focus on identifying national histories. In recent years, however, any previous tendency toward national isolation seems to be shifting toward a broader, transnational community of Caribbean creators and consumers of science fiction.

At the 2022 Feria del Libro de Santo Domingo (Santo Domingo Book Fair), the ADFE sponsored a number of events related to Latin American and Caribbean speculative fiction. One of them was particularly significant: *Prietopunk 2.0*, held in the Centro Domínico-Alemán, was an exhibit of visual artwork inspired by "Afrofuturist" literary works, many of them from the recently released anthology *Prietopunk: antología de afrofuturismo caribeño* (Prietopunk: Anthology of Caribbean Afrofuturism, 2021). Self-published by Aníbal Hernández Medina, the collection's Dominican editor and a member of the ADFE, the collection includes an introduction by Hernández Medina, a critical essay by Cuban author Erick Mota, and eighteen pieces of short fiction by authors from Cuba, Puerto Rico, and the Dominican Republic, as well as a Spanish translation of Dominican American writer Junot Díaz's story "Monstro." To date, the anthology and its accompanying art exhibition represent the first explicitly Afrofuturist group project in Hispanic Caribbean cultural production.

The term "Afro-futurism" (hyphenated) was first introduced by Mark Dery in "Black to the Future," a 1993 interview with the writers Samuel R. Delany, Greg Tate, and Tricia Rose, in which Dery questions the relative absence of African Americans in science fiction, both as creators and as characters. "Why do so few African-Americans write science fiction, a genre whose close encounters with the other—the stranger in the strange land—would seem uniquely suited to the concerns of African-American novelists?" (179–80). Afro-futurism is the term Dery uses to describe future-focused (science fictional) narratives centered on the stories of African Americans, and he (retroactively) identifies the American writers Delany, Octavia Butler, and Charles Saunders as Afrofuturists. Since Dery's essay, writers and artists have consciously adopted the label of Afrofuturism (which now appears unhyphenated). Choreographer and filmmaker Ytasha Womak, herself a declared Afrofuturist, sees Afrofuturism as encompassing critical, narrative, aesthetic, and even activist practices: "Whether through literature, visual arts, music, or grassroots organizing, Afrofuturists redefine culture and notions of blackness for today and the future. Both an artistic aesthetic and a framework for critical theory, Afrofuturism combines elements of science fiction, historical fiction, speculative fiction, fantasy, Afrocentricity, and magic realism with non-Western beliefs. In some cases, it's a total re-envisioning of the past and speculation about the future rife with cultural critiques" (9). Womak's definition of Afrofuturism relates to what critic Yomaira Figueroa-Vásquez has called "worlds/otherwise," which she understands both as "fashion[ing] new possibilities for Black life and ways of being in the world" and as "engaging the apocalyptic ends of worlds birthed by the non-ethics of modernity, coloniality, and settler colonialism" (148). While Womak's Afrofuturism may be more utopian in its aims and more specifically focused on technology and science fiction, both concepts are concerned with engaging the imagination in the sense that Arjun Appadurai understands it, as "a staging ground for action" (7).

Although literature from the Anglophone Caribbean by writers such as Nalo Hopkinson and Tobias Buckell has been recognized as exhibiting

Afrofuturist characteristics, many of the early science fiction texts from the Hispanophone Caribbean do not explicitly engage with issues of race or racial identity.[22] The desire of *Prietopunk*'s contributors to overtly identify their anthology as Afrofuturist and to engage with race or racialized culture in their narratives is thus significant. Yet as I examine in greater detail elsewhere, the *Prietopunk* anthology puts forward an idea of Afrofuturism, both in its introductory essays and in the short fiction selected for inclusion, that diverges from Womak's understanding of Afrofuturism as "redefin[ing] culture and notions of blackness for today and the future."[23] The stories in *Prietopunk* generally reflect racially mixed scenarios, and the "Afro" of these future imaginaries is frequently represented through African-derived religious elements rather than through the explicit racial identification of its protagonists.

Cuban author Erick Mota suggested in a recent lecture that the Hispanophone Caribbean's unique racial and cultural constructions have produced an Afrofuturism that differs from the US version, "una CF mestiza, que se centra en la mezcla [cultural]" ("Afrofuturismo") [a *mestiza* science fiction, centered on the (Caribbean's) cultural mixture]—thus explaining the use of the term "prieto" in *Prietopunk*. Yet if it fails to be a completely Afrocentric project, *Prietopunk*'s creation nonetheless reveals the willingness of Caribbean writers and artists to use science fiction to engage challenging questions around cultural identity, just one of the issues that science fiction texts explore. The anthology also stands as a testament to the presence of an increasingly collective spirit among Cuban, Puerto Rican, and Dominican creators, as well as to the ways in which creative imaginings are centered on the region. No longer confined to single island spaces, these writers, artists, directors, and musicians are increasingly drawing on multilayered collective histories as they explore collaborative and dialogic ways to engage the future possible. In the next chapter, I examine just what some of those future projections do and how their temporal disruptions function.

2

The View from the Future Possible

The first frame of the music video for Cuban jazz pianist Harold López-Nussa's version of "El buey cansao" ("The tired ox," 2020) informs the viewer that the year is 2220.[1] Instead of music, we hear a low hum, similar to a computer fan. Against a cloudy white backdrop of undulating, neon-like lines, three young women, clad in futuristic, metallic-looking ensembles, snap to attention, as if by mechanical command. They move forward in unison through the luminous void, and we see that they are being pulled forward by a VHS videocassette tape whose worn label has "El buey cansao" written in red marker. The stickers covering its outside—for the Pac-Man video game; the film *Back to the Future* (1985); Naranjito, the 1982 World Cup mascot; and the original cover of Cuban supergroup Los Van Van's album *El baile del buey cansao* (The dance of the tired ox, 1982)—firmly date the object to the 1980s. The videocassette and the women are all propelled forward toward a mysterious figure, face hidden, seated on a throne-like chair whose wavy outlines echo the shape of the void. A move of the figure's hand pauses this forward movement. Another move of the hand activates the tape, and—seemingly without need of a machine—it begins to broadcast into the air in front of them. The tape replays the recording of a dance competition show, "*Tira tu pasillo*" (Show off your steps). Three couples compete in front of a live band (López-Nussa's trio, plus the singer Cimafunk) playing "El buey cansao" whose members wear clothing suggestive of the early 1980s. As the pairs dance for the show, the three women in 2220 echo the dancing, their movements strangely automated, and the viewer soon recognizes the robot women from the future as the physical doubles of the female dancers in *Tira tu pasillo*. The show's competition progresses and two of the couples are gradually eliminated; their robot doppelgängers then freeze and are erased, as if fading from a computer screen. After the remaining couple on the taped show has celebrated their win, the seated figure in 2220 slowly stands to eject the tape. Dressed in a strange, ragged, egg-shaped garment that moves around her almost independently, she turns to face the audience, revealing herself as Cuban actress and dancer Rebeca Martínez. The camera moves in for a close-up, and Martínez raises her head to look directly at the viewer with a knowing smile. The camera then cuts abruptly to the end credits and to Martínez, now dressed in a costume identical to the one worn by the female robot dancers. She begins to imitate the stylized footwork of the dancers as she dances off alone into the void.

López-Nussa's video for "El buey cansao" gestures toward the past through the vision of a possible future. The spare, almost dreamlike, setting of the video's 2220 metanarrative stands in stark contrast to—and makes a further spectacle of—the performances of Cimafunk, López-Nussa, and his trio in the videocassette, whose "1980s" setting recalls the first version of the song released by Los Van Van in 1982 as "El baile del buey cansao" on their eponymous album.[2] (As if confirming this reference, an image of Los Van Van's original leader Juan Formell flashes on the screen just as the *Tira tu Pasillo* begins broadcasting.) The seamless, nearly invisible technology of the 2220 setting emphasizes the scruffy, "retro" feel of the videocassette tape, which López-Nussa's video highlights by reproducing the effect of a tape's scratchy playback.

Yet both the past and the future seem tinged with nostalgia. There is a certain longing inherent in revisiting the idyllic space of the 1980s dance show, set as it is at a moment in Cuba's history before the abrupt break in prosperity and the revolutionary narrative created by the arrival of the Special Period. In this context, the videocassette, today an outmoded technology (few of us still own VHS players) appears as a kind of technological Proustian madeleine, covered with evocative mnemonics for a viewer alive in the 1980s. But the 2220 setting also contains a nostalgic longing in its retrofuturist aesthetic, as its clean white setting recalls the interior of the space station in Stanley Kubrick's *2001: A Space Odyssey* (1968); it is the future imagined from a space-age past. The appearance of Martínez connects these two nostalgic moments, especially for Cuban viewers of a certain age. In the video, Martínez is the protagonist of the 2220 world, yet her own career as a dancer took off when she was "discovered," in the 1980s, on the dance show *Para Bailar* (on which the fictional *Tira tu Pasillo* is undoubtedly based), dancing to Los Van Van. Her presence in the future scenario, like the aesthetic references to Kubrick's film, keeps the supposedly future moment looking backward.

Svetlana Boym reminds us that nostalgia, though seemingly a longing for place, is always about time, specifically about a rejection of "the time of

Figure 2. Robot dancers in the video for Harold López-Nussa's "El buey cansao" (2020).

history and progress": "The nostalgic desires to obliterate history and turn it into private or collective mythology, to revisit time like space, refusing to surrender to the irreversibility of time that plagues the human condition" (xv). As a device designed to hold a performance in wait for a future spectator, the videocassette (and, indeed, the video recording) would seem the perfect vehicle for the nostalgic enterprise. The futuristic metanarrative in López-Nussa's video effectively stages a giving in to those nostalgic desires, creating a scene in which Martínez, as a kind of stand-in for the viewer, dwells on and, through the robot dancers, "re-creates" the 1980s dance. The technology of 2220, which manages to "play back" the 1980s cassette without the need for a VHS player, allows the tape to function as a kind of time machine.

Yet if the past and future scenes in López-Nussa's video are tinged with nostalgia, so, too, are both the past and the future performances in which the present is implicated, if invisible. For the video's 1980s are not purely the 1980s. The jazz elements of López-Nussa's cover of the song, along with Cimafunk's vocal improvisations, elongate the song's tempo; even from within the "retro" framework of the videocassette staging, this new version of the song declares its contemporariness, its temporal and sonic distance from Los Van Van's version. Cimafunk comments in an aside, "Este es un clásico" [This is a classic], a statement that separates the staged moment of this "1980s" setting from the song's actual release in 1982. Martínez is, in a sense, the key to the video's temporal play, for she does not remain merely a passive viewer, using the video's performance to linger on daydreams about the past. Present in all three times, her character at the end frees the music to circulate in the future moment of 2220, reminding the viewer that it is the music that matters and that we are more than passive listeners.

López-Nussa's video provides a primer for understanding the function of science fiction's future possible temporality. Nostalgia and science fiction share a similar impulse, a desire to break away from the fixity (and certainty) of the present, to inhabit an alternative time. Nor is nostalgia always focused exclusively on the past; as Boym notes, "it can be retrospective but also prospective" (xvi). But if nostalgic time "is that time-out-of-time of daydreaming and longing" (Boym xix), science fiction's future possible, "what has not [yet] happened," as Samuel Delany terms it ("About 5,750 Words" 11), moves forward, widening the horizon for the new (and unexpected), and shifting our view of the present and the nature of *this* moment in the process. Combining the "daydream" of the 1980s with the futuristic metanarrative, López-Nussa's video allows the viewer raised in the 1980s their moment of nostalgic "recreation" but does let them linger there. When Martínez breaks the video's fourth wall with a knowing wink and dances off into the distance, the very openness of the void both returns the viewer to the present and reminds them of their own potential for action. As it does so, the video shifts the viewer's perspective of not only the recent past but also their fixity in relation to the present. Taking the video's temporal exchange as a starting point, this chapter explores the ways in which recent Caribbean narratives use science fiction—specifically, the presence of a future possible—as a tool to destabilize narrative temporality.

Scholars since Aristotle have recognized temporality as a constitutive element of narrative structure. Mikhail Bakhtin signals to the fundamental relationship between time and narrative through his term "chronotope," which for him encapsulates "the intrinsic interconnectedness of temporal and spatial relationships that are artistically expressed in literature" (84). Paul Ricoeur sees narrative in a larger sense as a way to understand and reflect on time: "[T]ime becomes human to the extent that it is articulated through a narrative mode, and narrative attains its full meaning when it becomes a condition of temporal existence" (52). But as Ricoeur observes, how stories are told and how they are received is culturally encoded: "To understand a story is to understand both the language of 'doing something' and the cultural tradition from which proceeds the typology of plots" (56). Narrative is the medium through which we mediate our relationship to time, but it also shapes the way in which we perceive temporal experience in the first place. Building on Ricoeur's conception of the relationship between time and narrative, in her study of the contemporary novel Ursula Heise argues that shifts in novelistic form reflect our changing relationship with time. Heise posits that the "postmodernist" novel is "a way of dealing aesthetically with an altered culture of time in which access to the past and especially the future appears more limited than before in cultural self-awareness" (67). At the same time, "postmodern novels in their turn help to create the cultural lenses through which we perceive and interpret social and technological developments" (6). It is easy to see how what we know is a framework for the possibilities we can imagine. Yet what we imagine also has a way of shifting how we (re)interpret what is in front of us.

As a genre not unrelated to realism, science fiction could also be said to reflect the temporal and cultural anxieties of its creators. Darko Suvin observes that the term "science fiction" "does not imply only a reflecting of but also *on* reality. It implies a creative approach tending toward a dynamic transformation rather than a static mirroring of the author's environment" ("On the Poetics" 377). Suvin's definition of science fiction as responding to our current perception of the real reaffirms the ways in which the genre's speculation and invention are always in relation—building upon or reacting to—our experience of reality. Yet the inherently subjunctive, speculative nature of the genre unlocks the potential of the text to push back against what is perceived to be, to suggest alternative possibilities. Because, as Samuel Delany notes, "[i]n science fiction the world of the story is not a given, but rather a construct that changes from story to story" ("Science Fiction and 'Literature'" 69), science fiction has greater freedom with which to reimagine these relationships.

In this chapter, I examine the temporally disruptive potential of science fiction in recent cultural production through the ways in which the genre functions as ab-realism, a term coined by the critic Sheryl Vint to describe the fiction of British writer China Miéville, a style that combines what might be understood to include both science fictional and fantastic narrative elements. Highlighting the definition of "ab" as "outside of" or "beyond," Vint defines ab-realism as "a narrative logic that simultaneously captures the absurdities of 'real' life under capitalism *and* points to the power of narrative to activate the utopian traces of another world that is possible and coexists with this one" ("Ab-realism" 41). Building on Miéville's assertion that science fiction is less about true scientific logic or cognition than it is about the text's own persuasive logic, "*something done with language by someone to someone"* (Miéville 238, emphasis in original), Vint argues that ab-realism reveals the ways in which much of the "reality" of our world is constructed, highlighting the "gap between mimetic realism and 'reality'" (41).[3] This "gap" is a gap both in terms of what is represented and in terms of how it is represented vis-à-vis narrative temporality; as Miéville notes, by calling attention to the constructed nature of the present, ab-realism thus turns the tables on the hierarchical understanding of "reality" as somehow opposed to—superior to—the future possible.

Caribbean texts that employ ab-realism are explicitly engaged in exposing the constructed nature of both our experience of the present and our understanding of the past. In this way, they intervene in Caribbean cultural production in temporally disruptive ways, pulling the reader or viewer out of their narrative comfort zones and creating spaces for imagining alternative possibilities. In the same way that Martínez's presence in the video's 2220 metanarrative acts to destabilize both the video's re-created vision of the past and our (invisible, elided) present, the ab-real in Caribbean narratives makes visible the collective fantasies that readers may have taken as truths and reveals their constructed nature. As it does so, it opens a space in the text for a new horizon of the future possible.

To further illuminate the ways in which the ab-real fashions a space for the future possible, in what remains of this chapter I examine three additional texts that, like López-Nussa's video, introduce science fiction into spheres in which it was not previously present: Dominican writer Odilius Vlak's short story collection *Crónicas historiológicas* (Historiological chronicles, 2017), Puerto Rican writer José "Pepe" Liboy's novel *El Informe Cabrera* (The Cabrera report, 2008), and Cuban director Arturo Infante's film *El viaje extraordinario de Celeste García* (Celeste García's extraordinary journey, 2018). None of these texts is set in a new world or on a different planet; all of them take place in a present or future Caribbean. Yet in each of these narratives, the introduction of science fiction's future possible becomes a retroactive, ab-real lens that troubles established understandings of national histories and events, plays with current ideas of the nation, and reframes the reader's perception of literary and cultural canons. Whether through a contrast between a future reality and a present one or the insertion of the future possible in what was an established historical narrative, science fiction in these texts calls into question the fixity of the collective constructions the reader or viewer has accepted as reality. As they do so, these texts shift our understanding of stereotypical national tropes and reframe national narratives, introducing possibilities for displacing, escaping, or altering these narratives, even when these possibilities are frustrated in a given text itself.

Reframing Dominican Histories: Odilius Vlak's *Crónicas historiológicas*

As the title makes clear, Dominican writer Odilius Vlak's *Crónicas historiológicas* is concerned with both what Édouard Glissant might call "History" and "histories": that is, with how the official record has characterized historical events, as well as with how those events are remembered and (re)interpreted (*Caribbean Discourse* 93). Vlak, the nom de plume of Juan Julio Ovando Pujols (b. 1976), is one of the most active members of the new generation of Dominican science fiction creatives. Although they can be read as single stories, the chronicles are referred to by Vlak as a "cycle" (Vilar Madruga). Interlocking pieces of a larger narrative, they are all set in the same world, the Dominican Republic in the twenty-second century. In Vlak's vision of the future, his country has become a part of the highly developed world run by a "mitotecnocracia" (mythotechnocracy), under whose governance the city of Santo Domingo is a model not only of technological development but also of aesthetic standards. Yet as the term "mythotechnocracy" might indicate, technological development in this future Hispaniola is a fascinating mix of what a reader in the twenty-first century might understand as the scientific alongside the mythical or the fantastic. Scientists are now "psientíficos," a title in which the inclusion of the "ps" (suggestive of "pseudo") denotes not only a shift in outlook or method but also, possibly, a position between an assertion of scientific reason and the reliance on those areas beyond science. Governmental institutions engage in "las políticas del *Realismo Fantástico*" (27) [the politics of *Fantastic Realism*], a term that seems to reference Carpentier's "marvelous real," with the stated goal of "diseñar un presente salido de las mentes que piensan en el futuro y rescatar los elementos míticos del material histórico registrado" (27) [designing a present from the minds of those who think about the future and rescuing the mythical elements from the registered historical material].[4] The desire to "rescue" mythical elements suggests that in this future Santo Domingo "myth" and "history" are granted something closer to equal status. Historical events are studied not only so that Dominican citizens can learn more about them but also so that interested citizens can experience them through the vivid simulations of a virtual reality network. *Historias Patrias,* the virtual reality game in which players can participate in historic events—a kind of *Second Life* version of what historical reenactors do now in real life—is not only extremely popular but is supported by the work of governmental institutions such as the Academy of Historiology. The use of the term "historiology" in the title of this institution is significant; as Samuel Ginsburg has observed, rather than—or in addition to—the study of historical events themselves, Vlak is profoundly interested in the construction of historical narratives ("Future Visions" 12). The creation of a future Dominican society preoccupied with the historical past allows him to creatively explore the relationship between the two eras, even as his own writing visibly inserts science fiction into the Dominican literary narrative.

Like Santo Domingo's "mythotechnocracy," Vlak's chronicles are a fascinating mix of the scientific, the science fictional, the mythic, and the literary. "Descargas de meteoritos en la batalla del 19 de marzo" ("Meteorite showers in the Battle of March 19th"), the first story in Vlak's collection, centers precisely on the tension between historical events, their material traces, and the historical record. The narrative's protagonists, Luís Eduardo Moquete and Blaise Reynord Deligne, are two researchers—*psientíficos*—tasked with investigating the possibility that the Dominican army won a crucial battle in the Dominican Republic's War of Independence from Haiti (1844–56) in part thanks to the possession of a powerful military technology in the form of a piece of meteorite capable of producing explosions similar to those of canon fire. The two researchers have obtained a rock fragment that is supposedly part of this meteorite. In addition to analyzing the stone itself, their job is to mine the historical record for evidence of the meteorite and its powers. Combing through historical documents, including eyewitness accounts of the conflict, which took place on 19 March 1844, in Ázua, in the country's southwestern region, they find references to the stone not only in the colonial record but also as far back as legends of the Indigenous Taínos. Historical documents suggest that the meteorite and its force field have been present at—and played a role in—crucial moments throughout Dominican history.

In creating the archival record of a fictitious meteorite, Vlak makes ingenious use of real historical sources. The "pscientists" find evidence of the powerful stone in Columbus's diaries, in Hernán Cortés's chronicles, and even in a (retouched) national anthem, with Vlak's text borrowing from these original sources. This play with history highlights the constructed—and fragile—nature of the historical record itself. Ginsburg argues, "By injecting speculative elements into such significant moments in Dominican history, Vlak critiques how histories are created, sold, and mythologized, while also highlighting the role of counter-narratives in contesting official accounts" ("Future Visions" 12). The deft and seamless way in which Vlak inserts a science fictional dimension into actual written history may leave readers asking how many other fictions may have been solidified as "fact" and made to form part of a historical record.

Yet "Descargas" is about more than questioning the construction of histories. In addition to what the existence of these science fictional elements within the historical narrative suggests about reframing Dominican identity or history, Vlak's story pushes readers to engage with the future possible in a concrete material sense. The story begins with the introduction of a purely science fictional object, what Suvin calls a *novum* (*Metamorphosis* 63), in this case, a piece of rock that has been determined to come from a meteorite. Although they will go on to explore the presence of the meteorite in the written record, as the story opens Luis and Blaise are engaged in a physical analysis of the rock itself. The story's first sentences emphasize what Seo-Young Chu would term the "high-intensity" description that pulls the reader into this new reality:[5]

> El enjambre de nanobots se extendió nuevamente sobre el espacio del ionograma que proyectaban desde el averno de moléculas alienígenas del pedazo de roca que analizaban. Ésta flotaba sobre una red de filamentos de plasma a mitad de una esfera cristalina dentro de la cual bullía un pandemónium de iones; los cuales, a manera de atmósfera, servían para reflejar las ondas electromagnéticas que los nanobots transmitían desde el interior de la roca y a través de la estructura atómica de la esfera de cristal. (9)

> [The swarm of nanobots extended itself again over the space of the ionogram that they projected from the abyss of alien molecules of the piece of rock they were analyzing. The rock itself floated above a network of plasma filaments in the middle of a crystalline sphere, inside of which a pandemonium of ions was buzzing. Acting like a kind of atmosphere, these served to reflect the electromagnetic waves that the nanobots transmitted from the interior of the rock and through the atomic structure of the crystal sphere.]

Here the text pauses to engage the reader in the performance of a "cognition effect," forcing them to consider the "scientific" elements of the process of analysis. The careful description of the swarm of nanobots and the sphere in which the meteorite is held are almost cinematic in nature.

In contrast to recent science fiction narratives (including some explored in this study) that focus on the human experience of new worlds rather than the functioning of technology and scientific gadgetry, Vlak's text takes great pains to both explain something of how the analysis of the meteorite works and to situate these processes within the narrative. Alongside the two pscientists' careful study of the meteorite's physical properties, the banter between them as they examine the object includes references to string theory, chaos theory, and the butterfly effect, as if to underline that *science is happening here*.

Yet while the text insists on the scientific nature of this future environment, the two colleagues introduce other information into their conversation; they mention both Frank Herbert (author of the science fiction novel *Dune*) and H. P. Lovecraft, treating these authors as if they were also disseminators of scientific knowledge. When Blaise observes that the legends surrounding the Dominican meteorite share something with Lovecraft's short story "The Colour Out of Space," a text that is, in fact, about a meteorite that crashes in a desolate part of Massachusetts and ends up poisoning or destroying everything near it, Luis responds that this is a, "[r]eferencia idónea para pasar a la fase histórica de la investigación" (15), [suitable reference to pass along to the historical phase of this investigation]. This would seem to indicate that the intellectual environment in which Blaise and Luis are operating is one in which Lovecraft's tales of horror have acquired something close to the same knowledge status as historical narratives. Indeed, as Blaise goes on to clarify, alongside *Historias Patrias*, the official immersive virtual game produced and sanctioned by the Academy of History, there exists a second game, *Mitos Patrios*, which offers a version of history that does not discount the "mythological, legendary, or paranormal" elements that might surround a historical episode (15). If not as respected as *Historias Patrias*, the existence of *Mitos Patrios* indicates that this new Dominican society reserves space for narratives that would have been previously rejected as plainly false.

As the two pscientists explore the history of the meteorite, they must indeed delve into the more mythic elements of the meteorite's story. The Taínos (the island's Indigenous inhabitants) referred to the stone as "la lagrima del padre Yúcahu" [Father Yúcahu's Tear], a gift from the god Yúcahu to the Taíno people. The Spanish conquistadors who come in search of the stone are following that legend. For the knowledgeable reader, the stone's connections to Taíno religious history link it to an important episode in more contemporary Dominican histories both political and spiritual. The place most connected to the meteorite in Taíno mythology is the kingdom of Maguana. (Vlak plays here with the fact that "Maguana" supposedly translates to "the first stone, the only stone" in the Taíno language.) In the early twentieth century, San Juan de la Maguana was home to Olivorio Mateo, a popular faith healer known as "Papá Liborio," whose healing practices formed the center of an alternative community. Believing him to be a threat to US security during the occupation of the country, US marines murdered Mateo in 1922, but Liborio served as the inspiration for another millenarian movement with anti-imperialist overtones in the same site in the early 1960s, and he continues to be a popular religious figure in the region.[6] Although Vlak's text does not mention Papá Liborio by name, the story of the meteorite reaffirms the national spiritual significance of San Juan de la Maguana.

The last step of Luis and Blaise's investigation adds an additional layer of subjectivity. Once they have concluded their investigation, their report is fed into the "Simulador Visual Semántico" [Semantic Visual Simulator], a machine that creates a version of the event in front of a live audience. If the audience responds favorably to the simulation, the event will have the opportunity to be turned into a part of the *Mitos Patrios* experience. In the case of the meteorite and the battle in Ázua, the experience is a resounding success; spectators are able to witness how the meteorite, upon coming into contact with the body of a Haitian soldier, "se expandió, devorando toda la carne en un relampagueante destello violeta" (33) [expanded, devouring all of the flesh in a violet flash of light]. The goals of the company sponsoring the performance are both pedagogical and financial: "La reacción positiva de los ciudadanos era la señal de que los aspectos fantásticos rescatados de tal trozo de historia serían rentables para la compañía y funcionales para el mantenimiento de la conciencia histórica nacional" (29) [The citizens' positive reaction was the sign that the fantastic aspects rescued from this slice of history would be profitable for the company and functional for the maintenance of national historical consciousness.] The vision of history produced by these games is thus shaped not only by what is deemed historically significant by experts but also by audience popularity, by what "replays well."

Even as it forces us to reckon with the constructed nature of historical narrative and the historical archive, Vlak's text forces us to reconsider the significance of the historical events themselves: What might it mean if the battle of March 19th really *had* been won with the help of a powerful stone from outer space rather than military strategy? What does it mean to consider that the stone was a fundamental part of the religious practices of the Taíno chiefs? Does knowing that autochthonous Indigenous ritual practice on the island was anchored in something otherworldly change our understanding of what might be understood to be "native" and what constitutes "religion" or "magic"? Could the "mythic" or "magical" be considered scientific when seen from another angle? This last question seems to be one of the conclusions that Blaise and Luis reach as they conclude their investigations into the meteorite. The stone's power, derived from space, not magic, explains many of the "magical" elements of both the legends and the historical narratives surrounding the stone. In exploring the complicated relationship between history and myth, Vlak pushes the reader to question the values they assign to certain "truths," to expand their understanding of the possible.

Vlak's narrative introduces a revolutionary idea: that nineteenth-century battles for independence were sites of space-age technology. The text's insertion of science fiction into a historical event, manipulation of the historical narrative, and expansion of what might be considered part of the scientific record all create space for thinking about new and different trajectories for Dominican histories. Despite these radical possibilities, however, I would like to point out the ways in which Vlak's vision of a future Dominican Republic hews to some quite conservative notions of Dominican identity. First, the narrative of history that Blaise and Luis are investigating—and which appears to be the one presented by the *Historias Patrias* game—seems to center on large national historical events and on "patriotic" moments. Given that the meteorite's story connects pre-Colombian Indigenous history on the island with the writing of Columbus and early Spanish conquistadors, the presence of the meteorite as the throughline that connects the two groups serves to legitimate the Spanish and their descendants as the "rightful heirs" of this Indigenous technology. As both Dixa Ramírez and Néstor E. Rodríguez have shown, beginning in the nineteenth century, Columbus became a kind of symbolic figurehead for a particular kind of Eurocentric Dominican nationalism: "Skipping over three centuries of Spanish disregard, these nationalists returned to the conquest as it reminded them and the rest of the world that Santo Domingo was the founding site of European 'civilization' in the hemisphere" (Ramírez 117). Despite the expansive presence of myth, the histories that are explored via the virtual reality simulation games seem to be those dominated by male, *criollo* elites, people of both name and stature.[7] It is not clear how much space these narratives give to women, enslaved Africans, and free people of color as protagonists or actors with their own agency. The story's references to art and architecture in the Dominican capital seem to indicate that similarly conservative ideas of classical (European) high culture have prevailed in the aesthetic construction of the urban space; the Dominican Obelisk has been retained (and recovered); it now gives the governmental complex "la apariencia de un ágora en una Grecia del futuro" (27) [the appearance of an agora in a future Greece]. This may be the future, but future ideas of cultural progress and harmony remain extremely close to Latin American fin de siècle ideas of what constitutes both history and high culture.

The focus on Dominican history—specifically, colonial and nineteenth-century Dominican history—points to another lacuna in this future vision: where is Haiti in relation to the Dominican Republic in the twenty-fifth century? Although Blaise's name suggests possible Haitian ancestry, the nation occupying the other half of Hispaniola is conspicuously absent, except as a battlefield rival five centuries previously. Has Haiti been absorbed into the Dominican Republic, creating a single island nation, or are conflicts between the two countries still sources of tension?

The virtual reality simulations of Dominican History are supposedly designed to win over the hearts and minds of young Dominicans, "cada vez más identificada con la historia que los pioneros espaciales estaban escribiendo con sus hazañas más allá de las fronteras del Sistema Solar" (29) [who identified more and more with the history that the space pioneers were writing with their deeds beyond the borders of the solar system]. What makes a maintenance of the national imaginary important in this future, globalized context? If young Dominicans in 2525 are looking toward the stars, the desire to return to and reanimate narratives from the nation's past would seem to reflect back to the anxieties of the Dominican present. Carl Freedman argues that science fiction is the genre closest to historical realism; both are concerned with historical development/temporality, yet unlike historical realism, science fiction has the advantage of being free (to a certain extent) of the weight of the past: "[science fiction's] primary orientation ... is toward the future; it is thus capable of engaging the matter of historicity without the same kind of post-1848 ideological baggage that the historical novelist carries" (57). Ramírez argues convincingly for the ways in which Dominican cultural performances are designed to create visibility in an international arena in which the country has been "ghosted," particularly by US awareness, and the insistence on the "Dominicanness" of Vlak's future environment could be read as another gesture in this vein.[8] With its mixture of the factual and the fantastic, "Batallas del desierto" reveals the way in which national histories are also (intimate) fictions. Yet, in the end, this imagined future also finds itself trapped by well-established collective fantasies.

Twisted Tales and Tangled Origins: *El Informe Cabrera*

Nothing is what it seems in *El Informe Cabrera*, Puerto Rican writer José "Pepe" Liboy's 2009 novel. The book begins as a letter from a Manuel Molina to his unborn son. However, Molina's son's birth is not, as it turns out, imminent; we soon learn that his son may not be born until perhaps a hundred years after his father's death, through a scientifically engineered conception in an advanced center for embryology in Puerto Rico's interior. We are in a future Puerto Rico, one in which families use genetic engineering to combat increasingly prevalent birth defects and where babies are planned and "born" in a center for embryology deep in the mountains of the island. Given this futuristic scenario, it becomes clear that Molina's letter to his son will be more than a simple epistolary memoir. Alongside the personal narrative culminating in plans for his son's birth, Molina lays out another, future genealogy: the creation of the *informe* itself, a text he identifies as "una especie de novela de ciencia ficción histórica, con algo de tremendismo biográfico" (12) [a kind of novel of historical science fiction, with something of biographical sensationalism]. In the letters, notes, and other diverse texts that make up his "report," he elaborates a list of the "precursors" of this kind of novel, creating his own (retrospective) genealogy of Puerto Rican science fiction. The corpus of Puerto Rican science fiction that he outlines involves nineteenth-century authors whose work was never recognized as science fiction as well as Liboy's own literary contemporaries, writers such as Rafael Acevedo (b. 1960), Aravind Adyanthaya (b. 1965) and Yara Liceaga (b. 1972). Molina's "report" on the planning and creation of his biological child thus becomes simultaneously a meditation on the tangled genealogies of literary inheritance, an exploration of the limits of genre, and a proposal for future creation both biological and literary.

Participation in alternative literary communities is nothing new for Liboy. Although *El Informe Cabrera* is his first novel, by the time it was published he was already well known in Puerto Rico for his short stories, both those in the collection *Cada vez te despides mejor* (2003) and single stories that had appeared in a number of anthologies.[9] According to Juan Carlos Quintero Herencia, Liboy is one of a group of writers who have rejected the dominant norms of the Puerto Rican literary scene, forming a literary community based on otherness (a kind of outsider status) and a divergence from both the discourses and the practices of the Puerto Rican literary scene. Juan Duchesne Winter, who has named this group—which includes the writers Yara Liceaga and Eduardo Lalo, among others—"los raros" [the strange ones], asserts that their writing intentionally challenges the Puerto Rican literary status quo (31). Duchesne Winter diagnoses the "strangeness" in their literary production as a survival strategy, one that responds both to the island's colonial condition and to the economic and financial crises that it is currently experiencing.[10] For him, work by "los raros" calls into question "las bases de la representación misma y hace de la dificultad de comprensión inmediata, es decir, de la opacidad, un arma estética y política" (33) [the very bases of representation itself, making the difficulty of immediate understanding—in other words, opacity—a political and aesthetic weapon], in this way producing a contestatory writing that resists the pressures of the dominant literary culture to conform to certain norms or conventions.

El Informe Cabrera exhibits several of the characteristics that Duchesne Winter identifies as typical of this "strange" Puerto Rican writing. The polyphonic construction of Liboy's text, which displays a dense intertextuality through the constant referencing of an extensive group of national and international novelists, poets, critics, and historians, produces a sensation of opacity, particularly for a reader not attuned to the details of local literary and cultural history. Another technique that Duchesne Winter highlights in the work of "los raros" is what he terms "lo real múltiple" [the multiple real], a style of writing that mixes or collapses realist and fantastic elements to produce "una articulación compenetrada de múltiples realidades y zonas de la experiencia donde nada deja de ser real" (36) [an interpenetrated articulation of multiple realities and zones of experience in which nothing stops being real]. Duchesne's definition of the "real multiple" resonates with Vint's idea of the ab-real. The subject matter of Liboy's novel—a child who will be conceived and grown "to term" in a laboratory in the middle of a Caribbean island years after the death of his biological father—offers an example of this narrative technique. Although the narrator is clearly identified as Manuel Molina, there are a number of moments in the text, particularly those that connect to Liboy's contemporaries, when the reader could be forgiven for thinking that the narrator is an alter ego for Liboy himself.[11] In its mixing of details from the author's own life with speculative fictional elements, the narrative uses the future possible to reveal new, speculative dimensions of what has been understood as the real.

Amid the general "strangeness" of Liboy's novel, I find it significant that Molina explicitly identifies the text he is crafting as *science fiction,* an intentional gesture that I argue sets both Molina's—and through him, Liboy's—project apart from narrative techniques that run toward the more simply "strange." Why does Molina (and through him, Liboy) insist on connecting his text with science fiction? Film critic Christine Gledhill observes that "genre is first and foremost a boundary phenomenon" (221), a practice that observes a text's conformity to a certain stylistic mode either to emphasize similarities between that text and others (whether literary or cinematographic) or to highlight differences. For Gledhill, genre's value as a concept resides precisely in what is revealed when a text "breaks" with the established rules of that genre or when it changes the definition of what a particular genre can be. In this way, the study of genre offers a point of entry for examining the connection between a particular text and its sociopolitical and literary context. That Liboy identifies *El Informe Cabrera* as science fiction is thus important for what it tells us about not only the borders between literary genres but also what science fiction represents both within Puerto Rican literature and for Liboy's own readers.

Latin American science fiction, Antonio Córdoba Cornejo notes, has used science fiction's temporal orientation—the gazing toward the future from a present that will soon be the past—to comment on and engage with the past, and Liboy's text would seem to follow this tendency (31). The genre's temporal characteristics give Liboy and his narrator the tools with which to engage problems from Puerto Rican history, but from the distance of a possible future. By explicitly identifying his text as science fiction, Molina (and through him, Liboy) also insists on seeing it as different from mere realism; he deliberately emphasizes its difference, its strangeness or *rareza*.[12] In this way, the characterization of the "report" as a work of "historical science fiction" highlights what separates this work from other narratives; deliberately identifying what we might call the text's deformations, it reflects back to the reader the twisted elements of other, more consecrated histories. Molina's twin narratives, that of his family's relationship to embryology (in the novel's present) and that of science fiction's presence in Puerto Rican literature, allow Liboy to highlight more sinister yet equally hidden histories tied to US control of Puerto Rico. By identifying his text and others as science fictional, Liboy offers science fiction to Puerto Rican literature as a kind of "escape route," a new way of reading (and, for him, writing) a Puerto Rican literature whose communicative capacities reach beyond mere realism. Tracing a canon of Puerto Rican science fiction within the novel, he suggests that this route is not a radically new one but rather an already established—if hidden—local trajectory.

From its first page, *El Informe Cabrera* reveals a preoccupation with origins even as it works to complicate the idea of parentage. In the letter that begins the text, Manuel Molina declares that he is writing to give his son "un informe de los beneficiarios que yo quisiera que tomaras en consideración" (9) [a report on the beneficiaries that I hope you will take into consideration], a statement that implies that Molina will proceed to sketch out a family tree. However, the letter and the documents that follow it reveal a family structure not organized by generation or bloodline. The first "important" person that Molina names is his grandmother. She will be important, however, not only as a matriarchal figure but as an expert on embryology. When it becomes clear that Molina will need the help of science to produce a child, it is his grandmother who informs him that despite the family history of birth defects ("deformities"), he will be able to become a father thanks to a girl who "sería el vaso que permitiría tu nacimiento en caso de que los tiempos fueran adversos a personas como nosotros" (10) [could become the vessel that makes possible your birth in case the moment were adverse toward people like us]. Molina never clarifies what defines "personas como nosotros" [people like us], but this hint of strangeness becomes all the more real for never being explicitly defined. However, the conditionality and indeterminism of his grandmother's statement proves prescient; the "mother" that Molina—or rather, his grandmother—chooses is a kind of false mother, given that she herself turns out to be unable to conceive, since she lives near a contaminated mine. Although another woman is introduced as the boy's future mother later in the text, it never becomes clear whether she will come to fulfill that responsibility. The "lineage" that Molina sketches thus remains hypothetical, indirect, not-yet-realized.

Molina further complicates the idea of genealogy by referring to both embryology and parentage as metaphorical states. He tells his son:

> La experiencia te demostrará que tu destino es más importante que tu sangre, y que la embriología verdadera tiene mucho que ver con esos destinatarios que no participan directamente de tu nacimiento, pero que son como padres silentes, sombras vivas que te rodean y acompañan más allá de la experiencia visible. (10)

> Experience will demonstrate that your destiny is more important than your blood, that true embryology has more to do with those who

don't participate directly in your birth but who are like silent parents, living shadows that surround you and who accompany you beyond visible experience.]

Here Molina appears to downplay the biological principles of genetic inheritance; our formation as individuals, he suggests, has less to do with our cells and genetic makeup than with our psychic formation, with the emotional and spiritual processes of development that we go through, guided by individuals who may or may not be related to us by blood.

Just as Molina presents the reader with divergent conceptions of "inheritance" and "family," it becomes clear that we are also dealing with two different ideas of embryology: the classically scientific practice, and another, which might be identified as local or autocthonous. Molina relates that his paternal grandmother practiced embryology together with *espiritismo* [spiritism], and that she considered "que la embriología insular era una costumbre, un dato folklórico de nuestra isla" (14) [that the island's embryology was a custom, a folkloric aspect of our island]. He describes this science as if it were a local practice, something not necessarily visible but common all the same. Molina says of his work to find Puerto Rican texts that "[t]odo lo que se hablaba de embriología en aquel entonces tenía el carácter de una cultura oral" (42) [everything they said about embryology at that time had the feel of an oral culture], a characteristic that explicitly contrasts with the understanding of advanced science as completely tied to written knowledge. Thanks to its "orality" and its connections to espiritismo, this second, local embryology operates as a "secret" practice—visible but not, perhaps, officially recognized. To think of embryology in this way asks the reader to expand their understanding of what a science can be. Indeed, its orally transmitted nature stands in contrast to the literary (textual) search that Molina himself undertakes to locate references to embryology in the island's literature.

In subverting common narratives of heredity and expanding the definition of embryology, Liboy is both playing with a regional fascination with what Rudyard Alcocer has named "hereditarian discourses" (*Narrative Mutations* 4) and expanding the temporal possibilities of his narrative world. Alcocer argues that Caribbean literature evidences a preoccupation with "kinship, biological origins, and/or racial purity" (4), such that "relationships of heredity and dependence pervade areas not commonly associated with these relationships" (4). As Alcocer has observed elsewhere, heredity itself "operates within a linear temporal framework" (*Time Travel* 4).

By decoupling embryology from the idea of simple linear heredity, Liboy opens the door for thinking about time in general in more flexible ways. If we are not locked into our heredity, we are not locked into other linear relationships of cause and effect. Although Liboy's text does not mention race explicitly, it is hard not to think that by privileging non-consanguine relationships he is sidestepping the Puerto Rican fascination with ideas of racial purity that Alcocer mentions.

Molina's connection of embryology to espiritismo further hints at the presence of alternative models of temporality. A popular religious practice with links to the work of the nineteenth-century philosopher Allan Kardec (né Hippolyte Léon Denizal Rivail), Hispanic Caribbean espiritismo posits a world with two realms of existence, the physical world and the world of spirits, the latter involving those recently deceased and enlightened souls who have remained in spirit form to aid and instruct the living (Espíritu Santo, "Turning" 269). These two worlds are connected by human mediums, who receive messages—knowledge—from the spirit world, either through *misas espirituales* (spiritual masses), spirit possession, or clairvoyance. As Diana Espíritu Santo explains, the knowledge that mediums receive is also a "substance" with its own temporality: "[R]elevant spiritual knowledge is not immanent within or performed by the medium(s) but must be punctually evoked, coaxed into becoming from a state of nonexistence: knowledge accrues, diminishes, is blocked, disappears, hangs suspended, is intermittent, becomes suddenly unavailable, and reacts to situations and people" ("Liquid Sight" 581). In contrast to the linear temporality of Western scientific experimentation and testing, the suggestion of a spiritist embryology suggests a more fluid production of knowledge and the construction of a set of relationships that may be less linear than rhizomatic.[13]

Through Molina's discussion of a Puerto Rican embryology tied to island practices and traditions, Liboy also engages with the history of family planning on the island and its relationship to US colonialism. Historian Laura Briggs argues that since the United States seized control of Puerto Rico at the end of the nineteenth century, "[R]eproduction and sexuality have defined the difference that makes colonialism in Puerto Rico possible and necessary" (4). On consolidating control of the island following the end of the Spanish-American War, the US leadership in Puerto Rico instituted a series of both political and social-control mechanisms, intended to discipline and subjugate Puerto Rican bodies (Santiago-Valles 20). These practices included a concerted effort to control the birth rate on the island through education on family planning and birth control. One of the most politicized methods of birth control was female sterilization. By the mid-1960s, Puerto Rico had one of the highest documented percentages of ever-married sterilized women in the world (Warren et al. 353). While the actual number of sterilizations performed remains unclear, as Briggs has shown, both female fertility and family planning became hot-button issues in the political debates dealing with Puerto Rico's relationship to nationalism, capitalism, poverty, and even modernity (75).

In his study of the relationship between nineteenth-century imperialism and the development of Anglo-American science fiction, John Rieder argues that colonialism is "part of the genre's texture, a persistent, important component of its displaced references to history, its engagement in ideological production, and its construction of the possible and the imaginable" (*Colonialism* 15). If a colonial mindset is responsible for shaping some of science fiction's most common tropes, in *El Informe Cabrera* Liboy turns the genre back on itself; the descriptive possibilities of science fiction become the very tools with which he launches a critique of US colonialism in Puerto Rico. *El Informe Cabrera* returns to the controversial issue of family planning on the islands only to present the ironic reverse of the historical situation; if political powers both external (the United States) and internal struggled to control female fertility and female bodies in the twentieth century, Liboy's novel defines embryology—and, implicitly, family planning—as a local, autochthonous practice, characterized by elements (like espiritismo) that have no connection to "official" external science. Instead of showing us a national birth rate that is out of control, the text presents us with a family who has struggled, apparently for generations, to produce viable, healthy offspring. The novel also replaces the "secret" of forced sterilizations with a "secret" laboratory in San Sebastián, the town in the western part of the island where Molino's son will be conceived and brought to term. This laboratory occupies the former site of the Central Soller, once one of the largest sugar plantations on the island (*La central azucarera en Puerto Rico* 45–49); what was a center of agricultural-industrial power (something frequently controlled by US, rather than Puerto Rican, interests) in the first part of the twentieth century will now be refashioned for another kind of biological reproduction.

In addition to playing with the historical controversies surrounding reproduction in Puerto Rico, Molina's situation refers indirectly to environmental problems stemming in no small part from US colonialism. Puerto Rico has been a production center for the US pharmaceutical industry for decades. Despite the economic benefits that this production brought to Puerto Rico, the industry has also been one of the main contributors to environmental pollution on the islands.[14] (Another large source of pollution has been the US military, in particular the Navy's use of the island of Vieques as a bombing range, a practice that only ended in 2001.) Although Liboy's text does not directly reference these sources of pollution, that Molina's son's first "mother" is unable to have children because she lives near a contaminated mine reveals that environmental degradation is present, if unnamed, in the story. The novel presents us with a scenario in which embryology is not only a local alternative but also a necessity for people like Molina who find themselves unable to conceive a child without intervention.

Even as Liboy's text explores the existence of a "national" Puerto Rican embryology, the novel explores the connection between this science and literature. In Manuel Molina's narrative, the story of the artificial conception of his son becomes completely interwoven with the idea and practice of literary creation. As Molina himself admits, "[N]o puedo hacer otra cosa que comparar las ideas de las embriologías científicas con las ideas literarias" (75) [I can't help but compare the ideas of scientific embryology with those of literature]. It soon becomes evident that the connections between literature and embryology are as much about method or praxis as they are about coincidental closeness. The "series of documents" that Molina compiles for his son in the report, rather than a collection of official documents or scientific texts, turns out to consist of the proposal for a novel, also titled *El Informe Cabrera*; what appears to be the correspondence between Molina and a series of writers and literary critics; and an elaborated bibliography of writers and texts that deal with embryology or genetics. As it happens, these are also the texts that Molina will recognize as examples of a Puerto Rican science fiction. The appearances of embryology that Molina finds in these texts thus serve as trail markers that guide us to a particular way of reading. They show us how Molina (Liboy) intends science fiction to be used as an altered way of reading and seeing.

The first writer that Molina recognizes as someone who has explored the topic of embryology is Pablo Morales Cabrera. Born in 1866 and active until the early twentieth century, Morales Cabrera was a journalist by profession but is best known as a writer of short fiction. Molina's characterization of Morales Cabrera as the first writer of embryology is particularly interesting if we look at the specific stories that Molina identifies as dealing with this science. In "El kleptómano" (The kleptomaniac, from Morales

Cabrera's *Cuentos populares*), Indalecio, a man of humble background, arrives in town with dreams of ascending the social ladder. He becomes involved with an attractive young widow who also happens to be financially well off. Yet when the widow acts as though she might be pregnant, only to suddenly become noticeably thinner, everyone in town not only suspects that Indalecio may have been the father but also that he may have helped the widow get rid of the baby. When a few of the townspeople discover Indalecio burying something one dark night, they assume it is the child's body and have Indalecio arrested. In the end, however, they discover that the "body" is nothing more than a doll that Indalecio—revealed as the "kleptomaniac" of the title—has stolen. Although Indalecio is eventually freed, the scandal and his penchant for theft rob him of his dreams of becoming one of the town's elites.

Where, one might ask, is the treatment of embryology in Cabrera Morales's story? The text's only possible connection to the science appears in the first description of its protagonist: "¡Pobre Indalecio! Creo que él no tenía madre; nació de un esporo y creció como un hongo, más, si un botánico lo hubiese catalogado, lo incluye entre las especias venenosas" (161) [Poor Indalecio! I believe he never had a mother; he was born of a spore and grew like a mushroom, but if a botanist had catalogued him, he would have included him among the venomous species]. This description is repeated at the end of the story, with the addition of the statement that Indalecio "ya estaba clasificado como parasitario" (164) [was already classified as a parasite]. If one reads these statements in a realist mindset, it seems clear that the description of the story's protagonist is a metaphor: Indalecio is so alone in the world that *it is as if* he had been born without a mother (living or present), *as if* he has no visible connections to a past. The observation is redolent of classist and potentially racist assumptions. By having "arrived out of nowhere," Indalecio has no connections, no socially situated family who can vouch for him. He is a nobody, aspiring to a social position the narrator implies he does not merit.

Molina, however, seems to intend this quote to be read literally: Indalecio is not the product of the human process of conception but has instead been produced asexually by spores. If this is the case, then his kleptomania, "producto morboso de la degeneración humana" [morbid product of human degeneration], has nothing to do with his race or family background and everything to do with the (scientific)—literally, nonhuman—way in which he was conceived. Seo-Young Chu explains that in "[o]ccurences of figurative language in science fiction texts and contexts have an interesting tendency to elicit literal interpretation almost as a matter of course" (10). Reading the metaphorical description of Indalecio as if it were literal generates a completely different meaning. Indalecio doesn't act the way he does for psychological reasons but because he has literally been bred this way; he is something other than human, a new kind of being. His story also shares with the laboratory creation of Molina's future offspring a rejection of classic models of human reproduction and heredity. By reading the metaphors in Cabrera Morales's text literally, by reading "science-fictionally" through a cognitively estranging lens, a whole new story emerges, one with a stranger tone. The marginalization of Indalecio might even remind the reader of Molina's grandmother's observations about "gente como nosotros." Reading "science-fictionally," this example suggests, can reveal a multiplicity of alternative stories (and histories) in Puerto Rican literature.

By identifying "El kleptómano" as science fiction, Molina (and, through him, Liboy) is not so much recognizing a particular way of writing as he is proposing a particular way of *reading*. As Molina observes: "Una novela explícita de embriología no funcionaría. El juego es descubrir textos donde el sujeto oculto no se haya desarrollado" (16) [A novel explicitly about embryology wouldn't work. The game is to discover texts where the hidden subject has not been developed]. To insist on "high-intensity realism," to read from a "science fictional" perspective, transforms the meaning of even well-known texts, bringing to the surface a series of previously unrecognized concerns and tendencies.

Molina will later apply this method to reading José Martí, arguing that in the Cuban writer's poetry, "las palabras de la libertad, las palabras éticas, están desnaturalizadas por la experiencia de una forma poética" (32) [words about liberty, ethical words, are denaturalized through the experience of a poetic form]. In Martí's poem "El padre suizo" (The Swiss father), a text based on the case of a Swiss immigrant in Arkansas who murdered his three children and then killed himself, Molina reads the mention of "estrellas luminosas" [luminous stars] as a clear reference to space. He argues that instead of seeing the poem's mention of stars (that will "guide" the dead father) as an example of "la astrología judiciaria" [judicial astrology], they should be read as "límite o condición" (34) [limit or condition]. Space in Martí's text thus expresses an "oscillation" between a freedom that stands against "lo venial, lo doméstico" [the venal, the domestic] and the understanding or consciousness that for this freedom "tampoco una exterioridad conviene, que se deshace en la ciudad y el espacio" (34) [an exteriority doesn't help either, since it is undone in the city and in space].

Reading the embryological metaphors in Morales Cabrera's story as literal produces an estrangement in the reader; on the other hand, reading the reference to space in Martí's poem as literal takes the reader to levels of interpretation that in some ways are more figurative and less literal.

If, as Molina declares, "Se puede decir que todas las épocas tienen su novela sobre embriología y en cada época la disciplina se relaciona al tema más importante del momento en que se escribe" (17) [It can be said that every era has its novel about embryology and in each era the discipline is related to the most important topic being written about at that time], Liboy's text similarly reveals a driving interest in the concerns of his own generation. Reading from a "science fictional" perspective allows Liboy to construct a new canon from a corpus of classic texts, but it also helps him to identify a community of contemporaries, to establish a dialogue with other "strange" Puerto Rican writers. The many "letters" that appear as part of the fabric of the novel reveal an active correspondence between Molina and contemporary Puerto Rican writers like Edgar Ramírez Mella, Diego Deni (Pedro Cabiya),[15] Yara Liceaga, Kattia Chico, and Carlos López Dzur. If embryology in the nineteenth and early twentieth centuries was connected to eugenicist ideals, the generation of the 1990s "no maneja el tema de la embriología negativamente" (17) [doesn't engage with the subject of embryology negatively], as Molina states. These writers serve as a community for Molina (and for Liboy), either because their writing makes possible a shared way of reading or because they, too, are reading from a point of view that doesn't follow the expectations of ordinary realist narrative. By tracing the outlines of this community, Molina lays out a future genealogy for Puerto Rican science fiction, signaling to his companions on this literary journey.

The references to embryology that Molina finds serve as a kind of code for this "deformed" way of reading, a code that indicates the potential for a particular text to be approached through the "literal" lens of science fiction. In a letter to Yara Liceaga, for example, Molina characterizes embryology in his work as "forensic embryology" (36), something that would present an oxymoron. To illustrate this idea, he gives a summary of one of Liceaga's own stories: "La protagonista sostiene relaciones amorosas con un andaluz y enseguida visita un cementerio importante. La idea de que hay un hijo enterrado de ambos no se dice, pues el cuento es muy sugerente, no directamente del tema" (36–37) [The female protagonist has amorous relations with an Analusian man and shortly after visits an important cemetery. The idea that a child of theirs is buried there is never stated, but the story is very suggestive of the subject, even if it's not directly expressed]. The idea of "forensic embryology" has various possible meanings in this example. That the story takes place in a cemetery and that the couple's son may be dead would seem to indicate that any scientific work would have to investigate or study dead things. However, since forensic science uses dead bodies to uncover hidden stories, to call Liceaga's writing technique "forensic" suggests that she has found a new way to communicate previously "dead" material—that she has an ability to reconstruct a hidden scenario. If one were to read this material "science-fictionally," a "forensic reading" would consist of creating a scenario in which various levels of realist "intensity" were possible (to adapt Chu's concept).

Liboy's novel wants to rewrite the past because it wants to re-envision the future; the novel's sociopolitical critique is also fundamentally a literary intervention and vice versa. In a statement in an early letter, Molina explains that his focus on embryology is really a distraction from his book's primary intention: El meollo del asunto no es en sí la maternidad compartida, ni el hecho feudal de quién hereda o no el código del viajero, sino la proyección temporal del texto. . . . Mi novela estudia la conducta fenotípica (las imitaciones, los plagios, los carnavales, las parodias), como elementos que de alguna manera guían la proyección temporal del viajero niño. (26–7) [The crux of the matter is not shared maternity in itself nor the feudal question of who does or doesn't inherit the traveler's code, but rather the temporal projection of the text. . . . My novel studies phenotypical conduct (imitations, plagiarisms, carnivals, parodies), as elements that in some way guide the temporal projection of the child traveler.] The phenotypical characteristics that will shape Molina's future child are as much literary and cultural as they are scientific. What Molina (and through him, Liboy) desires to create is not only a new, flesh-and-blood son but also a new kind of text, both of which will be marked by play and deviation more than by origin. Thus the need to go back to rewrite the history of Puerto Rican science fiction; by inserting "deformations" into our reading of the past, other scientific fictions and other kinds of "high-intensity realism" are made possible in the future. If Puerto Rican reality is full of distortions, then the alteration of these alterations can offer new solutions, a new way of reading both the islands and their cultural history.

Familiar Aliens and Alien Familiars

Arturo Infante's *El viaje extraordinario de Celeste García* begins with the revelation of an illusion: "Mirar al cielo es ver el pasado" [To look at the sky is to see the past], says Celeste García (María Isabel Díaz), the film's protagonist. A guide at the Havana Planetarium, she is explaining to a planetarium audience how the light from distant stars must travel millions of light-years before becoming visible from Earth. The constellations that we see in the night sky are actually a reflection from the past, finally arrived in our present. Yet seeing the present as the past made visible could also be an accurate description of Celeste's own life. A shy, mousy, and late-middle-aged widow, she has never recovered from her years of marriage to an abusive husband, a situation that forced her to leave teaching, her real love and vocation. As a planetarium attendant, she hides behind the shapeless formality of her company uniform, and the severe bun in which she wears her hair makes her look older than she is. The film's opening scenes show her going through the motions of her daily routine, moving back and forth between work and her elegant but decaying Centro Habana apartment, which she shares with her adult son, with an occasional stop at the neighborhood shops. But Celeste's uneventful existence changes one night when she is awakened to the sounds of her neighbor, Polina, leaving in the company of some strange-looking people. The next day, a government news broadcast explains this unusual nighttime departure; aliens from a distant planet, Gryok, have been living among the Cuban population for years disguised as ordinary citizens. They have now all returned to Gryok, but in a gesture of thanks for the hospitality of their Cuban hosts, the Gryokites have invited a select group of Cubans to visit their planet. Celeste discovers that the strange writing on a card Polina slipped under her door before leaving is a special invitation to form part of the delegation to Gryok. She suddenly has a chance to leave everything she has known behind to travel to a distant planet.

With its introduction of alien visitors and space travel, *El viaje extraordinario,* Infante's first feature-length film, takes one of the most common tropes of Cuban cinema of recent decades, the question whether to emigrate, and gives it a provocative and expansive twist.[16] Since the 1959 Revolution that overthrew dictator Fulgencio Batista, the island has experienced several significant waves of emigration. While Cubans leaving the island in the 1960s and '70s were largely understood to have left for political reasons, those leaving since the beginning of the post-Soviet economic crisis of the Special Period, when the country saw a 28 percent increase in the number of emigrants, have left for a complex series of reasons, many of them economic (Lamrani).[17] The decision to leave the island and the process of leave-taking has been the subject of everything from feature films—*Nada +* (2001), *Habana Blues* (2005), *Personal Belongings* (2006), *Últimos días en la Habana* (2016)—to documentaries—*Balseros* (2002), *Suite Habana* (2003)—to zombie movies (*Juan de los muertos,* 2011, examined in chapter 4). Although fictional cinematic narratives and documentaries alike explore the expectations and fantasies that those leaving have about their new destinations, the idea of leaving Cuba for a whole new planet magnifies the challenges implicit in these earthbound migration journeys. If emigration has always meant leaving the known and familiar for the unknown, the option to travel to a different planet where no Cubans have ever been exponentially opens the dimensions of possibility. Even compared to those leaving Cuba for the United States or Europe, the travelers to Gryok are truly letting go of everything they know. What does it mean to leave behind not only your own country but also your own reality for a world that is, quite literally, alien? "Hay que ser anormal" [You have to be abnormal], says Celeste's boss of those who want to go, to which Celeste replies, "O no tener nada que perder" [Or have nothing to lose]. Brief clips reveal the current situations of Celeste's future travel companions: a pregnant woman attempting to relax in her small wood-frame house, an aging tango singer at a night club, a woman pausing from giving a man a blow job in the cab of his truck to listen to the announcement of the invitation from Gryok on the radio. All of them are eager to give up their current life for the possibility of a new and different future.

Celeste's declaration at the beginning of the film is not only a reflection of her own life; it is also an ironic commentary on Cuba's current situation. The remaining socialist nation in the Western Hemisphere, Cuba's economy has never completely recovered from the challenges of the Special Period, when it lost its favored trading relationship with the Soviet Bloc. An agreement with Venezuela that allowed for the importation of billions of gallons of crude oil and a brief opening to US tourist visits under President Obama both came to an end with the collapse of Venezuela's economy under President Nicolás Maduro and the restriction of both travel and remittances from the United States under President Trump. Although it does not explicitly identify Havana as a ruin, the cinematography in Infante's film lingers on the age of the city: the faded colors of a city street, the rugged faces of the elderly men playing dominoes on a street corner, the peeling plaster walls of Celeste's apartment. The material decay points to a place in which the past has become the present, in which the new—and more especially, the new and welcome—is rare.

The chance to leave Cuba—and Earth—for Gryok injects new energy into the emigration enterprise, and into Celeste's outlook in particular. Celeste may feel that she has nothing to lose, but the film reveals how much life she has in her once she decides that she will go to Gryok. She gets a haircut that makes her seem years younger. She unpacks old teaching supplies to take with her (Polina had reported that Celeste would be a good candidate to help educate the Gryokites about Earth) and buys a new travel bag. While those around her react to the news of Gryok's discovery with cynicism or skepticism, the possibility of exploring a world that is nothing like the one she knows awakens not only her enthusiasm for life but also a kind of innocent curiosity about the world around her. "¿Tendrá mar?" she muses at the office lunch table. "¿Y las leyes? ¿Tal vez un planeta tan civilizado no necesita leyes?" [Does it have an ocean? And laws? Perhaps such a civilized planet doesn't need laws?], all this to the great disgust of her two lunch companions, one of whom announces, "Yo lo que quiero saber es hasta cuándo la candanga esta" [What I want to know is how long this mess will last]. Celeste is undeterred by her colleagues' cynicism; the realization that she has a chance to explore not only a new life but also a new reality energizes her. After she announces her decision to travel in a TV interview with planetarium staff, she becomes a minor celebrity for her neighbors.

Just as the announcement of a new planet reorients Cubans with dreams of escaping their island reality, the science fictional twist in Infante's film begins to shift the viewer's perspective. The revelation that "aliens have been living among us" opens a space for strangeness and difference in what were expected narratives and visual scenarios. Although much of the film's cinematography captures ordinary elements of daily Cuban life, the information that aliens not only exist but have already been present imbues even the most quotidian of scenes with the possibility of the unexpected and unimaginable. Could ordinary (Cuban) reality in fact contain things beyond our conception or perception? The viewer begins to inspect each scene for signs of things that are other. The machines that the government agents use to examine Polina's apartment make noises that sound like robots or spacecraft. Future travelers to the planet look like aliens themselves when they don headsets that allow them to experience simulations of life on Gryok. The possibility that the strange and novel might be hidden within the ordinary shifts the viewer's approach to images that might otherwise be seen as familiar or even clichéd within Cuban cinema.

Infante's film is, at its core, a comedy in the guise of a travel narrative. Even as the viewer is awakened to the potential for the unexpected or unexplained in the formerly ordinary, one of the film's larger jokes is the way in which Cuban state bureaucracy (and, through it, Cubans themselves) assimilates what should be the most radical of events into the governmental machine. The irony of the journey to Gryok is that while most emigration from Cuba is not encouraged—nor even, in many cases, sanctioned—by the Cuban government, the trip to Gryok, as an official visit, becomes a bureaucratic event. (It is also described as "a visit," even though the temporal distance makes a return to Earth far from likely.) Although Celeste has received a special invitation, most of her fellow travelers are chosen by lottery. The government sets up "Offices for Interplanetary Travel" where people can register for the lottery to select the travelers. Cubans join long lines outside these offices just as one might wait in line for the bus or at the bank. Within this bureaucratic framework, the novel event of interplanetary space travel becomes just one more thing for which Cubans must queue up and wait.

As part of the official preparation for their interplanetary trip, those chosen as part of the Cuban delegation must travel by train to a special training camp, where they receive instruction on the basics of life on Gryok and practice getting ready to board the spaceship, an endeavor that must be carefully timed, since the ship can only land for thirty minutes. The bulk of the film's action takes place at the training camp, the Escuela Secundaria Básica en el Campo (ESBEC) Batalla de Mal Tiempo, a former *escuela al campo* (country school). Begun in 1965, the escuelas al campo brought high school students from urban areas to the countryside to perform agricultural labor in settings that were institutional, if not close to carceral. The waiting travelers are housed in the dormitories of the school, an experience in which, as Ileana Margarita Rodríguez observes in her review of the film, "[l]a disciplina militar del lugar remeda el régimen disciplinario de estos centros ya desaparecidos" [the military discipline of the place is reminiscent of the disciplinary regime of those now-disappeared centers].[18] In short, although the expectant travelers are ostensibly on their way to a new (freer?) life, both the location and the training regimen treat them to more, not less, governmental control in their exit process. Once they arrive at the training camp, the Gryok-bound Cubans are assembled in military lines, given an electronic bracelet that will be their ticket onto the spaceship, and assigned to one of three dormitories. Housed several people to a room, they are kept to a rigid schedule of mealtime, physical exercise, and lessons, and must remain in their rooms after "lights out." Of course, an added irony to the bureaucratic process that has been devised for the travelers is that they are watched over by other Cubans who may themselves want to leave yet do not have the opportunity. The largest difference between the training camp and the school as it was in its heyday is the throngs of hangers-on clustered outside the gates, many of them hoping to find some way through the bureaucracy in order to secure a place on the departing spaceship at the last minute.

The setting of the training camp at first stimulates a pleasant sense of anticipation and suspense, feelings that are enhanced with the introduction of a romantic twist to the plot. Augusto (Omar Franco), a butcher at Celeste's neighborhood meat market, just happens to have scored a seat on the spaceship to Gryok. A longtime insomniac, in part because of his experiences during the Angolan Civil War, he hopes that the change of environment will allow him to finally rest. Augusto has clearly had his eye on Celeste for a while; in one of the film's early scenes, we witness him trying to make conversation with her at the market as he helps her with an order, attention to which she seems oblivious. Their new circumstances spur him to more direct action and give Celeste the freedom and space to reciprocate. Encouraged by Celeste's bunkmates, the pair exchange flirtatious conversation in the dining hall and later escape from the physical training exercises to share a clandestine drink of water and conversation. Although Celeste remains coy, it's clear that she is pleased to receive his attentions.

Even as they heighten the viewer's sense of anticipation for Celeste's journey to Gryok, the scenes at the training camp also introduce a sense of frustration with the film's temporal trajectory: shouldn't we already be in space by now? In truth, the training camp sets up the film's central joke (among many small jokes): the longest journey that the viewer will witness in the film is the trip to the training camp itself. When one of Celeste's bunkmates dies of a heart attack during a practice drill, his bunk—and his place on the spaceship—is taken over by Yunier, a young man who reminds Celeste of her son. Unbeknownst to her, however, Yunier has bribed his way into being the first on the waitlist and is looking for a way to steal his girlfriend on to the flight as well. When the siren announcing the spaceship's arrival sounds, he sees his chance; he knocks Celeste out and grabs her bracelet, leaving Celeste tied up in a closet. Although the guards are alerted to the crime and Celeste is freed, it is too late; she runs on to the airfield just in time to see the ship, presented on screen (via CGI) as a kind of giant cephalopod in spaceship form, in lift off. This is the closest the film comes to showing the viewer anything from Gryok. We see only four short takes of the spaceship: the flash of the lights on its underside as it passes overhead; a panoramic shot showing it hovering over the school; a shot showing one "arm" in profile as passengers are individually "beamed up," and a final shot of its underside as it rises into the sky. Rather than follow the other characters on to the spaceship, Infante chooses to keep the viewer with Celeste. We never get a chance to glimpse the ship's interior or its crew and never learn what happens to the Cuban travelers after they are sucked into the ship's depths. In a subversion of the alien trope in many science fiction films in which an encounter with extraterrestrials proves to be an epiphanic experience or a moment of consciousness expansion, Infante's whole film turns out to have been setting the viewer up for a transition that never happens. There is, in fact, no science fictional journey shown in this supposedly science fiction film. Despite Celeste's heavenly name, her "extraordinary journey" has only taken her as far as the next province.

By a twist of fate—and a seeming question of seconds—Celeste has missed her chance to leave Cuba and start over. But would this new start have been the happy opportunity she imagined? Even as it plays up the hopes and dreams of the travelers, Infante's film also includes details that cause the viewer to wonder whether this intergalactic encounter will turn out exactly as advertised. To begin with, the school where the training camp is located is named for the "Batalla de Mal Tiempo" (which, depending upon how you translate it, could read the "Battle of Bad Timing" or the "Battle of Bad Weather"), an important conflict in Cuba's War for Independence that somehow also feels like a bad omen. This feeling is enhanced by the fact that, as Ginsburg notes, although the school's dormitories are all named for pioneers of flight (Yuri Gagarin, Arnaldo Tamayo, etc.), the dormitory in which Celeste and her friends are housed is named for Matías Pérez, a Cuban balloonist who reportedly "boarded a hot-air balloon and was never seen again" (126). Then there is the fact that at no point in the film do we meet an undisguised inhabitant of Gryok in the flesh. (The shot of the extraterrestrial visitors at the beginning of the film is what Celeste can see through her door; the viewer gets a hazy impression of people dressed in eighteenth-century wigs but has to assume that the visitors are disguised.) The absence in the film of any concrete visual representation of the Gryokites or their planet—beyond giant chickens— leaves it completely open for the audience to imagine what life on Gryok and its inhabitants might be like. The most suggestive moment occurs when a strangely dressed, wild-eyed man (Jorge Molina) who has found his way into the training camp confronts some of the would-be passengers in a hallway and urges them not to board the spaceship, screaming, "¡Ustedes, abran los ojos! ¡Los Gryokitas son aliados de los reptilianos! ¡No se monten en las naves! ¡Les van a chupar el cerebro!" [All of you, open your eyes! The Gryokites are allied with the Reptilians! Don't get on the spaceships! They're going to suck your brains!].[19] Given the man's dress, his desperate manner, and that he waves a piece of two-by-four as if it were a sword, it is easy to dismiss him as mentally ill, a spreader of meaningless conspiracy theories. Yet the disruption he creates opens a space for considering alternative versions of the scenario. What if the information the Cubans are receiving at the training camp is all propaganda? Is Gryok truly an advanced, nearly utopian civilization, or could the Gryokites have ulterior motives for their hospitality? In his conversation with Celeste, Augusto also expresses some skepticism about the training they are receiving. "¿No te da miedo?" [Doesn't it scare you?], he asks her, adding, "Yo todavía no me lo creo, Celeste. Tal vez porque estoy acostumbrado a que cuando te dicen que algo está tan bueno lo mejor es salir huyendo" [I still don't believe it, Celeste. Maybe because I'm used to hearing that when something's too good, it's best to run away.]. Finally, Celeste awakens the morning after the spaceship's departure to discover that the travelers' luggage is still piled up next to the landing strip. Was this an accidental oversight? Are these earthly possessions incompatible with life on Gryok? Or is this a sign that the travelers to Gryok are destined for a situation in which they won't be needing their belongings? Whatever the answer to these questions, Infante leaves open the possibility that this emigration journey is not what it appears.

Indeed, regardless of what awaits the travelers to Gryok, the film allows the viewer to see how the government radio announcements, the Offices of Interplanetary Travel, Celeste's invitation, the trip to the training camp, and the special wristbands the travelers are given all contribute to the construction of a space for the future possible, not only for Celeste and her fellow Cubans but also for the film's audience. The viewer never learns what awaits the travelers to Gryok, but we see how evidence is marshaled so that when the ship arrives, we are ready, like Celeste, to believe in the possibility that Gryok is real and that the trip could be everything she dreams.

When the Gryokite spaceship departs, the viewer, like Celeste, must return to what remains: Cuba. Although Celeste has been denied her voyage into space, the trip to and from the training camp for Gryok has been a kind of travel in time. Despite having been away from home for only a matter of days, she returns from the training camp to find herself estranged from her old reality. This distanced perspective is something akin to what filmmaker Carlos Lechuga describes experiencing as he prepared to leave the country: "Me paraba en la avenida 23 una hora antes de la cita acordada y veía a la gente pasar. Como si fuera un extranjero o un extraterrestre. Miraba con extrañeza a los que pasaban . . . Todo me parecía ajeno" [I stood on 23rd Ave. an hour before the agreed-upon meeting time and watched people pass by. As if I were a foreigner or an extraterrestrial. I looked with strangeness at those passing by . . . Everything seemed separate from me]. Having supposedly "left" Havana for Gryok, Celeste returns to her old neighborhood almost as a ghost. She discovers upon her return that things have moved on without her, as if she had been gone for much longer. Building on her local celebrity, her son Pedrito and her sister have turned her apartment into *Celeste*, a space-themed *paladar* (private restaurant) complete with night sky-blue walls and a menu that includes "Gryokite mojitos." Her job at the planetarium has been given away to a younger woman, who goes through the formality of her monologue with all the excitement of someone reciting a history lesson. Celeste can't let go of her dreams of Gryok. She spends her days back at the planetarium, this time as a spectator, watching the stars move around her, whispering the word "Gryok" to herself over and over, as if it were a kind of incantation that could spirit her away.

Yet if the stars remain inaccessible for Celeste, it turns out that she is not the only traveler who did not go to Gryok; Arturo, on realizing that Celeste was not on board the spaceship, forced the Gryokites to let him off. He reconnects with her at the planetarium and invites her out to his farm for the weekend. "Te trataré como una reina" [I'll treat you like a queen] he tells her, to which her playful response is, "Más te vale" [You'd better]. With this hopeful romantic ending, Infante's film seems to reveal yet another play on the viewer's expectations; Celeste's "extraordinary journey" is not a trip into space but rather a voyage of self-discovery. The preparations for her trip to Gryok were the beginning stages of a journey to self-confidence, love, and hope for the future.

Given the film's suggestively romantic ending, it is possible to read *El viaje extraordinario* as a romantic comedy that merely gestures toward science fiction as a comic device. Despite the simplicity of the film's romantic arc, however, I don't think we should dismiss the importance of the film's science fictional elements. Although she never leaves Earth, the presence of Gryok—as novum, as space of possibility—is what grants both Celeste and the film's viewers the distance from which to observe her contemporary Cuban environment with new eyes. The existence of the extraordinary—and the possibility of meeting it—changes the perspective and disrupts familiar trajectories. That Celeste and Arturo find each other after not boarding the spaceship is qualitatively different than if they had begun a relationship without ever leaving their neighborhood. It is different to have taken leave, to have let go, and to then return than to have never left at all.

What the Ab-Real Reveals

In the video for López-Nussa's version of "El buey cansao," the introduction of a futuristic metanarrative does more than simply allow the song to circulate between the video's two distinct time frames. The contrast created by the temporal disjunctiveness of the two moments (augmented by the fact that "1980" is not actually 1980 but rather 2020) opens a space for imagining other possibilities; neither the future nor the past is as fixed as they appear to be. The 1980s moment of performance (and its material traces) is as much a calculated construction as the future moment of listening in 2220, and in making this visible the video liberates the music from connection to one particular narrative. Martínez's dance at the end proposes an avenue for escape: neither dance competitor nor robot, as she dances off into the void, she offers the viewer the possibility to create something new as well.

With the stark division of its two temporal moments, López-Nussa's video provides a clear illustration of the way in which the ab-real functions in the other texts I examine in this chapter. Through the introduction of science fictional elements, narratives by Vlak, Liboy, and Infante destabilize established ways of viewing Caribbean history and reality, revealing the constructed nature of these concepts. This does not mean that their individual visions are completely liberatory or utopian. Although Vlak's future Dominican Republic gives equal space to historiography and myth, it remains attached to established ideas of Dominicanidad as well as long-standing national anxieties. Infante's film casts space travel—or at least the visit to Gryok—as a dubious solution to what ails its Cuban protagonists (and implicitly, Cuba more broadly). And while Liboy's novel is suggestive of the ways in which both Puerto Rican literature and Puerto Rican scientific narratives can be rewritten and expanded, it also highlights the scars of the islands' colonial relationship to the United States and the challenges of recovering from this history. Yet by estranging the reader from previous assumptions of what is real or possible, these works create a space for further reflection on the way in which other stories are told and on the accepted norms of possibility. The contrasts they establish between these alternate realities and our present expand the reader or viewer's idea of what is (not yet) possible, creating a space for things to be—and to be seen—otherwise.

3

The Countertimes of Caribbean Cyberpunk

On 29 November 2021, Frank Achon, a Cuban-born cryptoartist living in Miami, minted an NFT he titled "Havana Cuba 2059."[1] Achon posted his artwork on Foundation, an online gallery for creators of digital artwork and collectors looking to purchase artwork in bitcoin, with the tagline "Futuristic Havana Cyberpunk Revolution," and he subsequently shared the image on Instagram and Reddit as "Havana Cyberpunk 2059."[2] Achon's piece presents the viewer with a night scene: an iconic row of nineteenth-century buildings from the Cuban capital set against an impossibly starry sky. The main elements of the cityscape, from the buildings' arched walkways to the two classic 1950s American cars parked out front to the laundry hanging from balconies, all speak to the visual language of tourist photos of present-day Cuba. What sets "Havana Cuba 2059" apart is Achon's use of neon; in his image, the architecture has been retouched so that the cornices and balconies of every building are outlined in pink or purple neon. Neon signs in various languages—English, Spanish, and Korean—also adorn building entrances, identifying restaurants, bars, and a tattoo parlor. The building in the center of the frame is identified as "Patria y Vida Hotel," a reference to the 2021 song "Patria y vida," a collaboration between Orishas' frontman Yotuel, the group Gente de Zona, Descemer Bueno, Maykel Osorbo, and El Funky that became an unofficial anthem for the widespread protests that took place across Cuba on 11 July 2021.[3] Both the piece's tagline and Achon's use of neon reference cyberpunk, a subgenre of science fiction concerned largely with the relationship between humans and technology; his neon additions make use of a key element of the genre's visual aesthetics. Playfully setting itself one hundred years after the Cuban Revolution of 1959, "Havana Cuba 2059" conjures an alternative Cuban capital, a city whose linguistic landscape speaks to a kind of global cosmopolitanism (and the introduction of certain freedoms of consump-

Figure 3. Frank Achon, "Havana Cyberpunk 2059" (2021).

tion and leisure), even as both the architectural backdrop and the neon signs harken back to Havana's nocturnal landscape of the 1950s. The result is a scene that identifies itself with the future, even if it carries a retro edge. Ana Dopico has written compellingly about how classic images of post-Soviet Havana circulate "as currency and tableaux," as well as the ways in which the seemingly transparent images become a projection screen for neoimperialist fantasies while obscuring "political conflicts that cannot be assimilated by narratives of tourism and foreign investment" (452). By offering "Havana Cuba 2059" as an NFT, Achon was clearly capitalizing on the market for images of the Cuban capital; the NFT was auctioned off on 1 December 2021, and eventually sold for 0.10 in Ethereum cryptocurrency (the equivalent of $269.14 at the time of this writing).[4] At the same time, his oblique reference to the political conflicts of 2021 through the use of "Patria y vida," a song that offers an explicit critique of the Cuban government and its censorship, suggests that his fantasy for the Cuban capital might be as much about imagining a new kind of political and discursive space as it is about consumption (nostalgic or otherwise).

In a resonant display of synchronicity, between November 2021 and January 2022, Erick Mota, a Cuban science fiction writer and Havana resident, published a series of photographic compositions titled "Habana Cyberpunk" on his Instagram page.[5] Like Achon's NFT, Mota's "Habana Cyberpunk" series features pieces of Havana architecture altered to look as if they are framed in neon. At the bottom of each image, the words "Habana Cyberpunk" also appear as if outlined in neon lights. Like Achon, Mota uses what Pawel Frelik has called cyberpunk's "incarnations of light" (83) to reimagine Havana's cityscape. Yet where Achon's NFT creates a future language that is almost retro, the neon shadings of Mota's images alter the city landscape so that it becomes almost unrecognizable. In Mota's picture of a corner in Vedado, the light emanating from the window of a house is so bright that it eclipses any view of the building itself. The last photo in the first series, identified as "5ta Avenida. Miramar" ("Fifth Avenue, Miramar"), uses the neon to highlight a crosswalk in the wide boulevard that runs through one of Havana's most elegant neighborhoods. The lampposts and a wall on the far side of the crosswalk also appear etched in neon. In a further estranging detail, the image has been retouched so that overhanging trees are touched with light, giving the image an otherworldly quality. Any elements that might reference a visual cliché of Havana's urban aesthetics—say, the railing of a Miramar mansion—have been removed, so that the crosswalk emerges as a bridge to a new scene. What kind of new city might this be, the viewer asks? Mota's use of light makes familiar landscapes other, removing them from known geographies and the viewer's expected associations with them. The images offer themselves as new spaces of possibility, creating an alternative Havana beyond the viewer's spatial and temporal coordinates.

Both Mota's and Achon's neon reimaginings of Havana attempt to relocate the Cuban capital from its current coordinates of time and space. Taking their works as some as some of the most recent examples to play with the cyberpunk genre, this chapter explores the temporal uses of cyberpunk in the Caribbean, where it has functioned as a genre that has allowed writers and artists to craft alternatives to their islands' current temporal emplotments. Cyberpunk was initially a literary phenomenon, begun in English-language fiction in the early 1980s by a group of mostly male writers loosely connected to the magazine *Amazing Stories*, among them William Gibson, John Shirley, Pat Cadigan, and Lewis Shiner.[6] The novels and short stories that have come to be labeled as cyberpunk—of which William Gibson's novel *Neuromancer* (1984) is arguably the paradig-

Figure 4. Erick Mota, "De la serie Habana Cyberpunk. 5ta avenida, Miramar" (2021).

matic exemplar—offer an intense exploration of the relationship between humans and technology well before the popularization of the internet as we know it today.[7] The dystopian worlds conjured by Gibson, Neal Stephenson, and others served as a way for these authors to expand upon the changes they observed in Anglo-American society: an increased global circulation of goods, people, and information, as well as the potential for change that the new computer interface offered. The genre's exploration of the future possibilities of capitalism led the Marxist critic Fredric Jameson to tellingly characterize cyberpunk as "the supreme literary expression if not of postmodernism than of late capitalism itself" (*Postmodernism* 419). Although it shares "hard" science fiction's interest in technology (in this case, of cyberspace), cyberpunk narratives often focus on technology's effect on human relationships rather than on the mechanics of technological objects or processes. For Caribbean creators, however, rather than serving as a reflection of the tendencies of the present moment, the genre's syntactic elements become a language with which to envision the region's place in a future not limited by the borders—or temporal conditions—of island spaces.

As it emerged in Anglo-American fiction, cyberpunk was originally a genre that focused more on space than on time. Early cyberpunk narratives are largely concerned with two kinds of spatial existence: life on a future (or futuristic), often dystopian Earth; and life in cyberspace, the "decentered spatiality" that exists "parallel to, but outside of, the geographic topography of contemporary reality" (Bukatman, *Terminal Identity* 105). Brian Hale refers to cyberspace as an "inset world," in that it can also be understood as a "world-within-world," occupying a different ontological plane as much as a different spatial one (11). Texts like Gibson's *Neuromancer* imagine cyberspace as a mappable area with its own concrete geography, yet as Sabine Heuser notes, that cyberspace can in some way be considered a metaspace also "highlights the very concept of space (or notional space) in fiction" (25). Sherryl Vint characterizes cyberspace's relationship to physical space in terms of Cartesian dualism: "In cyberspace one *is* the mind, effortlessly moving beyond the limitations of the human body. In cyberpunk fiction, the prison of the 'meat' is left behind" (*Bodies of Tomorrow* 103–4). Both separate realm and metaphor, cyberspace presented a separate—but not unrelated—plane with its own rules that the characters of early cyberpunk narratives had to learn to navigate.

In addition to the creation of cyberspace as an experiential reality, cyberpunk fiction is also marked by what Bruce Sterling, another of the genre's progenitors, called "the unholy alliance of the technical world and the world of organized dissent—the underground world of pop culture, visionary fluidity, and street-level anarchy" (xii). With the growth of the internet, some of this antiauthoritarian attitude became associated with cyberspace itself, which was seen by many of its developers and early proponents as a universal space, distanced not only from the constraints of the material world but also from the control of nation-states. In his iconic "Declaration of the Independence of Cyberspace" (1996), cyberlibertarian political activist John Perry Barlow, addressing himself to the "Governments of the Industrial World," announces, "I declare the global social space we are building to be naturally independent of the tyrannies you seek to impose on us. You have no moral right to rule us nor do you possess any methods of enforcement we have true reason to fear" (18). Despite this promise of political freedom, cyberpunk texts often depict future societies in which corporate capitalism has triumphed and corporations, rather than governments, wield social control over both physical and cybernetic spaces. In response to this capitalist control, the protagonists of these narratives tend to be morally ambivalent characters who resist control of any kind: hackers, hit men, and cybercowboys, or characters with a foot in both the physical and virtual worlds and a resistance to authority.[8] It is this mixture of "high tech and low life" (Ketterer 141) that makes cyberpunk texts from this first Anglo-American wave stand out. Indeed, some critics have asserted that the genre differs from other kinds of science fiction more in style than in substance. Cuban writer and critic Yoss characterizes it as "más bien como un estilo de escribir y una manera de abordar la realidad que una auténtica corriente" ("Marcianos" 77) [more a style of writing and a way of approaching reality than an authentic current]. Authors like Gibson crafted narratives that were distinctive as much for the ways in which their protagonists engaged with society as for how they engaged with this new, virtual space.

Cyberpunk's association with space was further cemented through the early connection it established with a specific set of visual aesthetics. Indeed, as Anna McFarlane, Graham J. Murphy, and Lars Schmeink argue (and as Achon's and Mota's work demonstrates), cyberpunk is now as much "a visual and aural phenomenon" as it is a literary one (2).[9] The genre truly entered the popular imagination through film; movies such as *Escape from New York* (John Carpenter, 1981), Ridley Scott's *Blade Runner* (1982), and later the Wachowski siblings' *Matrix* trilogy (1999, 2003) gave a particular visual feel and tone to the contours of both the virtual and the material worlds in cyberpunk narratives. *Blade Runner*, in particular, as Scott Bukatman has observed, is "all about vision" (15). Scott's film introduced a visual-aesthetic language that would come to be the genre's hallmark, an ultraurban landscape composed of "a profusion of simulations"— "synthetic animals, giant viewscreens, replicants, memory implants, and faked photos" (Bukatman, *Blade Runner* 19)—as well as "virtual realities, holographic interfaces, and neon-saturated urban sprawls" (Frelik 83). The total aesthetic impression of the first *Blade Runner* film—one continued by subsequent visual texts such as Laeta Kalogridis's adaptation of Richard Morgan's novel *Altered Carbon* (2002) into a TV series (2018)—manages to both posit a future time and inject a kind of retro feel into the visual landscape. As Heuser observes, the "junk and refuse" that litter the urban landscapes of cyberpunk cinema present a contrast to the "streamlined futures" envisioned by earlier science fiction writers (33). The result is a cityscape that feels grungy, lived-in, and in keeping with the scruffiness of "punk."

The hacker is the emblematic protagonist of cyberpunk narrative. With a talent for understanding and manipulating technology he—or she, though, as Karen Cadoga and others have noted, the protagonists of early cyberpunk texts are overwhelmingly male—is perfectly adapted to the highly technological world in which he finds himself.[10] The hacker figure in early cyberpunk narratives tends to be someone using their talents in a less-than-legal manner: entering locked spaces within the Matrix, stealing information, and selling their services to the highest bidder.[11] Despite their prodigious talent for navigating advanced technology, hacker characters are often located on the social margins, whether because of their youth, illicit dealings, or disdain for dominant society. The hacker is often the personification of the "punk" within cyberpunk narratives. Bruce Sterling, explaining the title of *Mirrorshades: The Cyberpunk Anthology*, the first collection of cyberpunk narrative, says: "Mirrored sunglasses have been a Movement totem since the early days of '82. . . . By hiding the eyes, mirrorshades prevent the forces of normalcy from realizing that one is crazed and possibly dangerous. They are the symbol of the biker, the rocker, the policeman, and similar outlaws" (xi). The connection Sterling's description establishes between the hacker (i.e., standing in for the "Movement") and the policeman is significant; cyberpunk has maintained strong ties to detective fiction and noir—above all to the work of Raymond Chandler—from the beginning. Bukatman even goes so far as to characterize cyberpunk as "a hybrid of science fiction and urban crime narrative" (141–42), though Joe Nazare has shown that the relationship between the two genres can be ironic or derivative (384). This connection is one that has continued even as cyberpunk has traveled to other parts of the world: protagonists frequently function as detectives, assuming responsibility for discovering the author of a crime or explaining a mystery. This work can be done within social laws or outside them, in cyberspace or anchored in real geographic coordinates. In these investigations, the hacker often occupies a morally ambivalent space within the text, operating both within and outside the law.

Cyberpunk's strong visual vocabulary and exploration of moral ambivalence were elements that appealed to Latin American writers who discovered the genre in the late 1980s and early 1990s.[12] If Anglo-American cyberpunk was, as Cuban writer Erick Mota observes, "una extrapolación de los miedos del ciudadano común de Norteamérica. Un espejo de la realidad de su tiempo" (4) [an extrapolation of the fears of the ordinary American citizen. A mirror of the reality of their time], writers from Mexico, Brazil, and Argentina were drawn to the genre for the ways in which it reflected elements of their rapidly urbanizing and unevenly developing contemporary reality. The genre allowed writers to meditate on the dystopian elements of their own societies, which M. Elizabeth Ginway describes as "past abuses and corruption, along with neoliberal policies that have stripped away state programs and protections in the name of global economic competition" ("Latin America" 392). Although these Latin American writers were in no way constitutive of a unified movement, for many of them cyberpunk spoke not to the future but rather to what was happening in the present: increased internal migration to urban centers in the region, technological advancement often controlled by political and economic elites, struggles for control between governments and extrastate agents. As a result, as Ginway notes in her survey of the genre, many of their texts are less interested in exploring "fantasies of disembodiment in cyberspace" (Ginway, "Latin America" 385) than in examining the changing relationship between technology and the body in alternative Latin American futures.

In Brazil, where novels with cyberpunk tendencies appeared almost parallel with the movement in Anglo-American literature, the genre was taken up by writers as the nation emerged from several decades of dictatorship. "Tupinipunk," as this wave of Brazilian cyberpunk came to be known, shares Anglo-American cyberpunk's preoccupation with urban space, but according to Ginway, "carnivalizes" the genre, resulting in texts that place greater emphasis on sexuality and the body (*Brazilian Science Fiction* 164). Novels such as Alfredo Sirkis's *Silicone XXI* (1985), perhaps the first Latin American cyberpunk novel, and Fausto Fawcett's *Santa Clara Poltergeist* (1990) also fuse cyberpunk aesthetics and Brazilian spiritualist religion to "resituate cyberpunk's preoccupation with New Age spirituality within a Brazilian tradition of religious syncretism" (King 37).

Cyberpunk writing appeared in Mexico slightly later than in Brazil, in the early 1990s. Critic Hernán García observes that in Mexico "la década del noventa perteneció al cyberpunk" ("Texto y contexto" 1) [the 1990s belonged to cyberpunk], as writers such as Gerardo Horacio Porcayo, José Luis Zárate, Bef (né Bernardo Fernández), and Juan José "Pepe" Rojo found the genre particularly responsive to engaging with Mexico's political and economic climate following the implementation of neoliberal policies including the North American Free Trade Agreement (1994). Porcayo's *La primera calle de la soledad* (Solitude's first street, 1993), considered Mexico's first cyberpunk novel, incorporates many of the genre's classic syntactic elements. Set in a dystopian future Mexico, Porcayo's narrative centers on Zorro, a hacker who finds himself playing the role of double agent in a power struggle between rival religious sects. Similarly incorporating elements of the noir thriller, Pepe Rojo's novella *Ruido gris* (Gray noise, 1996) features an "ocular reporter" (with camera ocular implants) who finds himself creating sensationalist events so he can be the first one to film them.

If the ethically ambivalent nature of typical cyberpunk protagonists also provided a perfect vehicle for Latin American authors to explore the gray areas of both political engagement and technology's role in politics, the genre was also adapted by authors in the region to engage with specific national literary traditions or to take on national anxieties. The protagonist of Argentine writer Eduardo Blaustein's novel *Cruz diablo* (Devil cross, 1997) is both a gaucho and a hacker, a fusion of national and cyberpunk icons that, as Edward King observes, allows Blaustein to "[set] up a parallel between the technologies and representational systems that achieved the consolidation of the Argentine nation and the cybernetic technologies and logic of control that form part of the assemblage of post-dictatorship neoliberalism" (98). Carlos Gamerro's *Las islas* (The islands, 1998) uses the literary apparatus of cyberpunk to explore another sensitive moment in Argentine national history; his novel centers on a hacker and video game designer who is also a veteran of the Falklands/Malvinas War, allowing for a metaphorical exploration of the effects of the war on the national psyche.

Like their fellow authors in Mexico, Brazil, and Argentina, Caribbean cyberpunk writers were directly influenced by Anglo-American examples of the genre, which circulated freely in Puerto Rico and began circulating— informally, and sometimes clandestinely—in Cuba in the early 1990s.[13] Drawn to cyberpunk as a literary form just as Cuba and Puerto Rico each found themselves in the midst of larger sociopolitical crises, writers from these islands used the genre as a means to engage with these conditions. Like their Latin American counterparts, Cuban and Puerto Rican writers were drawn to cyberpunk in this post–Cold War decade in part for the ways in which the genre removed them from their current temporal coordinates. Yet this was less because they saw cyberpunk as a reflection of their changing societies than because of the ways in which cyberpunk did not reflect them.

In certain ways, the worlds inhabited by Cuban and Puerto Rican writers in the 1990s could not have been more different; one island was the last bastion of socialism in the Americas, combating an economic and sociopolitical crisis engendered by the fall of the Soviet Union. The other was for all intents and purposes a US colony, dependent upon and limited by its subordinate relationship to the American economy. In Cuba, a state-funded literary apparatus supported writers and artists even as material constraints limited books' production and circulation. In Puerto Rico, literary initiatives were constrained by individual economic circumstances and the dictates of foreign publishing markets. Despite the stark differences between the political structures of each island, however, the changes to the sociopolitical landscape that Cuba and Puerto Rico experienced in the 1990s positioned both islands as increasingly marginalized from and peripheral to larger narratives of globalization and prosperity.

Cyberpunk offered Caribbean writers a venue not only for reflecting on these narratives but also for repositioning the Caribbean within them and beyond them. In this sense, for Cuban and Puerto Rican writers who incorporate cyberpunk elements in their works, the genre's engagement with time becomes as important—if not more so—than its treatment of space. In her article on Cuban cyberpunk, Maielis González argues that cyberpunk "se ofrece ante los estudios literarios como un constructo simbólico de la contemporaneidad" (240) [offers itself to literary studies as a symbolic construct of contemporaneity]. However, Caribbean cyberpunk texts do not necessarily portray a future toward which the islands appear to be heading. Rather, they construct future narratives whose most salient characteristic is their radical difference from both the present *and* possible futures. When these texts conjure globalized dystopia, they place Caribbean spaces in the center of this future reality. In this way, the world(s) of the texts themselves—both the cyberspace the texts conjure and the flesh-and-blood future worlds they portray—become temporal heterotopias: spaces both logistically and temporally removed from readers' current realities.

Michel Foucault, who coined the term, understands heterotopias as "counter-sites": "a kind of effectively enacted utopia in which the real sites, all the other real sites that can be found within the culture, are simultaneously represented, contested, and in-verted" (24). Foucault uses the example of the mirror to explain the relationship between a heterotopia and reality. The mirror is a kind of utopia, a "placeless place" (ibid.). But it is also a heterotopia, since, as he puts it, "The mirror ... makes this place that I occupy at the moment that I look at myself in the glass at once absolutely real, connected with the space that surrounds it, and absolutely unreal, since in order to be perceived it has to pass through this virtual point which is over there" (ibid.). Like the reflection in a mirror, which is both real and unreal, the versions of Cuba or Puerto Rico that appear in cyberpunk texts are not (yet) real; even as they act as a foil for real places, reflecting certain aspects of these islands' present-day physical places, they explore other conditions that are completely fabricated or foreign. But Foucault also points out that heterotopias maintain an intimate connection between space and time, such that they might equally be termed "heterochronias" (26). The conventions of the cyberpunk genre offer Caribbean writers a means to fashion literary and artistic heterochronias, expanding the possibilities for imagining things outside dominant temporal narratives and structures of power.

Cyberpunk's often dark extrapolation of future possibilities might seem to mark it as an antithetical generic language for constructing a heterotopia. Yet as Anne Dvinge notes, heterotopias "contain both progressive and utopian possibilities as well as more regressive, even dystopian elements" (2). Indeed, while many Caribbean cyberpunk texts could be considered dystopian, these dystopias are often unusual for the ways in which they do not extrapolate from the present conditions of their authors. To understand the possibilities—and the limits—of what cyberpunk brought to Caribbean literature, this chapter examines the heterotopias crafted by two very different books, Cuban writer Michel Encinosa Fu's short story collection *Niños de neón* (2001) and Puerto Rican writer Rafael Acevedo's novel *Exquisito cadáver* (2004). Rather than viewing the islands as marginal peripheral spaces or as natural landscapes to be consumed, Encinosa Fu's and Acevedo's narratives move past the static moments of the current crises during which they were written to imagine the Caribbean islands as incorporated into a globally interconnected future. In keeping with cyberpunk's recognizable syntactic elements, these texts emphasize urban topography, locating the region as an integral part of a technologically advanced urban world whose organization is not defined by the boundaries of the nation-state. Yet while technology can sometimes be a tool for resistance, Encinosa Fu's and Acevedo's texts maintain a critical stance in relation to both technological development and sensorial phenomena; though the physical body is often at the center of any liberatory possibilities, it is also ultimately the limit of both spatial and temporal interaction. The separation of these textual worlds allows Encinosa Fu and Acevedo to play with heterotopias in two different ways: even as they offer up imagined environments different from Caribbean reality, they also showcase characters engaged in their own construction and maintenance of heterotopic spaces. In different ways, these cyberpunk narratives are temporal escapes that meditate on the finite possibilities of escape itself.

A Late Capitalist Future Seen from a Post-Soviet Moment: Michel Encinosa Fu's Ofidia

When Michel Encinosa Fu's *Niños de neón* was published in 2001, Cuban science fiction was perceived by both its creators and the broader national audience as a peripheral genre. Disparaged and abandoned during the "Quinquenio Gris," the most stringent years of governmental censorship in the early 1970s, science fiction had re-emerged slowly as an acceptable—and publishable genre—in the 1980s. *Niños de neón* was only the second Cuban book with any stylistic or thematic resonances with cyberpunk to be published, following Vladimir Hernández Pacín's short story collection *Nova de cuarzo* (1999). Although cyberpunk came late to Cuba, it emerged very much within Cuba's state-supported literary scene. Encinosa Fu was a member of the El Establo, a state-sponsored writing group whose members also included Hernández Pacín, Yoss (whose novel *Timshel* had been the first science fiction book to win the Premio David in 1988), Fabricio González Neira, Ariel Cruz, and Raúl Aguiar.[14] Yoss, Aguiar, and Encinosa Fu would go on to help found another writing workshop, Taller Espacio Abierto, focused exclusively on science fiction.[15] The appearance of cyberpunk thus coincided with the consolidation of a distinctly Cuban science fiction "fandom," made up of both readers and writers.

Yet writing in Cuba had been fundamentally altered by the so-called Special Period, the deep economic crisis that began in 1990 with the collapse of the Soviet Union—and the end of the Soviet Bloc as Cuba's primary trading partner—and which lasted in some form until the beginning of the new millennium.[16] The sudden end of Soviet trade subsidies and the absence of imported goods and materials from Eastern Europe forced a radical contraction of Cuba's economy. A lack of access to oil and gas led to frequent electricity blackouts, often for six to seven hours a day, resulting in the closure or partial closure of many places of work (Eckstein 95–96). Public transportation was severely limited, and breakdowns of buses and machinery for lack of parts were common. Food was rationed and supplies of other basic goods such as soap, cooking oil, and toilet paper were scarce.

Due to these material shortages, the publishing industry nearly shut down as well; newspaper publishing runs were reduced, and many books written during the leanest years of the Special Period were not published until years later (Eckstein 96). The lack of resources for books may also have been at least partially responsible for a shift away from long novels toward shorter forms, or toward narratives that could be consumed as both a longer novel and as related short stories (Sklodowska 18).

Although the Special Period most visibly altered the Cuban economic and material landscapes, it also marked a significant change in the island's relationship to time. In the language of Cuba's revolutionary government, the Revolution is never referred to as a finished event but rather as an ongoing present; the "completion" of the Revolution as a utopian future is never viewed as having occurred. However, the crisis of the Special Period forced many Cubans to question both the achievements of the Revolution and the possibility of the fulfillment of the revolutionary project. José Quiroga notes that "Cubans could not quite make sense of a logic where revolution and collapse could be put onto the same grid" (10). As Odette Casamayor-Cisneros puts it, after 1989, Cubans found that "ni su presente ni su futuro [estaban] en sus manos" [neither the future nor the present was in their hands] (38). Ironically, like the Revolution itself, the Special Period was another supposedly exceptional "moment" that has never officially ended. Cubans on the island were conscious of this temporal disconnect; in the preface to his anthology *Cuba in Splinters* (2014), writer Orlando Pardo Lazo speaks of the Revolution as a "national narrative that distances us from the rest of the planet—the Doppler Defect. What has caused us Cubans to be less contemporary: strange vermin forsaken by God and capital" (7). The revolutionary government's primary solution to the economic problems of the Special Period—to reopen the island to foreign tourism—only made this material and narrative temporal dissonance more noticeable, as Cubans found themselves sharing space with visitors who had access to all the material comforts and technologies of capitalist society in their home countries.

The writers who began publishing cyberpunk in Cuba in the late 1990s were not out of step with their literary peers more broadly. As González Fernández observes, cyberpunk in Cuba "participa de igual manera en el repertorio de leitmotivs que se suelen enumerar al hablar de la narrativa de los novísimos" (250) [participates equally in the repertory of leitmotifs that are often enumerated when speaking about the work of the *novísi*-

mos (writers who came of age in the 1990s)]. For González Fernández, this means that cyberpunk fiction shares with the production of writers such as Zoé Valdés, Ena Lucía Portela, Ronaldo Menéndez, and Ana Lydia Vega Serova, among others, a tendency to focus on marginalized elements of society: prostitution, AIDS, drug use, disaffected youth. I would argue that it also shares with literature of the 1990s a tendency toward what Odette Casamayor-Cisneros has called a "una ingravidad ética" (292) [an ethical weightlessness], a kind of floating existence, a refusal to engage with either older revolutionary messages or the current political stasis. Rather than rejection, the "weightlessness" that Casamayor-Cisneros ascribes to writers of this generation is an attitude of distanced observation.

Although Juan Carlos Toledano Redondo asserts that cyberpunk offered the Cuban writers of Encinosa Fu's generation "a literary style suitable for the representation of the decadence of that Cuban reality" ("From Socialist Realism" 448), the world that Encinosa Fu presents us with in the pages of *Niños de neón* re-creates an urban aesthetic that has more to do with the societies of what Fredric Jameson terms "late capitalism" than with the conditions of the Cuban Special Period under which Encinosa Fu's stories were written. Elana Gomel argues that rather than understanding cyberpunk in general as "dystopian" we should see it as "post-utopian," given that "the collapse of communism and other 20th century ideologies has left neo-liberalism and global capitalism without conceptual rivals" (Gomel 2). Certainly, at the time at which Encinosa Fu and his compatriots were writing, Cuba was still attempting to position itself as a surviving socialist alternative, despite the economic hardships its population was enduring. In Cuban literature, the very capitalist dystopia that Encinosa Fu conjures is thus notable for the contrast it offers both to the technologically impoverished Cuba of the 1990s and to the temporal narrative advanced by revolutionary discourse. Toledano Redondo argues that this apparent aesthetic conflict allows Cuban cyberpunk writers to construct a counter-narrative to socialist realism even as they offer a critique of late capitalism ("From Socialist Realism" 451). Indeed, as a closer look at the postutopian environment of three of Encinosa Fu's stories shows, the outlines of cyberpunk's late capitalist decadence allow him to craft a textual world, despite its gritty, even tragic elements, that is liberating in its radical difference to the Cuba of the late 1990s. The central tenets of that difference can be seen in the sense of interconnection produced by technology, resulting in a "shortening" of space and time; an urban setting that is notable for its excess and anonymity; and a social world shaped by both simulacra and the carnivalesque.

Like its companion volume *Dioses de neón* (2004), *Niños de neón* is largely set in Ofidia, a future, mirror-image of Havana that shares many of the aesthetic and structural features of classic cyberpunk settings. The island on which Ofidia is located is no longer really an island, thanks to the "Trans-Caribbean Highway," a superhighway that extends all the way from Florida in the north to the Amazonian city of Belém in the south. Technology has made travel quicker and has made everything seem smaller and closer. Ofidia itself is a highly developed, technologically dependent city, in which everything is connected to the *RED (Network)*, and where computerized systems control all aspects of the environment, including the climate. At the same time, cities in this future world are rigidly segregated; Ofidia's three sectors—Pueblo Alto, Pueblo Medio, and Pueblo Bajo—seem to be divided largely by social class, as well as function. The highly segregated, class-oriented world of which Ofidia is the center is profoundly capitalist in nature; as one character observes, "si no puedes consumir, eres inútil en la sociedad" (112) [if you can't consume, you are useless to society]. The state appears to have largely disappeared, its functions taken over by several generic, totalitarian corporations—e.g., Consumption Corporation, Transportation Corporation—that govern and organize much of urban life. As the "neon" in its title indicates, the dystopian atmosphere of Encinosa Fu's collection remains aesthetically indebted to the work of films like *Blade Runner* and *The Matrix*. The reader may assume that Ofidia is Havana, but the truth is that the city in these texts is devoid not only of the Cuban capital's major historical landmarks but also of anything that could be seen as colloquially "Cuban." Indeed, the urban world Encinosa Fu conjures follows Scott Bukatman's observation that "[c]yberspace arises at precisely the moment when the topos of the traditional city has been superseded" (121–22). If the Havana in which Encinosa Fu penned *Niños de neón* was engaged in marketing its well-preserved, uniquely "Cuban" historical areas, the city that emerges in his stories is defined by its ultra-urbanness, but also by its anonymity, which is both physical and temporal.

In keeping with cyberpunk's antiauthoritarian ethos, Encinosa Fu's stories illuminate the marginal corners of the world of Ofidia and the liminal subjects—hackers, thieves, gangsters, contract killers, and prostitutes—that inhabit these spaces. As Toledano Redondo has noted, however, there is a distinct lack of emphasis on technology in Encinosa Fu's narratives, which are consistently more about "humans with human problems" ("From

Socialist Realism" 457). The atmosphere of his narratives, as I have argued elsewhere, is notably noir, both physically and emotionally: many of the stories take place at night, in spaces that are literally or figuratively dark (night clubs, the city sewers), and there is a pessimistic—if not nihilistic— tone to many of the narratives.[17] Violence is omnipresent, whether in the form of calculated contract killings, street-gang warfare, crimes of passion, or more casual acts that speak to a disregard for life. The stories' protagonists are survivors, both the authors and victims of some of these violent acts as well as witnesses to more generalized violence and degradation around them. What is notable, in addition to this climate of violence, is the focus on the text's temporal present. Even as Encinosa Fu's narratives offer a heterotopian escape in their simultaneous separation from and relationship to Cuban temporality, they also focus on characters engaged in their own construction or maintenance of heterotopias, creating spaces of sanctuary and respite, however temporary, from the harsh world beyond. This can take the form of refuge in virtual realms, in fantasy and simulacra. But it can also mean taking momentary refuge in physical spaces or experiences that offer temporary respite, if not permanent salvation.

Enmeshed in a world in which technology can isolate and separate, Encinosa Fu's characters search for sensual, physical connection to the present moment. "Ángel," the third story from *Niños de neón*, centers around a short-lived romantic triangle that goes awry. The story's narrator-protagonist, Katrina Kowalezcu, is a hacker who works with her girlfriend Laura, nicknamed Puño de Hielo [Ice Fist]; Katrina disables corporation-security software from her computer, allowing Laura to steal materials and documents on site. Their perfect balance is upset when Katrina picks up Ángel, a beautiful drifter, on a business trip for new software, and brings him home to Ofidia. Although Laura is at first jealous of her partner's new lover, she, too, eventually takes him to her bed. Thus begins an unusual threesome and a new dimension in Laura and Katrina's relationship.

Although she recognizes that Ángel is "un vagabundo que vendía su cuerpo y sus poemas a cualquier perdularia falta de afecto como yo que se atravesara en su camino" (34) [a vagabond who sold his body and his poems to any love-starved scatterbrain who crossed his path], both Katrina and Laura bond with Ángel in a way that they have not bonded with each other. Katrina's description of the night she finds Laura and Ángel in bed together is particularly revealing of these changes: "No sentí enfado alguno, sólo una alegría purificadora. Me acosté junto a ambos, hecha un ovillo; besé la oreja de miel de Ángel y me dormí. Soñé con una iglesia, donde un conjunto de lobunos feligreses rezaban a un Cristo de sal. Soñé con un viaje de intrusión donde no existían para mí barreras ni hielos" (38) [I felt no anger, just a purifying happiness. I lay down next to them, curled into a ball; I kissed Ángel's honeyed ear, and I fell asleep. I dreamed of a church, where a group of wolflike parishioners prayed to a Christ of salt. I dreamed of a hacking excursion with no barriers or ice]. True to his name, Katrina sees in Ángel something of the angelic, a kind of mythical savior. The hacker who has nicknamed herself "the Virgin"—"porque hasta ahora nadie ha logrado jamás penetrar mi hielo y acceder a mis secretos en software" (35) [because so far no one has ever penetrated my ice and accessed my software secrets]—finds that Ángel accesses a new dimension of her inner being. Instead of dividing Laura and Katrina, he brings them closer together, as the three create a kind of new relationship, "un paraíso en la tierra" (39) [a paradise on earth], a shared love among three individuals.

If cyberpunk offers itself as a kind of heterochronia, Ángel's presence temporarily creates an alternative reality for both Katrina and Laura, a time away from their quotidian, technologically mediated experience. Part of his attractiveness for them seems to be his difference from their world. As Nazare notes, cyberpunk characters are frequently "potentially alienated not just from society but from their own minds and bodies" (386), and Katrina and Laura make their living from manipulating the omnipresent technology. Although they work "together," their division of labor—Katrina hacks the security systems; Laura carries out operations in situ—creates a separation within this close cooperation. Ángel's engagement with pretechnological modes of creation like poetry and collage seems to generate a nostalgia for a simpler, more connected life. Indeed, the text contrasts the cold precision with which Katrina narrates the various steps of a hack with the tenderness with which she narrates her relationship with Ángel and Laura. When the trio graffiti a wall one night, their drawing shows "tres figuras humanas, concebidas como por hombres de las cavernas" (39) [three human figures, as if drawn by cavemen], a visual representation of both the primacy and the centrality of their relationship. If Katrina's life before Ángel was an "existencia gris" [gray existence], his presence allows them to imagine other, more lively and embodied ways of being.

Yet just as Ángel's arrival opens them to other ways of relating, his departure threatens to forestall these possibilities. Like the celestial being his name references, he is not of this world, only passing through, and his decision to move on destroys the fantasy in which the two women have been living, provoking a crisis in both women as well as in their relationship with each other. The structure of Encinosa Fu's text parallels the combustible encounter between these two realities. Katrina and Laura's relationship with Ángel, relayed in a series of flashbacks, alternates with a moment-by-moment narration of a job that Katrina and Laura appear to be finishing, with Katrina watching from the computer as Laura breaks into a building. Only at the end do we realize that this is a setup; Katrina has Laura trapped in the building, deactivating the security system only to reactivate it once she is inside. Katrina's betrayal of her partner is an act of revenge; spying on Laura through her artificial-eye implant, she was a silent witness as Laura murdered Ángel by strangling him with her bare hands: "Yo he muerto ya una vez, Laura, cuando a través de tu implante ocular vi tus manos—que parecían las mías—fundirse al cuello de Ángel, en un callejón de Pueblo Bajo donde lo habías seguido, y apretar y apretar y apretar" (43–4) [I died again and again, Laura, when, through the ocular implant I saw your hands—that seemed to be mine—tighten on Ángel's neck, in an alley in Pueblo Bajo where you had followed him, and squeeze and squeeze and squeeze]. Laura, the cold, methodical thief, kills her lover because she can't bear to be without him. Yet in Katrina's description, it is hard to tell whether her own horror stems from the wrongness of Laura's actions or from the way in which they intersect with her own passionate desires; when she witnesses the murder through Laura's eyes, the hands encircling Ángel's neck become her own as she becomes simultaneously both witness and perpetrator.

In the story's last moments, Katrina, her job done, her relationships with both Ángel and Laura irrevocably finished, passes by the wall the three lovers had painted. The mural is no longer visible; only one of Ángel's feet can be glimpsed, hidden under a "holoposter," the pretechnological creative moment erased by technology. She leaves some flowers, as if it were a memorial, observing as she does so, "*Consumatum est:* dijo alguien famoso que no recuerdo. Que para bien—o para mal—sea. Ya eso no importa" (44) [*Consumatum est,* said someone famous, I don't remember who. May it be for good—or ill. That no longer matters]. Her plan to avenge Ángel's death is indeed finished. Yet while Christ's death on the cross, referenced in "Consumatum est," was a sacrifice to save humankind, the doorway to a new kind of temporality, Ángel's death seems to open the door to far more ambivalent ways of being. His presence revealed new possible ways of loving and living to both Katrina and Laura, and the tenuous harmony created by their relationship with him is gone completely. Indeed, in the end Katrina finds herself completely alone, truly free from the limitations of her previous mode of existence but without a clear path to follow. That the "ending" of her revenge tragedy "no longer matters" suggests that an open future may be less than desirable.

If the heterotopian relationship in "Ángel" is built around intimacy, "Mi nombre es nadie" (My name is no one), the fifth story in *Niños de neón*, constructs a cyberpunk heterotopia through the use of anonymity. The narrative is one of the few that does not take place in Ofidia; the central action of the story occurs in Prague. The story follows the unnamed protagonist, an aging contract killer, over the course of a day as he accepts and carries out a hit. The job, presented as a routine killing of a wealthy target, proves to be harder than he had anticipated; he survives but is wounded in the process. A visit to a backdoor doctor also proves dangerous when she, too, tries to betray him. The protagonist finally seeks solace and momentary safety with a young prostitute he met briefly in the bar where the killing took place, only to discover the morning after their encounter that she is a replicant who has been infected with a lethal sexually transmitted disease. As the story closes, the hit man accepts his impending death, returning to the bed where the prostitute is still asleep.

As the title indicates, the sense of anonymity in "Mi nombre es nadie" is conveyed first and foremost by its characters. The story's unnamed protagonist is not only anonymous for the reader; when placed in a situation where he must introduce himself to another character, he states only, "Yo soy" [I am] (53). The only crucial details that the reader learns about the hit man are that he is originally from Ofidia, and that he is no longer "hacha joven" (64) [a young axe]. But many of the other characters are also unnamed, referred to only by titles referencing their function or typology: "the prince" (the wealthy target), "the gorilla" (the bodyguard), and "the girl" (the prostitute). The only characters that have names are "Noria" [Water wheel], the man who pays for the hit, and "La Estrella" [The Star], the clandestine doctor who attempts to silence the hit man after she tends to his wounds, and even these names sound like aliases. The last words exchanged between the dying hit man and the woman who has infected him are, "No me has dicho tu nombre" [You haven't told me your name], to which the response is, "Tu tampoco . . . pero eso no importa" (66), [You neither . . . but that doesn't matter]. Indeed, the text leaves it unclear whether the prostitute remembers who her companion is or whether she has confused him with someone else. The lack of identifying details, of backstory, ensures that the reader's attention remains focused on what is happening in the narrative's present moment. The emphasis is not on *who* these characters are, but on how they engage with one another. When the hit man says, "I am," his statement is an affirmation of his existence in this moment. Even if the characters have a past, they are living within—and for—this one day.

In keeping with its anonymous characters, the setting of "Mi nombre es nadie" stands out for its very lack of particularity, from its separation from anything that might be recognized as colloquial, folkloric, or novelistic. Although the city in which the action unfolds is identified as Prague, it really could be any large urban environment. The text gives us just one glimpse of Prague's skyscrapers, shining in the distance "cual estilizadas mazorcas de luz" (53) [like stylized corncobs of light]; nowhere is there any mention of the Czech capital's historical landmarks. From the reflections of the protagonist, the reader is given to understand that it is now a peripheral city that suffers in comparison to Ofidia in both size and complexity, but this is a Prague divorced from its history. The text's descriptions of place focus largely on tactile details, many of which would be applicable to any large urban environment. In the reader's first view of the protagonist, he is crouched in an alley, "la espalda contra la mugre de una pared" (52) [his back against the grime on the wall], contemplating the rats and spiders that keep him company in this marginal space. The indoor spaces are similarly generic; as the hit man contemplates the prostitute's room, he observes it contains, "[n]ada notable, solo la clonada mediocridad de una puta novata" (65) [nothing notable, only the cloned mediocrity of a novice prostitute]. Ironically, it is the very ordinariness of his surroundings that allows the protagonist to lower his guard, a mistake that he will pay for with his life.

The anonymous nature of "Mi nombre es nadie" also, significantly, gives the narrative an out-of-timeness and an out-of-placeness. Indeed, read against a corpus of Cuban literature from the 1990s in which the intimate geographies of a Cuban setting—most often the capital city—are omnipresent, the generic urbanness of "Mi nombre es nadie" provides an almost shocking difference.[18] Without knowing more about the characters, it is impossible to measure the significance of the events of the night for anyone except the participants. Was the "prince" someone important? Will his assassination alter the course of this world? This anonymity also helps to lend the story its ambivalent, bittersweet quality. While the contract killer looks his target in the eye, the disease he has contracted kills its victims indiscriminately. The actions of the story's eighteen hours have life-and-death stakes for these individuals, yet the rest of the city goes on. This very anonymity reveals the expendability of these lives. On the other hand, as Toledano Redondo observes, anonymity offers the protagonist a kind of solace, a protection; unrecognized, he is allowed the final encounter with the prostitute who is "another nobody, another shadow in the city" (458). The attraction of the space (and moment) in which the protagonist takes his final refuge may be precisely that he is not required to be a hit man or a prince; in its lack of specificity, it is a space in which he can just be.

If stories like "Mi nombre es nadie" and "Ángel" focus on characters who have been able to manipulate the technology of Ofidia to their own ends, whether that technology comes in the form of weapons or computers, "Niños de neón," the eponymous and last story in the collection, centers on those who live on technology's margins. The story's protagonist is an eight-year-old street urchin, known only by his gang nickname, Abeja Ceñuda [Scowling Bee]. In truth, Abeja has no other name; he is one of a population of unregistered children, abandoned by their parents and without the money to pay for digital documentation that would confirm their existence. Although he has neither the space nor the funds for the necessary equipment to be a professional hacker, Abeja is a "hacker" of the city itself; he and the other child members of his gang, the Bastardos Rojos [Red Bastards], have learned to navigate the city's physical underbelly, traveling from place to place through underground tunnels and plumbing pipes that serve as on-the-ground connection to digital crime. In the interest of survival, they have crafted a true counterspace to the above-ground city, an alternative city that allows them to live on what is discarded or stolen from the world above.

In contrast to the underground world of the sewers that it will shortly introduce to the reader, "Niños de neón" begins with another kind of heterotopia: a children's carnival in the wealthy section of Pueblo Alto seen through Abeja's eyes:

> Hubsie; la mascota PA infantil del momento, reina sobre el carnaval y sus labios de jerboa holográfico cantan la rima de turno: "Sé feliz en el sueño del día; sé feliz, más feliz todavía". Y miles de niños, obedientes hasta la adicción del comando subjugante de la felicidad, se desgañitan en un coro frenético, mientras una catarata de caramelos se les obsequia desde el cielo, desde las fauces abiertas del dragón-zeppelín, y las anfetas invaden sus organismos privilegiados. (107)

[Hubsie: the infantile PA mascot of the moment, reigns over the carnival, and his holographic gerbil lips sing the verse in turn: "Be happy in today's dream; be happy, even happier still." And thousands of children, obedient to the addiction of the subjugating command of happiness, scream their heads off in a frenetic chorus, as they are rewarded with a waterfall of candy from the sky, from the open jaws of the zeppelin-dragon, and the amphetamines invade their privileged organisms.]

The description, with its overtones of addiction and subjugation, is ambivalent; as Hubsie's song intones, the scene is indeed a temporary dream, an escapist fantasy for children who can afford to participate in the carnival. And yet the fantasy does provide at least a momentary happiness for these "privileged organisms." The contrast between the Pueblo Alto children's celebration and Abeja Ceñuda's life in the tunnels sets up the temporal atmosphere of the story. Having snuck away from guard duty to watch the festivities—and gather fallen candy—Abeja Ceñuda is aware of the ambivalent nature of this fantasy, just as he is aware of his own desire for any temporary respite that this world might provide him, should he have access to it.

Abeja Ceñuda's dalliance at the children's carnival turns out to have been a costly mistake: while he was away, a rival gang—the Detritos Espaciales, known colloquially as the *espaciomierdas* [space shits]—attacked the Bastardos Rojos's stronghold, severely wounding several gang members and carrying away Maravilla, a severely disfigured girl whose knowledge of digital security allows the Bastardos Rojos to carry out their small criminal jobs. The espaciomierdas want to exchange Maravilla for control of a key piece of the underground geography. Feeling that Maravilla's kidnapping is his fault, Abeja Ceñuda attempts to rescue her on his own. The rest of the story is the narrative of this ill-fated rescue attempt. Abeja is amazingly able to find Maravilla thanks to a lucky break; Maravilla's older brother, a full-fledged hacker, gives Abeja a complete printout of the plans to the city's tunnels. Working in analog, Abeja is thus able to ambush the espaciomierdas, surprising them long enough to run off with Maravilla. However, it becomes clear that they may not make it back to the safety of their home "territory" before being overtaken.

Midway through Abeja and Maravilla's escape, the story takes an unusual temporal hiatus; seeking to rest and recoup their strength, the pair climb into what appears to be an abandoned maintenance room. In a room covered with erotic posters, Abeja finds a newspaper from the year 1999. "Uf, vaya si estamos en una caverna primitiva" (122) [Wow, what a primitive cave we're in] he exclaims. In a narrative that has been largely distinct from the reader's temporal moment, this encounter with material remains from a date in our recent past pulls us closer to the dystopian time of the story. Ofidia's dystopian violence and class segregation has seemed an invention; suddenly, we are not so far away—there but not there, as in Foucault's mirror. This sense of connection is only reinforced when Maravilla offers to tell Abeja a story. "¿Conoces el cuento de Peter Pan y Wendy, Abeja?" (123) [Do you know the story of Peter Pan and Wendy, Abeja?] she asks. Up until this point, the stories in *Niños de neón* have carefully avoided temporal references, even when they refer to geographic coordinates—Florida, Prague—with which the reader might be familiar. It is as if, in this last narrative, Encinosa Fu brings the reader in to the possibility that Ofidia may be a/our future, confirming its identity as a heterotopia, there and yet not (yet) there.

The mention of *Peter Pan*—and, more significantly, the Lost Boys—creates another significant point of intertextual connection and comparison. Neverland was a kind of heterotopia, one that the Lost Boys chose to dwell in indefinitely. Member of another tribe of "lost boys," Abeja has never been given a choice of when to grow up; rather, he has been forced to face adult responsibilities and consequences too quickly. For children of the tunnels like Abeja, childhood itself is a kind of purgatory. As the text observes, "Esto era sólo una muerte miserable y cotidiana, hasta que hallabas la entrada a una irrealidad distinta con un puñal clavado en el pecho o la sonrisa de aceptación de algún jefe de las calles" (113) [This was only a miserable and quotidian death, until you found an entrance to a different irreality with a dagger to the chest or the smile of acceptance from some street boss]. Abeja has no family and no past to return to. Faced with either death or acceptance into an older gang as the only possibilities, his focus, like that exhibited by characters in many of the other stories in the collection, is on time in the present. His only option, if he wants to live, is to keep going.

In the end, Abeja and Maravilla's need to keep going forces not only an end to this temporally limited heterotopia but also a radical encounter between the world of the tunnels and the world outside. Just when it appears that they are trapped between a sewer grate and the advancing espaciomierdas, they manage to push through the grate and exit into the middle of the children's carnival in Pueblo Alto. The rival gang follows them, still firing their lasers, sowing chaos in the heart of the city's inner sanctum: "Gritos infantiles. Ecos de sirenas legales. Murmullo aéreo de turbocópteros de prensa. En vivo y en directo, desde el corazón de Pueblo Alto, desde la médula de Ofidia, desde el núcelo neural del mundo" (126) [Children's screams. Echoes of legal sirens. The aerial murmur of press turbocopters. Live and direct, from the heart of Pueblo Alto, from the marrow of Ofidia, from the world's neural nucleus]. The careful segregation of worlds has been breached, revealing the fragile nature not only of the carnival's heterotopian fantasy but also of Ofidia's own social organization. The police arrive, and Abeja Ceñuda is shot with a tranquilizer dart. His last act, as he falls to the pavement, is to grasp at some fallen candy, a kind of last reach for one of the few momentary pleasures he has known.

As Abeja's tragic end exemplifies, the characters in Encinosa Fu's stories rarely find lasting respite or escape. The heterotopias they discover or construct are fleeting and imperfect. The heterotopia of Encinosa Fu's own book is similarly imperfect, there and not there. In his elaboration of the world of Ofidia, Encinosa Fu sticks to many of the stylistic and thematic elements of cyberpunk. The result is a dystopian landscape whose high-capitalist degradation creates a contrast with the Cuba of the 1990s. Yet these very elements—an ultraurban, highly technological and morally ambivalent environment, a largely masculine gaze—replicate some of cyberpunk's own silences, especially with regard to gender and race. In his fidelity to the aesthetic language of cyberpunk, Encinosa Fu creates a spatiotemporal landscape that offers an escape for readers grappling with the challenges of Cuba's Special Period. But in doing so he sidesteps a deeper consideration of what a future Cuba might look like.

Bodies in and out of Time: *Exquisito cadáver*

The 2001 publication of *Exquisito cadáver* marked a new direction for its author, Rafael Acevedo, as well as for Puerto Rican literature. The novel was Acevedo's first foray into narrative fiction after four highly regarded books of poetry, and the first of his two science fiction narratives to date.[19] Although other Puerto Rican writers—notably Marta Aponte Alsina, José Liboy Erba, and Pedro Cabiya—had begun contemporaneously incorporating speculative elements in their fiction (and would continue to do so), *Exquisito cadáver* stood out for its explicit use of syntactical and thematic elements from cyberpunk even as it was marketed within "mainstream" literature on the islands.[20] The daring nature of Acevedo's project was recognized when the book was subsequently awarded the prestigious Casa de las Américas Prize. While Cuban cyberpunk writers were, to some extent, writing for a local community of other writers and enthusiasts of science fiction, a similar community did not yet exist in Puerto Rico at the time of publication for *Exquisito cadáver*. Acevedo's text thus brought the genre's elements into a cultural sphere that was not (yet) habituated to them. Ángel Rivera observes that science fiction begins to be cultivated as a genre on the island only after the publication of Acevedo's novel (74–75). The novel marks a significant moment in the broader science fictional turn in Caribbean literature even as it occupies an exceptional position in the Puerto Rican corpus, making its strategic employment of the cyberpunk worthy of closer examination. *Exquisito cadáver* did not set off a cyberpunk "scene" in Puerto Rico, but it certainly initiated what has become a sustained interest in science fiction on the island.

The 1990s inaugurated an extremely dynamic moment in Puerto Rican arts and letters. After a kind of "integration" in the 1980s of what Puerto Rican cultural critic Elsa Noya describes as, "lo que era, podía, o debía ser, un sistema literario y cultural nacional frente a la situación de dependencia colonial" (768) [what the national literary and cultural system was, could, or should be in the face of the situation of colonial dependency], the 1990s witnessed a diversification of critical viewpoints—thanks in part to the influence of poststructuralist criticism—and an explosion of publications by a group of younger writers. In tandem with this expansion of the space of cultural debate, there was a diversification of political views, as the traditional connections between left-leaning intellectuals and a support for Puerto Rican independence was no longer a given. Rivera identifies Acevedo, along with fellow science fiction author Pedro Cabiya, as members of a group of writers who "escapan del efecto centrípeto de los debates de corte nacional o nacionalista" (77) [escape the centripetal effect of debates around national or nationalist topics]. Acevedo's deployment of cyberpunk may have been novel, but his engagement with a broader set of intellectual questions was in step with the time.

Although it was not immediately apparent, like Cuba, Puerto Rico in the late 1990s also found itself at the beginning of a significant economic crisis, but in a vastly different context. A "Free Associated State" of the United States since 1948, the island was effectively a US colony. Its economic stability and development were largely dependent upon US regulations. The year 1996 saw the beginning of the phasing out of Section 936 of the US tax code, which had provided tax incentives to US businesses—especially pharmaceutical companies—operating subsidiaries in Puerto Rico. The removal of this incentive resulted in the gradual flight of foreign investment from the island, leading to a stagnation of Puerto Rico's economy and the beginning of a series of economic crises as the government attempted to make up for the loss in revenue by issuing more and increasingly fragile bonds.[21]

The ability of Puerto Ricans, as holders of US passports, to travel freely to and from the American mainland has produced what the sociologist Jorge Duany refers to as "a nation on the move" (3) and what writer Luis Rafael Sánchez, in a 1983 short story, more colloquially named "la guágua aérea" ["The Flying Bus"]: a population of transnational subjects who engage in a circular migration between island and mainland with relative ease.[22] But this very mobility has meant that in times of economic crisis or downturn, those with the means to do so can leave the island for other opportunities. The first mass exodus of Puerto Ricans to the United States occurred in the post–World War II era. The 1990s saw the beginning of a second large exodus that ran parallel to the aforementioned economic changes. As Duany notes, between 1991 and 1998, almost a quarter of a million Puerto Ricans left the island, such that by 2000 there were more Puerto Ricans residing in the United States than in Puerto Rico itself (Duany 13). In the years following the 1996 changes to the tax code, the drain of skilled citizens leaving the island was a shadow exodus that ran parallel to the flight of US and foreign capital. *Exquisito cadáver,* and the world Acevedo creates, provide an interesting refraction of this economic uncertainty.

Set in Urbania, a futuristic San Juan in which state bureaucracy and actual governing power reside in a state-corporation and "máquina administrativa" [administrative machine] called The System, Acevedo's novel maintains the fusion of science fiction and the detective genre that marks many Anglo-American cyberpunk narratives. As Rivera has noted, the outlines of the novel's central plot are heavily influenced by *Blade Runner* (80). The unnamed narrator-protagonist secures a job at a privatized detective agency where he engages in advanced surveillance techniques that involve "scanning" the eyes of the recently deceased. In keeping with the detective framework, the text begins with the mysterious appearance of two dead bodies: one an anonymous cyberpirate whose corpse is left in the street, the other a high-profile System Administrator, shockingly presented as the main course at his own banquet. Yet the detective narrative is ultimately undermined, first when the nature of the crimes themselves is thrown into doubt, then when the narrator begins to question his job responsibilities and his own behavior. His search to understand leads him to reject both the System's repressive practices and its stranglehold on narrative, an act of rebellion that finds him disconnecting from Urbania's omnipresent technology and finally engaging in a romance with a mystery woman who may also be a replicant revolutionary.

As with Encinosa Fu's Ofidia, Acevedo's Urbania has an identifiably dystopian edge; it is a technologically advanced society in which the state and private corporations have merged in decidedly totalitarian ways, in which humanity is rigidly defined (and replicants easily expendable), and in which the scarcity resulting from environmental degradation leads to both social unrest and increasingly rigid state control of both humans and material resources. Yet where Encinosa Fu's narratives present Ofidia as a closed alternative universe, the environment of *Exquisito cadáver* stands out for its porosity. Guillermo Irizarry notes that in its creation of a futuristic, dystopian Puerto Rico, the novel "construye un espacio social liminal, ubicado entre lo vivo y lo muerto, entre la posnación y la nación" (203–4) [constructs a liminal social space, located between the living and the dead, between the postnation and the nation], but the same description could be applied to Acevedo's text itself. Taking its name from a surrealist parlor game in which players take turns writing on a piece of paper to produce a collaborative text, the novel reproduces the game's playful spirit of pastiche and collage, first intertextually—interweaving quotes from other writers into the text as epigraphs, direct quotes, and dialogue—then, perhaps more significantly, through the narrative's fusion of elements of science fiction with philosophical parable, slipstream, and noir.[23] In this way, as Melanie Pérez Ortiz observes, "Es una reflexión sobre el acto de representación y sus instrumentos o medios posibles más que sobre la escritura en sí" (158) [More than a reflection on the act of writing, it is a reflection on the act of representation and the instruments or media available]. Like the mirror in Lewis Carroll's *Alice through the Looking-Glass*, Acevedo's narrative creates a constant slippage between physical, lived reality and what is virtual, imagined, fantasized, or even staged, destabilizing the sense of a linear timeline as it does so. Indeed, as the narrator begins to question the System's linear narrative of events, the experience of other (virtual) realities, made possible through technology, pushes the narrator—and the reader— away from a blanket acceptance of historical, linear time and toward a focus on the present moment and the ethical interpersonal encounters to be found therein. Countertimes, the novel's multiple small heterotopias, emerge from these moments of engagement.

Exquisito cadáver's play with linear time begins in the novel's two epigraphs. The first is taken from Cuban writer José Lezama Lima's prose poem "Muerte del tiempo" ("Death of Time," in *La fijeza*, 1949): "La gravedad no es la tortuga besando a la tierra" (87) [Gravity is not the tortoise kissing the earth]. Lezama's poem explores the way in which perception destabilizes our understanding of time, and the verse Acevedo includes as the epigraph enacts this destabilization, recalling both a concrete sense of time and space—the turtle's kiss a slow, steady approach to the ground, an encounter between the animal and the earth—only to reject it. The second epigraph, drawn from Stéphane Mallarmé's dramatic poem *Hérodiade*, is a long apostrophe that echoes Foucault's description of the mirror as a heterotopia. Hérodiade (Herodias) recalls how she searched in the depths of the mirror's reflection for her memories, only to find that, "Je m'apparus en toi comme une ombre lointaine" (44) [I appeared in you as a distant shadow]. Her experience of finding herself "there and not there" foreshadows the process the protagonist—and, with him, the reader—undergoes over the course of the novel. These epigraphs gesture not only toward a general sense of temporal instability but also toward the text—and, implicitly, the lyric in particular—as its own space of temporal capture, its own heterotopia.

The sense of temporal and spatial destabilization suggested by the epigraphs from Lezama and Mallarmé would seem to dissipate with the first scenes of the novel. In the first chapter, related in the second person, the narrator finds himself in New York City's Harlem in winter, in a moment of indecision and ambivalence: "Caminas por la Duke Ellington Boulevard. Ha caído el Muro de Berlin y no te importa" (7) [You walk down Duke Ellington Boulevard. The Berlin Wall has fallen, and you don't care]. Wandering west, he finds himself in a Cuban café, where he orders "arroz amarillo, pollo, café expreso. Café, dices, como quien dice droga" (8) [yellow rice, chicken, espresso. Coffee, you say, like someone says drugs]. This description gives the reader concrete temporal and spatial coordinates; the "recent" fall of the Berlin Wall places us in 1989, while Rosita's (or La Rosita, as it was formally called) was a restaurant on Broadway and 108th Street in the Morningside Heights neighborhood of Upper Manhattan. The desire for the food, the experience of it, the pungent warmth of the café in contrast to the wintry landscape, coupled with the narrator's desire to return home—"Tienes que regresar, volver allá" (8) [You need to return, to go back there]—all contribute to a vivid sensation of concrete reality. The warmth of the Caribbean is invoked from a nostalgic position of diaspora; travel is physical, by foot and then by plane, as the narrator struggles to find a way to JFK Airport.

Yet this initial temporal and spatial solidity is later revealed as illusory; just as the first chapter locates the reader in a concrete reality, the second chapter places this in doubt. The narrator is back in New York City in winter. Speaking in the first person now, he visits a Buddhist monastery (a heterotopia in New York City if ever there was one), where he stays for three years. On leaving the monastery, he emerges back on to the Harlem streets, disoriented, only to then observe, "Entonces me quito las gafas de mi máquina de visión y miro el contador de tiempo. Llevaba casi tres horas conectado" (11) [Then I take off the glasses of my vision machine and look at the timer. I'd been connected for almost three hours]. His experience in the monastery is itself revealed to be a fabrication, created through a virtual reality simulator. This suggests that the narrator's "memory" of walking through Harlem in 1989 was also a virtually staged experience. Indeed, in that first scene, the narrator tells a street watch salesman, "[E]l tiempo se queda, yo soy el que pasa" (7) [Time stays in place; I'm the one passing through], a statement that seems to reference the experience of using the vision machine. The machine fuses the temporal and the spatial; each moment is a "place" to visit, a distinct heterochronia.

The visual may be the gateway to heterochronic moments, but it is also the primary mode of both narrative perception and social control. In the narrator's professional life, sight is a means to glean information; as a detective, he is being trained to read thoughts by looking into the eyes of an individual, either when they are alive or shortly after they are deceased. The narrator's rejection of The System begins when the separation between the "real" and the "virtual" ways of seeing is called into question. Two events initiate his pulling away. In the first instance, the narrator discovers a corpse on an unprogrammed rainy day:

> Miré nuevamente el cuerpo de Gonzalo Fernández. Miré su rostro y no pude dejar de leerlo. Comencé a sentirme terriblemente angustiado. Alguien tocó mi hombro izquierdo. Era un extraño ente al que conocería más tarde como Johnny Walker. "Don't you ever look at a dead man face," dijo en tono paternal. Yo lloraba, quizás por la muerte, quizás por el olor a piña recién cortada, o por ti. (20)

[I looked again at the body of Gonzalo Fernández. I looked at his face, and I couldn't stop reading it. I began to feel terribly anxious. Someone touched my left shoulder. It was a strange being that I would later come to know as Johnny Walker. "Don't you ever look at a dead man face," he said in a paternal tone. I was crying, perhaps because of the death, perhaps because of the smell of ripe pineapple, or because of you.]

Against his training, the narrator begins to connect emotionally with the dead man. Yet when he asks his boss, Claris, about the body, he is told that the man was "un biopirata de poca monta" (21) [a petty bio-pirate], and that he died of natural causes. But then, how to explain the lingering sense of unease and angst, not to mention the evocative scent of ripe pineapple?

It is hard not to see this ocular connection as an instance of the experiencing of what philosopher Emmanuel Levinas has called "the face of the Other." For Levinas, an encounter with the face of the other establishes a deep state of relation, out of which can be born a pure ethical response: "The face opens the primordial discourse whose first word is obligation" (*Totality and Infinity*, 201). The technique through which the narrator is charged with carrying out his repressive task is also how he achieves a coming to consciousness.[24] In any case, the profound relationship established by this face-to-face contact demands an ethical action. Rather than "reading" the dead man for information, the detective forges a connection with him through his gaze, which in turn stimulates an emotional response.

In *Exquisito cadáver*, taste and smell are the senses that serve to structure the novel's heterotopias; as we have seen in the narrator's experiences with the vision machine, they anchor the narrator in the present moment of an experience, whether real or virtual.[25] The narrator's encounter with Gonzalo Fernández's body is not the only time that the sensorial experience of taste or smell functions as something more than the gathering of information; Acevedo's text is rife with both literal and figurative mentions of taste and eating, often described in ways that produce similarly unexpected connections. The smell of pineapple that surrounds Fernández's body is important for the emotional response that it evokes in the narrator, a sadness and anxiety that is unconnected to his personal experience. (It is the anti-madeleine, emotional presence that emerges unconnected to an actual memory.) It is not a direct synesthesia, in that a smell is still a smell, yet the sweet odor of pineapple is not indicative of the tropical fruit itself, but rather a whole range of experiences.[26] When this scene comes back to the narrator later in the text, as perhaps a dream, perhaps a memory, it is the pineapple smell that "le añade una escala a ese mapa de ficción" (191) [adds a scale to this fictional map]. By extension, the smelling, tasting, and particularly preparation of food become both mediators and metaphors for relationship. The smell of ripe pineapple emanating from the body of Gonzalo Fernández signals that the narrator will begin to relate to him not merely as an object but as a human being. The sensory experience pulls the narrator into a moment of relation in a profound way.

The text adds a further dimension to the detective's sensory experience of the pineapple when it includes a description of the pineapple from Spanish chronicler Gonzalo Fernández de Oviedo's *Historia general de las Indias* (1535) as if it were the narrator's own observations of the fruit. Fernández de Oviedo's description is the sixteenth-century version of a vision machine. Writing for a reader who would likely not have seen a pineapple before, the Spanish chronicler is attentive to all the ways in which the fruit can be perceived and experienced. The result is a kind of parenthesis in Acevedo's text, a temporal suspension in which the reader contemplates a pineapple—via colonial history—before returning to the anonymous corpse in front of the detective.

Gonzalo Fernández's body is just the first instance in which experiences of taste and smell reflect the narrator's increasing conflict between his inner desires and his participation in the System's structures of control. After he is ordered to deactivate a replicant who is supposedly "a public threat," he plays out a scenario in the vision machine in which he is on the run in Southeast Asia, experiencing tremendous hunger: "[E]l estómago me pedía exilio. Sólo pensaba en arroz. Una taza de arroz. Y con aquel olor de mariscos en el aire hubiera sido suficiente" (115) [My stomach was asking for exile. I only thought of rice. A cup of rice. And with the smell of shellfish in the air, that would have been enough]. The ambivalence that the narrator has experienced about shooting the replicant—he suspects that the man may not be guilty, or not guilty as charged—plays out in the sequence staged by the vision machine as a sense of lack, an absence of food.

The second point at which both the narrator and the reader begin to lose sight of the border between what is real and what is not occurs when he is called to serve two replicants with a "yellow ticket," a warning that they are under surveillance for possible conduct violations. His interaction with the replicants, a couple who identify themselves as Frederick and Windows, goes beyond the limits of his job description; indeed, Windows spirits him away to another—virtual?—space, where she gives him a small box covered with Chinese characters. Their interaction is intimate and flirtatious; looking into her eyes, he finds himself attracted to her: "Me sentía atado a ella, su voz era como una ruta de seda, su mirada luz de luna" (38) [I felt tied to her, her voice was like a silk route, her glance moonlight], even though he knows she is a replicant, even though the reason for their conversation, as well as its location in time and space, is far from clear.

The detective's emotional connection to Windows is not the only part the incident that unsettles his understanding of what is so. Seeing that the narrator has deviated from the job he was sent to do, Claris and two agents step in, shooting and deactivating Frederick. The narrator finds himself emotionally affected by the replicant's death: "Aquellas gotas de aceite derramadas por Frederick me deprimieron. No era sangre, estaba claro. Pero algo había muerto. Era como una metáfora de aquello en lo que nosotros nos estábamos convirtiendo" (40) [Those drops of oil Frederick had spilled depressed me. It wasn't blood, that was true. But something had died. It was like a metaphor for what we were turning into]. Rather than reaffirming the difference between human and machine, the detective's experience of the replicant's death minimizes the separation between them.

The narrator's emotional responses to Windows and Frederick make him question the nature of what is happening to him and what he has been asked to do. Yet as the novel progresses, visual technologies themselves begin to "malfunction," revealing the constructed nature of temporal narratives. The narrator has become what he refers to as a "cyberjunkie" (65); as we witness firsthand in the second chapter, his primary method of escape in his free time is his "vision machine," a *Perceptron III* (refurbished) that allows him to construct alternate realities and explore historical events. At first these historical episodes are recognizable for the reader. But then the machine, which has some technical problems, begins to mix elements from different historical scenarios. In one significant experience, the 1989 protests for democracy at Tiananmen Square are invaded by stone-wielding Germans (presumably from the moment of the toppling of the Berlin Wall) and a researcher from the Human Genome Project. What were initially designed to be discrete heterotopian experiences now bleed into each other.

If the narrator's interaction with replicants causes him to question the nature of his job, the appearance of the second body in the novel highlights the irreal nature of the System itself. The System Administrator has not simply been murdered at his own dinner party but prepared as part of the meal: "[E]l cuerpo del personaje principal de la fiesta apareció en la cocina, crudo, pero aderezado como si fuera parte de la gran cena. El cadáver estaba rodeado de pasta, *spaghetti ai frutti di mare*" (49–50) [The body of the party's main celebrity appeared in the kitchen, raw, but seasoned as if it were part of the great feast. The cadaver was surrounded by pasta, *spaghetti ai frutti di mare*].[27] The narrator recognizes the antiauthoritarian gesture as allegory: "Alguien había transformado la ciudad en cena. Un ojo caníbal. Un hambre de cambio" (63) [Someone had turned the city into supper. A cannibal eye. A hunger for change]. Considering the place of taste in the text, the desire to turn the city into a meal suggests an attempt to undo systems of control to alter the timescale of relation; to ingest the city would be to create a momentary experience out of indefinite bureaucracy. Despite the clarity of this exquisite cadaver's visual message, however, it fails to be fully understood. Although the Administrator's death will be investigated, he is immediately replaced by another functionary. As Pérez Ortiz observes, "Mientras que los humanos son desechables y reemplazables, la máquina social sigue funcionando" (161) [While human beings are disposable and replaceable, the social machine continues to function]. Indeed, the investigation into the Administrator's death, an act that should anchor the plot and motivation of the "detective story" at the heart of the novel, is revealed to be a kind of performance. Although a replicant cook confesses to the crime, it is not clear that he is guilty; evidence appears to indicate that his brain was tampered with. Other details of the crime are similarly called into question.

As his encounter with Windows and Frederick reveals, the detective's job, particularly the act of gathering this information (a kind of mental invasion, albeit postmortem), becomes gradually repugnant to him. He begins to be haunted by the vivid scenes of replicant interrogation and "deactivation" that he has witnessed, including killings in which he may or may not have participated. This haunting becomes a full-scale rejection of The System's repressive methodology when his friend STB is killed for ostensibly maintaining terrorist thoughts, something the narrator knows not to be true. This crisis of conscience leads the narrator to "go rogue"; with the assistance of the replicants, he removes the neurochip that grants him the ability to read others. He returns to the street, no longer a part of the system of digital information but instead an embodied human: "Con la conciencia del cuerpo. A su merced. Ésa era la subversión. No un plan. Un estilo de vida" (167) [With the consciousness of my body. At its mercy. That was the subversion. Not a plan. A lifestyle]. He attempts to find in the purely corporeal another way of reading, a more ethical way of being.

The narrator's literal "unplugging" from Urbania's System signals his decoupling from its temporal narrative. This is echoed by the structure of Acevedo's text itself. The novel is divided into three parts. The first and longest section centers on the events previously described: the detective's hiring and training, his experiences on the job, his eventual rejection of what he is being asked to do, and a dramatic final scene in which he himself attempts to escape arrest. In the third and final section, the narrator is rescued by the replicants, learns that he has been unknowingly an agent for the system, has his neurochip removed, and begins a new life beyond this programming. In between these two parts of the detective's story, however, is a second section, which chronicles the Proyecto Orión, in which a crew of replicants is sent to the Orion Nebula in search of a planet with water, which has become scarce on Earth.[28] The project fails; the crew does find water, but they ultimately refuse to complete the mission and return to earth, preferring to explore the wonders of the new world they have discovered. What was to be an extractive mission becomes a voyage of existential discovery: "En este océano perfecto en todos los sentidos se confirma la existencia de los deseos. El agua es un deseo que se extiende por décadas y lugares" (140) [In this ocean, perfect in all ways, the existence of desires is confirmed. Water is a desire that extends through decades and places]. The crew of the Proyecto Orión have found that recognition is utopian in its realization of their projected desires.

The defection of the crew of the Proyecto Orión finds a kind of parallel in the narrator's experience in the last section of the novel. Without connection to the electronic data that register his presence in the System, his new life in Urbania occurs in a kind of heterotopia, a new, mobile city. The center of this new world is a romantic relationship, the culmination of a love affair between the narrator and an unnamed woman, who may or may not be Windows. Their emotional connection is carried out through an exchange of glances: "Ahora no puedo dejar de leer tu rostro ... se olvida uno a otro, quieto y puro, por completo potente y vacío" (169) [Now I can't stop reading your face . . . they forget each other, quiet and pure, completely potent and empty]. In love, the face produces not merely ethics but transcendence. Pérez Ortiz characterizes this section—correctly—as prose poetry (169); this is the lyric subject in love and in relation. The use of the second-person and the third-person plural in these last chapters creates a slippage between the narrator's love interest and the reader: "Estábamos en aquel lugar alejado del Centro. Y estábamos bien. A veces alguien llegaba por allí" (207) [We were in that place away from the Center. And we were fine. Occasionally someone would arrive]. The space and time of this new countersite is undefined, but in that indeterminacy, the text seems to suggest, lies possibility.

Cyberpunk Past and Future

In his elaboration of the concept, Foucault understood heterotopias as relating to real spaces in one of two ways: either the heterotopia creates "a space of illusion that exposes every real space, all the sites inside of which human life is partitioned, as still more illusory," or it offers up "another real space, as perfect, as meticulous, as well-arranged as ours is messy, ill-constructed, and jumbled" (27). The textual heterotopias that Encinosa Fu and Acevedo construct with cyberpunk's syntactical elements illustrate these different relationships. *Exquisito cadáver* seems most aligned with Foucault's first definition; the text's porous narrative seems designed to move the reader to question the nature of experience, the division between human and machine, and even the nature of perception itself. Through an exploration of how "embodiment" can be experienced physically and, paradoxically, virtually, the narrator's journey both creates and removes illusions, ultimately providing a meditation on the constructed nature of reality. Encinosa Fu's "neon" fictions, on the other hand, offer a refracted vision that, if not about social perfection, is perfect in its articulation of capitalist dystopia and degradation, offering a window into late capitalism as an alternative to Cuban socialism. In this sense, both *Exquisito cadáver* and *Niños de neón* provide the reader—particularly the Caribbean reader—with a spatiotemporal escape from the writers' present. Yet in their proximity to real Caribbean spaces and times of crisis, these heterotopias provide a distance from which to critique those adjacent presents.

Beyond the moment of its emergence in Cuba, on the cusp of the new millennium, cyberpunk has had an uneven trajectory in the Hispanic Caribbean. It has never become a "Movement," as Bruce Sterling called the first Anglo-American rise of the genre. The last narrative to remain fully committed to many of cyberpunk's most notable aesthetic and thematic preoccupations may be Erick Mota's alternate history *Habana Underguater* (2008), analyzed in chapter 5. Yet the cyberpunk stylings of *Exquisito cadáver* and *Niños de neón* initiated the recent science fictional turn in Caribbean literature that this book explores by revealing the potential in its shifting temporalities, particularly its expansive conditions for engaging "otherwhens" as well as the critical potential of those new worlds. As a result, while Toledano Redondo is right to conclude that the genre never became "a mainstream style among many sf authors on the island" ("From Socialist Realism" 396), neither has it completely gone away. Cyberpunk elements can still be found in more recent fictions from the region such as Miguel Pruné's *Cosmos Burlesco* (2012), Elaine Vilar Madruga's *Bestia* (2015), Maielis González Fernández's *Sobre los nerds y otras criaturas mitológicas* (2016), and Daniel Burguet's *Cuando despierte* (2019). Indeed, Achon's and Mota's returns to the genre in visual form, using neon as a heterotopian overlay, speak to the power of the subgenre and its aesthetics to remove us from our current place and time and to create the conditions for an escape from the here and now.

4

In the Time of the Zombie

Remaking a Caribbean Icon

"All zombies are inherently remakes," Sarah Juliet Lauro observes, tongue in cheek, in her study *The Transatlantic Zombie* (148). Lauro's statement can be understood in two ways: As human beings that have been separated from their human consciousness (pre- or postmortem), the undead are literally remade from formerly living humans. More metaphorically, the zombie is now an international icon with a vast literary and cinematic corpus, every new example of which necessarily draws on and responds to the preceding models.[1] The renewed interest in zombies has created no shortage of these "remakes"; the last decade has witnessed the appearance of an increasing number of films, TV series, novels, and graphic novels in not only the United States but also places as diverse as Hong Kong, Korea, Pakistan, Norway, India, Indonesia, Chile, and Colombia.[2] The zombie as a popular figure clearly travels well, with each "remake" often operating simultaneously within both international and regionally specific realms of signification.

This chapter investigates the presence of the zombie in recent cultural production in the Caribbean, for the region has not remained immune to the vogue in narratives about the undead. In the case of the Caribbean, however, the zombie's (re)appearance is not an arrival but a return; the figure's historic connection to the region gives its flexible liminality an added significance. The modern concept of the zombie is drawn from Haitian folklore rooted in African belief systems (Ackerman and Gauthier). The Haitian *zombi*, a recently deceased body reanimated by magic to serve one master, exists in "that misty zone which divides life from death" (Métraux 282), in complete subservience to the person who made it. Although I argue for reading the zombie in Hispanophone Caribbean cultural production as a science fiction trope, the zombie's Caribbean origins and significant history mean that the undead that appear in Cuban, Puerto Rican, and

Dominican novels, short stories, and films can't help but reference aspects of these other, earlier zombies from the region. In these Caribbean texts, zombies thus function, science-fictionally, as "a locus of radical *alterity* to the mundane status quo" (Freedman 54) while signaling critiques specific to the region's historical and cultural circumstances.

In contrast to the cultural artifacts that I examine elsewhere in this study, which take up science fiction as a mode with which to imagine new ways of being, zombie narratives employ the undead as a temporal haunting, causing them to intrude on the world of the text as a physical reminder of histories, mindsets, or systems that have not (yet) been cast off in the push to create new futures. As beings who have been radically, artificially severed from the rhythms of biological life and death, zombies exist in a state of temporal suspension, a *destiempo* or "untimeliness" with respect to the humans around them; they do not evolve, they do not age, and they are neither passing through life nor moving toward death. This metaphorical connection to death—for, as Sara Lauro and Karen Embry remind us, the zombie is an "ontic/hauntic object," both an actual and a symbolic presence—has helped connect the zombie to the past and, specifically, to Haiti's past ("Zombie Manifesto" 86). M. Elizabeth Ginway observes that zombies "are the ultimate expression of an intermediary state" in that in their undeadness "they embody the paradox of a present haunted by an embodied past" (*Cyborgs, Sexuality, and the Undead* 1). Through their radical alterity, Caribbean zombies incarnate the remains of the past and point to time out of joint.

The temporal dissonance that zombies incarnate in the texts in which they appear is not unlike the temporal disjunctures that film critic Bliss Cua Lim has observed in Filipino films with fantastic or supernatural elements. For Lim, the presence of the fantastic reveals the fracture between a dominant (Western, colonial) worldview and another that has not yet been subsumed or subordinated. Like the supernatural elements that Lim analyzes, I argue that zombies are also evidence of "immiscible times." Yet unlike the fantastic in Filipino cinema, zombies are not a reference to precolonial temporal forms. Rather, they are evidence of what is left behind from those very colonial processes. Serving as symbols of temporal, ideological, or discursive stagnation, they highlight some fundamental characteristics of Caribbean societies and their lingering effects. Specifically, they reference the region's historical relationship to slavery as well as the histories of labor exploitation and racialized social exclusion that have emerged as slavery's aftereffects.

As a being forcibly bound to serve another, the Haitian zombie is both a symbol of and a metaphor for the experience of chattel slavery, a reflection of the plantation system that was at its height in colonial Saint Domingue before the Haitian Revolution. Building off Orlando Patterson's characterization of slavery as a form of social death (2008), Natalie Belisle argues that the zombie is "the most iconic representation of social death" (26). Haitian zombies were described as sent to do undesirable tasks, to work odd hours or to labor late into the night, thus incarnating slavery's dehumanizing effects. The zombie's *destiempo*, its out-of-timeness, is part and parcel of its connection to slavery. As Saidiya Hartman has observed, for postslavery societies that have never fully reckoned with the weight of that violent history and the grief it engendered, the past is very much still present, particularly for the descendants of those who were enslaved: "[T]he 'time of slavery' negates the common-sense intuition of time as continuity or progression; then and now coexist: we are coeval with the dead" (759). This is the state of being that Christina Sharpe has described as "in the wake": "to occupy and be occupied by the continuous and changing present of slavery's yet-unresolved unfolding" (13). The Caribbean zombie is the incarnation of this spectral past that is not past, not fully alive but shambling along all the same.

The zombie's historical connection to slavery in the Caribbean also makes it an inherently racialized figure. Although, as we shall see, contemporary Caribbean zombies are not always explicitly racially coded, the appearance of the undead in a Caribbean text often has something to say about racialized systems of social stratification both present and past. As human bodies that are considered "not human," zombies illuminate various kinds of exclusionary social borders. If monsters, as critic Mabel Moraña argues, generally signal the biopolitical (123), the zombie, in the words of Aalya Ahmad, "remains redolent of the subaltern" (131), despite its many travels and transformations. In their representation of biological "bare life," they can also represent those who have no agency within a current system.[3] As Gerry Canavan observes, "Zombies are always other people, which is to say they are Other people, which is to say they are people who are not quite people at all" (432). The zombie's function as a marker of biopolitical bare (un)life has been useful for Caribbean writers and directors who have used zombie fictions to reveal the ways in which racialized colonial systems of exclusion remain active into the present.

Through its connection to the figure of the slave, the zombie offers a postcolonial critique that ties this foundational labor system in the Caribbean to subsequent models of labor exploitation in the region. As Kerstin Oloff reminds us, "The zombie's continued relevance as a figure that encodes alienation is rooted in the Haitian experience of the emergence of modern capitalism, which depended on, and was propelled by, the exploitation of the colonies" ("'Greening' the Zombie" 31). In its controlled docility, the zombie has been seen as a worker who is literally incapable of resistance.[4] At the same time, as a myth associated with the only country in the Americas founded as the result of a successful slave rebellion, the Haitian zombie also maintains a connection to rebellion from slavery. In this sense, the zombie in the Caribbean paradoxically speaks both about social death and about modes of survival (Arroyo).

To show how Caribbean fictions use the zombie's temporal liminality and its connection to foundational Caribbean systems of exploitation to critique current situations of stasis and highlight continued exclusionary or exploitative practices, this chapter explores four recent zombie narratives. Both Cuban director Alejandro Brugués's film *Juan de los muertos* (Juan of the dead, 2011) and writer Erick Mota's short story "That Zombie Belongs to Fidel!" (anthologized, in English translation, in *Cuba in Splinters: Eleven Stories from the New Cuba*, 2014) chronicle zombie epidemics or invasions in Cuba as a way of highlighting the friction between revolutionary narrative/state discourse and daily life on the island.[5] Puerto Rican author Pedro Cabiya's novel *Malas hierbas* (2009; *Wicked Weeds*, 2016), which plays liberally and literally with making and remaking zombies, returns to the zombie's place of origin, where the figure provides a fertile vehicle for exploring Haiti's position with respect to the Dominican Republic and the status of Caribbean narrative. Finally, Puerto Rican author Pabsi Livmar's short story "Golpe de agua" ("Water Strike," in *Teoremas turbios*, 2018) provides us with a stripped-down version of the zombie that both returns the figure to the essence of the enslaved worker and strips away the borders separating human and zombie. In these narratives, the zombie's temporal and biopolitical "otherness" makes them flexible, visible vehicles for highlighting the connections between historical traumas and contemporary social borders, particularly those associated with race and ethnicity as well as neoliberal structures of power. In their fact of being liminally "stuck," they show us what around them has also been unable to move forward.

From Folklore to Science Fiction: The Zombie Journey

To understand how the zombie has come to be understood as a science fictional figure, it is helpful to review the transformations it has undergone in literary and cinematic cultural production. Within the Haitian context, the *zombi* is an undeniably national symbol, one that maintains strong symbolic ties to the various dimensions of the country's history.[6] Yet the Haitian zombie also has a long history as a transnational figure. Its connection to Vodun and other folkloric traditions made it the object of considerable interest to early travel writers to Haiti who arrived on Hispaniola during the US occupation of Haiti (1915–34) and the Dominican Republic (1916–24). Drawn to the island as the repository of an "exotic" Caribbean otherness, these travelers exploited this element in their texts. Travel narratives from the 1920s and '30s, such as William Seabrook's *The Magic Island* (1929) or Zora Neale Hurston's *Tell My Horse* (1935), present an image of Haiti as the locus of an enigmatic realm of non-Western magic, in contrast to Western (North American) reason.[7] These supposedly real accounts of zombies, which were hugely popular, became fodder for fictional publications, where zombies added an exotic touch to pulp novels' exaggeratedly dramatic tales.[8]

As it migrated to popular US print and film culture in the early twentieth century, the zombie came to be seen as symbolic of the Caribbean region more broadly. Early Hollywood zombie movies, which appeared around the same time as their pulp fiction counterparts, borrowed from the content and tone of these early narratives to present Haitian—and, by extension, Caribbean—culture as darkly mysterious, dangerous, and "other" to Western logic and order. As Lauro observes, "The zombie myth itself became a kind of slave when it was abducted by American and European filmmakers, voided of its previous associations, branded as a new signifier, and made to bear a very different psychic load" (135). In films such as Victor Halperin's *White Zombie* (1931) and Jacques Tourneur's *I Walked with a Zombie* (1943), both of which feature white women (one American, one Canadian) who become zombies after traveling to the region, Caribbean culture appears as menacing and contagious and zombies serve as both vehicles for and symbols of contagion.

Of course, there is another kind of zombie. Director George Romero may have drawn on the Haitian type for his first zombie film, *Night of the Living Dead* (1968), but as Peter Dendle notes, Romero also "single-handedly re-defined the zombie" (50). The zombie introduced by Romero's horror films is the ultimate cannibal monster, driven by the need to consume human flesh, or, failing that, bite humans and thus transform them into other zombies. These "post-Romero zombies" (2), as David Dalton has termed them, are no longer magically "made" from the dead and buried to serve a master; instead, they are drawn from the ranks of the infected living, who, bitten by zombies, are "reborn" as undead and proceed to infect others through their desire to feed on human flesh. Romero-type zombies roam in packs, which grow in number as their victims rise again to become other zombies.[9] Unlike the Haitian zombie, whose living death might be intimately connected to the life experienced before, Romero's zombies (and those that have followed his model) are almost always seen as an enemy or an evil to be fought against. Narratives about a zombie epidemic often deal less with how the zombies came to be created than about how humans must now deal with them. Dalton notes that the cannibalistic zombie of recent Latin American cinema "threatens to invert the roles of colonizers and colonized" (3). If the Haitian zombie's enslavement was understood as potentially temporary, contemporary zombie hordes represent a radical challenge to the status quo.

In giving zombies a rational reason for their existence, Romero's construction of the zombie clearly draws from science fiction rather than from the fantastic. In contradistinction to Haitian undead, post-Romero zombies are no longer generated through magical enslavement; instead, they are literally contagious, the product of an illness such as a virus or an extreme dose of radiation. Despite their monstrousness, their existence has a scientific explanation, even if it could be argued that the lack of a known origin for the virus "represents the failure of science and rationality" (Ballina 205). Haitian zombies are created to serve a human master's demands; Romero's zombies instead respond solely to biological drives, principally the desire for human flesh.[10] In this form, zombies simultaneously "embody physical corruption, reminding us of our own mortality" (Boon 35), and represent contagion; the fear is not that of being killed by a zombie but of eventually becoming one.

Since *Night of the Living Dead*, zombies on screen have often been viewed more as examples of the horror genre than as science fiction, and there is no doubt that the divisions between the two popular genres can be difficult to parse. In an early essay, Bruce Kawin asserts, "Both horror and science fiction open our sense of the possible," but he differentiates between the genres by observing, "Most horror films are oriented toward the restoration of the status quo rather than toward any permanent opening" ("Mummy's Pool" 294). Indeed, zombie-apocalypse films that follow Romero's model largely exemplify Kawin's assertion that "[h]orror is fascinated by transmutations between human and inhuman (wolfmen, etc.), but the inhuman characteristics decisively mandate destruction" (*Horror Film* 81). However, Kawin's early definition is based on the differences he observes between classic American science fiction cinema and horror films of the 1950s. In his later work on horror, he acknowledges that a film can fit into the "crossover" or "shared" subgenre of science fiction horror, "[i]f there is a strong science fiction premise *and* if the burden of the picture turns out to induce horror" (*Horror Film* 73). The Caribbean zombie narratives I analyze here depart from a science fictional premise but complicate the attempt to distinguish between science fiction and horror in other ways. Although some of these fictions, such as *Juan de los muertos*, do deal with a zombie "invasion" or "apocalypse," most of them do not present a clear return to the status quo (assuming the identity of what constitutes the "status quo" is even clear or attainable). Indeed, they often signal a fundamental corruption of the body politic; there is no healthy body—or time of origin—to which to return. Furthermore, these narratives show how an "us-vs.-them" stance is ultimately neither successful nor, in some ways, possible to sustain. Indeed, as autochthonous Caribbean bodies, the zombies in the fictions examined in this chapter problematize the division between national bodies and other bodies, between self and other, and between past and present realities. Through the ways in which they signal an inability to move beyond foundational trauma or temporal stasis and a continued engagement with exploitative systems, the undead make visible the unending temporality of contemporary Caribbean dystopias.

Capitalizing on the Zombie Apocalypse: *Juan de los muertos*

When Alejandro Brugués's *Juan de los muertos* debuted at the Havana International Film Festival in 2011, Cuban audiences were treated to something unprecedented: a zombie movie set and filmed in Havana, by a Cuban director, with a largely Cuban cast. This was a new kind of film for Cuba; Brugués's comic imagining of a zombie apocalypse on the island offers a direct departure from the realist tradition that has largely dominated Cuban cinema since 1959.[11] Through both title and plot, *Juan de los muertos* identifies itself as a Cuban version of *Shaun of the Dead* (2004), British director Edgar Wright's spoof of the zombie film genre in which two English slackers take on a zombie apocalypse. In *Juan de los muertos*, the slackers are Cuban, but like their British counterparts, they rise to the occasion to fight the zombies when the crisis presents itself.

It would be wrong, however, to characterize *Juan de los muertos* as simply a Cuban remake of its British predecessor. As Dunja Fehimović observes, Brugués's film "cannibalize[s] foreign products to create something new" (149).[12] *Juan's* humorous intertextual references tie it to the corpus of English-language zombie movies, even as its references to classic Cuban films work to reframe the Cuban cinematic canon. If *Shaun* satirizes the zombielike existence of the British consumer capitalist, *Juan* is an exposé of the rottenness of the Cuban revolutionary state and its narrative of temporal progress. The staging of a zombie apocalypse in Havana allows Brugués to satirize some particularly Cuban issues: the changing relationship between the individual and (collective) society, the post-Soviet climate of "getting by," the prevalence of what Cubans call *el doble moral* [double morality], and the question of and anxiety over diaspora. The context of the zombie epidemic also allows the film to return to the fraught figure of the New Man and the socialist project from very different perspective. If zombies are a radical otherness, *Juan* shows how very strange and "other" to itself Cuban society has become.

A brief comparison between *Juan de los muertos* and its British predecessor reveals the ways in which Brugués adapts the now-international model of the "zom-com" to the Cuban context.[13] Both *Shaun* and *Juan* make use of the cognitive dissonance of a zombie outbreak to humorously critique certain aspects of their respective societies. Yet while *Shaun's* zombies reveal the lethargy and conformity at the heart of British society, Brugués's film gestures toward the death of socialist ideals, celebrating the survivor instinct—the emergence of a new kind of laboring body and its emerging guerrilla capitalism—as much as it parodies it.

Shaun, Wright's protagonist, is a contemporary British everyman: a nice guy with a decent but unexciting job (managing an electronics store) and a decent, if unexciting, life. His idea of a night out is to spend an evening down at the local pub, the Winchester, with his juvenile best friend Ed and his girlfriend Liz. Liz wants their life together to be more exciting, but Shaun can't seem to find the energy to make a change. When Liz decides she has had enough of Shaun's inertia and dumps him, the arrival of the zombie outbreak the following day gives him both the motivation and the opportunity he needs to redeem himself. He and Ed discover how to fight off the zombies, "rescue" Shaun's mother and Liz, and lead a small group of survivors to the Winchester. It takes the arrival of the zombies—creatures even more conformist than Shaun himself—to reveal the brave and determined leader underneath Shaun's modest, apathetic exterior.

Shaun's opening credits present the key to the film's humor. The camera engages in several wide shots that show ordinary Londoners engaged in their daily lives, riding the bus, sorting groceries. The joke is that these people *already look like zombies;* they go about their day in an automatic, unconscious fashion. So closely do they resemble zombies that when the zombie epidemic begins, the undead are indistinguishable from uninfected humans. Shaun himself, at the beginning of the film, is equally zombielike; we see him enter the corner store to grab a soda and fail to notice the bloody handprints on the refrigerator. Through these scenes, *Shaun* pokes fun at how twenty-first-century urban capitalist labor turns us all into zombies. Only the dire straits in which humanity suddenly finds itself are finally enough motivation to rouse Shaun from the stupor in which he lives his life. In this way, *Shaun* traces, in humorous fashion, the transformation of a capitalist "zombie" into a supposedly more "awakened" citizen.

Although J. Andrew Brown is to some extent right that Brugués "hangs his film on the narrative of the earlier film" (7), *Juan of the Dead* does not chronicle a similar awakening. Juan, the protagonist, might be seen as an antihero rather than an everyman. In contrast to Shaun's days of drudgery, Juan spends his days drinking rum, romancing his upstairs neighbor, and illegally fishing in Havana Bay, accompanied by his friend Lázaro, an even more uncouth slacker than Juan himself. The film's seemingly idyllic first scene makes clear Juan's cavalier attitude toward work. Juan and Lázaro sit on a homemade raft, gazing at the afternoon sun shining on a turquoise blue Caribbean Sea. "¿A veces no te dan ganas de irte remando a Miami?" [Don't you sometimes want to set out rowing to Miami?], asks Lázaro. Juan shakes his head and answers: "¿Para qué, chico? Allá, yo tengo que trabajar . . . Además, yo soy un sobreviviente. Sobreviví a Mariel, sobreviví Angola, sobreviví al Período Especial y la cosa esta que vino después . . . Esto es el paraíso, y nada lo va a cambiar" [Why, man? Over there, I'd have to work . . . Anyway, I'm a survivor. I survived Mariel, I survived Angola, I survived the Special Period and this thing that came after. This is paradise, and nothing will change that]. As it ironically references the tourist's characterization of the Caribbean as a "paradise," this exchange identifies Juan as "a weightless character," a protagonist literary critic Odette Casamayor-Cisneros sees as typical of recent Cuban fiction (315–16). Indifferent to the myth of heroic Cubanness, having already survived a series of previous national trials or crises, Juan lives in a "floating" state, planning nothing, attached to nothing, taking what comes day by day. If Shaun is unconscious of his time, Juan is aware that time is a good part of what he has, something made clear in the ironic reference to paradise. As we see in the film's first exchange, he readily admits that he prefers not to go to Miami because there he would have to work, adding, "Aquí soy un recolector, como los taínos. Es cuestión de sentarse a esperar" [Here, I'm a gatherer, like the Taínos. It's just a question of sitting down to wait], a description that emphasizes his identity as an autochthonous Cuban. Juan's floating state is also a kind of temporal stasis where he privileges "waiting" and inaction, for most aspects of his life seem to have ground to a halt. Juan is divorced, and his ex-wife lives abroad in Spain. His attractive adolescent daughter Camila, back in Havana to visit her grandmother, wants nothing to do with her father, whom she perceives as an alcoholic failure with criminal tendencies. The zombie outbreak allows Juan to redeem himself in the eyes of his daughter, but not because he rescues her nor because he undergoes a radical change in outlook; rather, the arrival of the zombies interrupts his "floating" state, temporarily giving his life the motivation it has been lacking.

Notably absent from *Juan's* opening credits is the vision of people at work presented in Wright's portrait of London. Certainly, the camera's slow pan reveals an older woman trundling down the street with a shopping cart and people moving in a slow, meandering fashion that could be described as "zombified." Yet no one seems to be working here. The scene reveals that many of Juan's compatriots also live in a floating kind of time. *Juan* uses the zombies' disruptive conformity to break open the placid nature of this urban landscape, to poke fun at both old revolutionary socialist fervor and the new opportunistic capitalist ethos.

Juan's conversion to "hero" after the zombie outbreak is in line with his unorthodox, unsanctioned habits of survival. If Shaun is blind to the zombie outbreak until one literally almost bites him, Juan is almost immediately aware that something is amiss and begins planning a way to work the situation. Brugués has observed that *Juan* demonstrates three distinctly Cuban survival strategies: "to try to carry on as if nothing had changed, to find a way to profit from the new situation, and/or, when all else fails, to leave the island" (quoted in Fehimović 156). Juan is motivated to action only when it becomes clear that he will no longer be able to continue with the previous status quo.

The zombies' arrival exposes the hollowness of some of the standard rhetoric of Cuban socialism. Despite the zombie's connection to the Caribbean region and its long history as a consumable product of US popular culture, when zombies begin appearing in Havana the city's residents, including Juan and Lázaro, have no idea what they are. The government responds by labeling the zombies "dissidents," thus fitting this new crisis into the old rhetoric. TV news coverage warns Cubans to stay away from these dangerous individuals who are "backed by the U.S. government."[14] The irony of calling zombies "dissidents" will not be lost on viewers; with their horde behavior, the undead are clearly the ultimate conformists. At the same time, the zombies *are* dissidents in the sense that their behavior represents a radical disruption of the status quo. Motivated by their hunger for human flesh, the undead cannot be swayed by ideology, coerced by fear, or tempted by greed.

The first appearance of a zombie in Juan's neighborhood underscores the irony of the government's response, as it is none other than Mario, the president of the local Committee for the Defense of the Revolution, the neighborhood Socialist Party office. When Mario begins wreaking havoc at a neighborhood meeting, lumbering down the front steps of his building and grabbing the first neighbor he can find to feed on, his appearance provides Juan with the first clue that the zombies are not, in fact, dissidents. After listening to the government news broadcast, Juan observes, "No me jodas, chico. Mario no es ningún disidente. En mi vida he visto un gordo más chivato y más maricón que ese" (You've gotta be fucking kidding me, man. Mario's no dissident. I've never seen a fat guy who was more of a rat and a faggot in my life). Mario has thus gone from figuratively feeding on people (accusing them of being "antirevolutionary" to benefit his own standing in the party) to literally eating them. The most "loyal" of Cubans, someone directly responsible for carrying out the dictates of the revolutionary government, has become a physical parasite.

The zombification of Mario and his fellow "good Cuban citizens" makes visible the ideological and temporal rifts in Cuban society. If Juan's "floating" life is at odds with both the revolutionary spirit and revolutionary "immanence," in Brugués's film it is the aging revolutionaries—and the discourses of the Revolution—that are framed as temporal anachronisms.[15] Despite the skepticism of people like Juan and Lázaro, the old revolutionaries like Mario—and, the film ironically suggests, revolutionary fervor itself—have not gone away; instead, they are present as monstrous, reanimated things. Zombification gives new meaning to the verse from the national anthem sung at the neighborhood gathering, "Morir por la patria es vivir" [To die for the fatherland is to live]. Those citizens who die are "reborn" to "live" as zombies; to be "dead" to the patria—outside the boundaries of Cuban national space and Cuban citizenship—may be the only way to live. At the same time, Juan now must literally kill these once-good-Cuban-citizens to save the country and himself, an uncanny echo of other sacrifices in the Revolution's history.

Juan presents the viewer with a temporal irony; if the revolutionary government is slow and static, unable to respond to change, zombies are all drive and action. As Mario's rampage at the neighborhood meeting reveals, the unchanging nature of socialist rhetoric is completely ineffective at containing the zombie epidemic. Later events in the film demonstrate that the historical models of socialist action are equally ineffective for dealing with the new crisis. Returning home one evening, Juan and his friends are "kidnapped" by a truckload of revolutionary-style commandos. Declaring that they are rescuing survivors to arm them and "raise the walls of a new community," they strip Juan and his friends naked (presumably to reveal any zombie bite marks) and chain them together in the back of a military-style convoy truck. The commander, a handsome man in fatigues, announces, "Quien no está con la comunidad está en contra de la comunidad" [Whoever is not with the community is against the community], directly echoing Fidel Castro's famous pronouncement in his 1961 speech "Palabras a los intelectuales," "Dentro de la Revolución, todo; contra la Revolución, nada" (12) [Within the Revolution, everything; against the Revolution, nothing]. This strategy turns out to be fatal when it is revealed that one of the enchained men is infected. His complete zombification leads to a mutiny in the back of the truck as the men try to escape being bitten, and this "new society" ends before it begins when the driver is accidentally shot in the chaos and the truck crashes.

As those who have previously "triumphed" in society become the zombie epidemic's first victims, Juan becomes the most unlikely of heroes, in that to a great extent he has given up on heroism itself. His early description of himself as a "survivor" is significant. To be a survivor is not to triumph; it is to get by, to live by making the best of a series of bad situations, to remain alive. The ability to *resolver* (literally, resolve), to cobble together a solution, allowed Cubans to make it through the worst scarcities of the Special Period, the post-Soviet economic crisis of the early 1990s. As Cuban writer Yoss points out, Juan "es la personificación de la resistencia del cubano 'normal,' de su capacidad para hacer de su necesidad virtud, para vivir del invento" (51) [is the personification of the 'average' Cuban's resilience, of his capacity to make necessity a virtue, to live by invention]. Ironically, the person who shows himself to be best able to deal with the zombie crisis is not a shining example of Cuba's "New Man," the model socialist individual envisioned by Ernesto "Che" Guevara, but someone Guevara might have viewed as a social failure.[16] Juan is no tireless worker, willing to sacrifice everything for the socialist project; he has no political ideals, zero ambition, and is motivated largely by self-interest rather than altruism. Despite his status as a failed "New Man," the parallel established between Juan and the socialist regime—which, some might argue, is likewise hanging on (surviving) through simple longevity—is impossible to ignore. Yet as the film reveals, Juan's capacity for invention, his ability to see through rhetoric, and his willingness to adapt to new situations in the present are precisely what allow him to avoid becoming a zombie. The implication, as Fehimović has observed, is that the zombie invasion is just one more crisis in Cuba's constant state of crisis (156).

A motley collection of similarly pragmatic social misfits joins Juan in his fight against the undead. In addition to Juan's daughter Camila and his friend Lázaro, they include La China, an effeminate, cross-dressing gay man who makes a living as a petty thief; El Primo, La China's large Afro-Cuban friend, who sports a Mike Tyson–like tattoo on his face but faints at the sight of blood; and Vladi California, Lázaro's son, a handsome hustler who spends his time romancing tourists and dreaming of escaping the island. As both Sara Potter and Maribel Cedeño Rojas observe, Brugués's film conforms to the norms of the zombie film genre in which the "heroes" of the film are society's underdogs (Potter 8, Cedeño Rojas 281). A thief, a gay man, a hustler, a tattooed Black man: the group represents many of the elements of Cuban society that the Revolution has at one time or another condemned or marginalized.[17] Yet like Juan, they are all "survivors" in the new post-Soviet Cuba.

Juan and his friends do not set out to fight the zombies. In fact, when Mario attacks the neighborhood meeting, his appearance provides a welcome distraction from the discussion of a recent rash of car-radio thefts for which La China is responsible. When the zombie epidemic reaches epic proportions and it becomes clear that the status quo will not be able to hold, Juan decides that the situation "requiere un plan" [requires a plan], words that echo Cuban socialist political discourse. The plan he has in mind, however, is not a plan for surviving the zombie apocalypse but a plan for capitalizing on it. Ever the canny observer, he sees the zombie outbreak as an opportunity for personal gain rather than heroism. As he explains, "Estamos frente a una crisis, y solo hay una cosa que podemos

Figure 5. "Surviving" in *Juan de los muertos* (2011). Production still from the film.

hacer... Cobrarles" [We're faced with a crisis, and there's only one thing we can do... Charge them for it]. He and his friends form a "company," hiring themselves out to families who need someone to kill off their zombified family members. "Juan de los Muertos: matamos a sus seres queridos" [Juan of the Dead: we kill your loved ones] is their slogan. When Camila, aghast at Juan's flagrant ability to take advantage of the situation, expresses her outrage, Juan explains, "Cami, somos cubanos, esto es lo que hacemos cuando se ponen malas las cosas" [Cami, we're Cuban; this is what we do when things get bad]. With this, Brugués pokes fun not only at the rigidity of the old Cuban order—the socialist rhetoric that fails to adapt to a novel crisis—but also at what Cubans call *el doble moral* [double morality], the egotism and self-interest of the new "do-it-yourself" Cuban capitalism. Juan and his friends do help people—a notable example being when Juan saves a young boy from his zombified father —but knowing that the situation with the zombies is likely to change, they are on the lookout for any way to come out ahead. When Vladi and Lázaro return from a scavenging raid pushing a wheelchair filled with cases of rum, Juan asks, "¿Y el viejo?" "Murió. Tuvimos que dejarlo" [And the old guy? He died. We had to leave him], declares Lázaro, but Vladi adds, "No necesariamente en ese orden" [Not necessarily in that order], the implication being that they have killed the old man (or left him to be eaten by zombies). Lázaro in particular uses the chaos to his advantage: when he comes across a neighbor who owes him money, he attacks him, even though the man is clearly not a zombie, confident that the chaos of the zombies will hide this settling of old scores.

Zombies at Work in Cuban Cinema

By showing how Juan and his friends—and the Cuban authorities—respond to the zombie crisis, *Juan* pokes fun at the mixed messages of Cuban society, particularly the way in which revolutionary ideals conflict with contemporary survival practices. But *Juan* does different work when examined in the context of Cuban cinema more broadly. Brugués's film establishes an intertextual relationship with Cuban cinema, using these (often parodic) references as a means of reshaping our understanding of specifically Cuban tropes. As Sara Armengot observes, these references demonstrate that *Juan* is not "an outlier in the Cuba film canon," but can in fact "be productively read within the robust national filmmaking tradition" (4). We might say that *Juan* "reanimates" these earlier narratives, shining a light on the changes that have occurred in Cuban society and highlighting the cognitive dissonance between the historical context of the original films and Brugués's movie.

Perhaps the most notable cinematic reference in *Juan* is to Tomás Gutiérrez Alea's classic film *Memorias del subdesarrollo* (Memories of underdevelopment, 1968).[18] As both Armengot and Ann Marie Stock have noted, Juan's use of a telescope to observe the city is a direct reference to Sergio, the protagonist of Gutiérrez Alea's film, who spends his days pondering the changing urban landscape visible through his telescope (Armengot 52, Stock 61). Sergio is also a kind of "untimely" figure: a disaffected pseudo-intellectual, he chooses not to leave for the United States with the rest of his well-to-do family, even though his bourgeois leanings make it seemingly impossible for him to fully participate in the Revolution's reshaping of society. Gutiérrez Alea himself envisioned *Memorias*—and film more broadly—as a medium that would allow viewers the space for their own political (revolutionary) coming to consciousness.[19] *Juan* plainly refuses to create the space for that work. Zombie-fighting is about practical action, not reflection. Where Sergio's mediated observations of the city emphasize his isolation and his inability to incorporate himself into revolutionary life, despite his albeit ambivalent desires to do so, Juan's scrutinizing of the city is practical and strategic: his vantage point on the roof of his building is a good view from which to safely survey the state of things, gauge zombie activity, and plan one's next move.

One significant interaction between Juan and Lázaro also references a later film co-directed by Gutiérrez Alea and Juan Carlos Tabío, *Fresa y chocolate* (Strawberry and chocolate, 1993).[20] The story of the friendship that develops between David, an idealistic college student, and Diego, a gay dissident writer, *Fresa y chocolate* contains an emotional climax that features a farewell embrace between the two men, a moment that signals the bonds they have formed despite their personal and ideological differences. Dara Goldman points out the temporal uncertainty in this final scene: "Although it stands as the final image of the film, thus gesturing towards a desired future, both the characters and the viewers are aware that Diego will be leaving the island shortly thereafter" (24). *Juan de los muertos* provides a strange restaging of this interaction. Lázaro, thinking he may be about to die, asks Juan for one more favor: will Juan let him perform oral sex on him? Juan, initially aghast, finally agrees, and only then does Lázaro admit the request was a joke. Brugués's film thus mocks the cathartic moment offered by *Fresa y chocolate*, making visible a homophobic strain of sexual anxiety that has been running through *Juan's* largely homosocial environment. Yet this mockery is also a commentary; despite—and in part through—Diego and David's melancholic goodbye embrace, *Fresa y chocolate* opens the way for the Revolution to learn from its mistakes, pointing toward the possibility of a redemptive future. Lázaro's joke signals the extent to which Cuban society has moved past the point of redemption for both revolutionary discourse and a certain kind of revolutionary future. The allusions to key moments in Cuba's cinematic narrative simultaneously recognize this zombie-filled Havana as Cuban and highlight its "radical alterity."

The climax of *Juan* comes back to a very Cuban question: should Juan stay, or should he go? Realizing that the zombies vastly outnumber them, Juan, Lázaro, Vladi, and Camila, the remaining members of the group, make a plan to escape. They turn a late 1950s American car into a raft and launch it into the Havana Bay, planning to head for Miami. But will Juan leave with them? This dilemma of diaspora has been at the heart of much recent Cuban cinema, including Juan Carlos Cremata Malbertí's *Nada +* (Nothing more, 2001) and *Viva Cuba* (2005), Benito Zambrano's *Habana Blues* (2005), and Brugués's own first film, *Personal Belongings* (2007).[21] In these films, the choice of whether to stay in Cuba or leave to start anew elsewhere is largely a question of personal volition or economic need. The zombie crisis in *Juan* gives that issue literal teeth, and the decision seems to be clear. Yet despite being vastly outnumbered, with no end to the zombie invasion in sight, Juan insists upon staying. As the car-raft with Lázaro,

Vladi, Camila, and a small boy they have saved—a symbolic nuclear family—floats off, Juan turns away from them and prepares to dive back into the fray.

In contrast to many zombie films, including *Shaun of the Dead*, the final scenes of *Juan de los muertos* leave little possibility for any restoration of the status quo, as they suggest that the zombies have overrun the island. Fehimović argues that a failure to exterminate the zombies indicates the continued existence of "indomesticatable difference within the nation" (164). Yet the zombies do more than exist within the Cuban body politic; they overwhelm it, seemingly forcing out most of the human citizens or converting them to the ranks of the undead. The shots of a horde of zombies running down the Malecón provide powerful visual contrast to the images of historic marches celebrating the Revolution. If the zombies make visible the remains of outmoded, disjunctive parts of Cuban society, their triumph would seem to be less an opening for a new kind of Cuba than a statement that these "remains" have suffocated the possible existence of any alternative. Is Juan so Cuban, so unwilling to step outside the island's disjunctive temporal state, that he prefers to conform, to become undead, in order to remain?[22] If this is the case, it would appear that Juan, the self-interested (if loveable) opportunist, has at the last moment decided to make "the ultimate sacrifice," to die fighting for a symbolic Cuba whose best hope for existence may be off the island.

Seen from another perspective, however, the zombie invasion of Cuba seems to be a true apocalypse, a radical break with the past that makes space for a new reality. From a logical standpoint, it seems clear that Juan will soon become a zombie; as one of the few remaining human "survivors," he will be unable to hold out against the zombies for long. His decision to stay—and become a zombie—can be read as an anticonformist gesture that marks the beginning of a radical new order, and Syd Vicious's version of the song "My Way," which plays against animated images of Juan fighting the zombies during the scrolling of the end credits, seems to suggest as much. In his exploration of the zombie as a metaphor for capitalism's exploited Other, Canavan suggests that there is an ethical position in seeking to become a zombie: "To become a zombie would be to obliterate the line dividing 'us' from 'them' by allowing ourselves to be fully and finally devoured by alterity" (450). Juan has lived by refusing to conform to Cuban socialism's tenets of masculinity and productivity. Ironically, he demonstrates both of these tenets in his last moments of separation from the zombie horde.

Zombies for the Revolution (The End Is Not the End)

Like *Juan de los muertos,* Erick Mota's story "That Zombie Belongs to Fidel!" features a Cuba that is identical to its real counterpart except for the presence of zombies produced as the result of a contagious supervirus. Yet there the similarities between the two Cuban texts end. Unlike in *Juan de los muertos,* the zombie invasion in Mota's story has not resulted in widespread chaos and destruction; though the text never makes clear exactly how long it has been since the outbreak of the virus, zombies have been around long enough to have become tolerated by the general population and to have been assimilated into Cuban bureaucracy and Cuban life. Mota's tale is set in a Havana marked by the spread of the Z virus, where the unnamed narrator works as a researcher at CIDZ, a government center attempting to find a cure for the disease. When, at the beginning of the story, the narrator sees a lone zombie shambling down the street, he observes that this sight used to be unusual, as zombies were previously required to be accompanied by a human escort. He ends by observing, "Since then things have relaxed, as they always do. . . . Zombies now roam freely through the streets and no one fears them. Everything will always be the same in this country: a mess" (134). What was first a crisis has now become an accepted part of the status quo. Or rather, as the narrator's statement implies, the status quo is and has been crisis, so that the addition of the zombies makes seemingly little difference. Cubans have adapted to the walking dead in their midst, as they have implicitly adapted to other social difficulties. Some people, like the narrator's brother Panchito, have even begun to pretend to be zombies so that the family can qualify for the extra meat ration reserved for those families with undead members.

Mota's portrayal of a Cuba post-Z-virus outbreak provides a different scenario for how the revolutionary state responds to a novum. The Cuban government has not responded to the zombie epidemic by attempting to kill all the zombies; rather, as the narrator observes, the Revolution has tried "to assimilate the zombie problem dialectically" (136), by working to find ways to incorporate them into the revolutionary project. The scientists at CIDZ, of whom the narrator is one, have developed a serum that suppresses the zombies' urge to eat human flesh. This has made it possible for zombies to be made to perform certain basic tasks, in particular harvesting sugarcane. They have become productive members of society, even if they still require a human escort and the proper paperwork. The parallels here between the language used to describe the zombies' domestication and the ways in which nineteenth and early twentieth-century writers described the expected assimilation of enslaved Africans and their descendants into Cuban society is difficult to ignore.[23] Through this process of chemical acculturation and social control, the Cuban zombies have been returned to the slave status of the Haitian zombie—to labor in the cane fields, no less!—only in this case they are working "for the Revolution."

As zombies are gradually integrated into the workforce, Cuban society itself is undergoing what can only be described as a process of transculturation.[24] Even as the CIDZ's serum allows zombies to (re-)acquire some minimal humanlike functions, people in the narrator's neighborhood begin to behave increasingly like members of the undead. Panchito observes that the neighbors playing dominoes on the street corner "have a lost look in their eyes and they move funny . . . They were all dead silent. A silence of the tombs, my brother" (138). In addition to adopting zombie mannerisms, some people begin to take on a zombie aesthetic. The teenagers that hang out on Calle G begin to make themselves up to look like the living dead.[25] Zombies are no longer dangerous; a zombie appearance is cool.

Just as humans appear to be "adapting" to the zombies in their midst, it becomes clear that both the zombies and the Z virus that produces them are evolving in response to their surroundings as well. When a mysterious bio-leak occurs at the CIDZ, the narrator and most of his colleagues are sent home and told to stay there. Sometime later, a "mosquito man," a health inspector charged with making sure city residents are taking appropriate measures to eliminate the places where mosquitos can breed, knocks at the door. Something is off about the inspector; he walks strangely, and his vocal modulation is too flat. The narrator suspects the inspector may be a zombie, so he tests the visitor's humanity by answering a question in a way a zombie cannot process; the inspector immediately loses his composure and attacks the family in true zombie fashion, revealing himself to be one of the undead. Horrified, the narrator realizes that the Z virus is continuing to adapt, allowing zombies to take on—or rather, retain—more human characteristics. Ironically, the serum developed by CIDZ is indirectly responsible for this development; by changing the zombies' brain chemistry, the narrator notes, the serum, "ended up giving the Z virus the tools to adapt itself to us" (146). Seeing humans as the zombies' "predators," the Z virus develops the ability to make its hosts (the zombies) increasingly indistinguishable from the humans that surround them.

Ironically, the discovery that zombies are becoming more like humans precipitates an increased state of social breakdown that only accelerates the two groups' resemblance. The narrator states: "We no longer bathe. We only go out to run errands and pick up Panchito's meat ration at the butcher's. Our movements are slow. Our words, monosyllabic. Just like the grocer, the butcher, the police and the neighborhood hooligans. They're all zombies now. Or they pretend to be zombies just to survive. Like we do" (147). Zombies and humans are mutually predatory. Just as zombies have become more humanlike, so humans begin to act more zombielike as a means of self-protection. Self and other become increasingly indistinguishable; it is no longer possible to tell who is human and who is zombie. Given that they increasingly behave the same way, the difference between the living and the undead may come to be just a question of biology or semantics.

Mota's vision presents the commingling of zombies and humans in Cuba in an ambivalent light. From a capitalist standpoint, zombies in Cuba may be exploited by the Revolution, but through their lack of resistance to this exploitation, they become its soldiers. In a system that conceptually leaves no room for the concept of exploitation—all individual work is a contribution toward the good of the whole—they are the ultimate "volunteers," true model citizens. As the narrator observes, "They don't mind working overtime, they don't balk at overflowing buses, they don't demand to be paid in dollars, they don't write dissident blogs, they don't stage riots" (149). Appetites controlled, the undead are absolute conformists, literally incapable of self-serving behaviors that might sabotage the system. The ongoing conditions of Cuba's revolutionary social system, the narrative suggests, are untenable for humans without some form of escape or resistance. To resist conformity is to subvert the system, to give in to the mess, but it is also to resist becoming one of the "undead." As examples of biological stasis, the zombies not only uphold revolutionary fixity but go one better. In fact, at the end of the story it becomes unclear whether any of the government leadership is still human.

In the end, the infiltration of the undead into Cuban society forces the human population to become increasingly conformist as a means of self-defense. Yet living "like zombies" forces human Cubans into a static, nearly undead existence, threatening to collapse the separation that exists between the unending horizon of revolutionary time and the rhythms of daily life in Cuba. In the story's last scene, the narrator and his grandmother watch as an army of zombies parade on national television: "They don't tire, they don't sweat, they don't fall out of step . . . We Cubans have never done anything with such precision. One might say this Zombie Period is our moment of glory" (149–50). A zombie military parade could be seen as the complete undead takeover of the Cuban system. (Of course, it is impossible to tell whether the marchers are all zombies or a mix of zombies and conforming humans.)

Mota's story exemplifies Michael Löwy's observation that the "critical viewpoint" of much what Löwy terms "irrealist" narrative "is often related to the dream of another, imaginary world, either idealized or terrifying, one opposed to the gray, prosaic, disenchanted reality of modern, meaning capitalist, society" (214). In this case, however, the disenchantment has to do not with "capitalist society" but with socialist revolution. Although it does not situate itself with respect to historical time, "That Zombie," like *Juan de los muertos,* can be seen as a commentary on the post-Soviet moment in Cuba, in particular the period of leadership transition, when Fidel Castro stepped down as Cuba's leader, handing the reins to his brother Raúl. What happens to a revolutionary mindset when the horizon of futurity has become foreclosed? The zombies' infiltration of the revolutionary apparatus in Mota's dystopia exposes the untimeliness of Cuban revolutionary time, revealing the Revolution itself as a kind of specter. Life under the zombies slows the passage of time, but then, the narrative suggests, the Revolution has also (already) been a way of stopping or slowing down time. Does the inhabiting of this specter by the undead reveal a total triumph of the Revolution in a new, terrifying way or expose the fragility of its facade? It could be argued that as the zombies assume these roles in socialist spectacle, they free human Cubans from having to do so. Within limits, the zombie takeover has created a space for ordinary Cubans to think outside of or beyond the Revolution. Yet within the confines of the island space, locked into at least the imitation of subservience, this freedom is illusory.

Return to Hispaniola

Brugués and Mota seem more interested in exploring the implications of the Romero-type zombie epidemic than in tying their Cuban zombies to a history of zombies in the Caribbean. Yet the idea of zombies as conformists, which both *Juan de los muertos* and "That Zombie Belongs to Fidel!" highlight, and the idea of conformity as a kind of slavery, particularly in Mota's narrative, establishes a strong—albeit indirect—connection to the Haitian zombie and the question of labor. Pedro Cabiya's novel *Malas hierbas* (*Wicked Weeds*), set on Hispaniola, takes that connection further, revealing not only a consciousness but a self-consciousness with regard to the zombie's historical ties to the island. Indeed, in Cabiya's text, the zombie's connection to Haitian history and folklore makes its flexible liminality a powerful device for engaging with Hispaniola's complicated present.

If the Caribbean zombie always carries with it echoes of its Haitian origins, that Haiti and the Dominican Republic share not only an island but also an intimate, often contentious history means that the zombie is a complicated figure on the Dominican half of Hispaniola. The Dominican Republic came of age as a nation in the second half of the nineteenth century, caught between Haiti, isolated on the world stage as the first Black republic in the Americas, and the United States, which at various moments has exerted political, financial, and military control over the country.[26] Lorgia García-Peña identifies the Dominican Republic—and *Dominicanidad*—as existing "in a geographic and symbolic border between the United States and Haiti" (3).[27] This complicated social and racial positioning not only has prompted a rewriting (whitening) of the national narrative at various moments of the country's history; it also demands the constant reinforcement of unstable borders. In the reinforcement of the borders of Dominican nationalist discourse, Haiti has often functioned as what Caribbean scholar Simon Gikandi terms a "negative sensorium," a poorer, darker country whose existence facilitates—makes possible—a narrative of Dominican success and Dominican whiteness (xiv). Regarding this instability, the zombie is a particularly volatile figure when it crosses the border into the Dominican context. On the one hand, since it originates in Haiti, the zombie is representative of Haiti as "negative sensorium," as well as exoticizing practices not unrelated to the treatment of Haitian culture (and zombies) in US literature and film in the 1920s and '30s. On the other hand, the presence of the zombie on "the other side of the border" has the potential to illuminate areas of Dominican culture and discourse, as well as Dominican-Haitian relations, that would otherwise remain obscured.

Cabiya, born and raised in Puerto Rico but a longtime resident of Santo Domingo, is aware of the charged nature of the zombie once it crosses the border.[28] Presented as the research journal of a Haitian-Dominican scientist, *Malas hierbas* contains the intertwined tales of two very different kinds of zombies: as a zombie narrator searches for a cure to his "zombieism" in modern-day Santo Domingo, upper-class Haitian émigrés in the wealthy suburbs of the Dominican capital traffic in "unconscious" zombies, providing the local elite with an ideal workforce of compliant undead from across the border. Tacking back and forth between Haiti and the Dominican Republic, the novel uses the juxtaposition of Dominican and Haitian perspectives, along with gradations of zombie consciousness/sentience, to show how modern-day affective sensibility in this Caribbean locale is both bolstered by and connected to more basic forms of capitalist exploitation, forms not so different from the systems of enslavement that marked the island's foundational history. The contrasting circumstances of these two kinds of zombies—the "free" and the enslaved—make visible historic Haitian precariousness within contemporary Dominican borders as well as the racialized nature of that precarity.

Malas hierbas begins with a clear reference to the fragmented, "remade" nature of both zombies and zombie narratives. In a brief paratextual preface titled "Advertencia," a "Pedro Cabiya," identifying himself as a kind of "curator" for the book, tells us that what the reader has in her hands is in fact a "scrapbook," put together by a Dr. Isadore Bellamy. "Cabiya" explains that Isadore's scrapbook, a diverse collection of texts, can be read either in the order in which they appear or according to the categories in which they are grouped in the index, à la Julio Cortázar's novel *Rayuela*.[29] This description of the text we are about to read as both fragmented and unfinished unsettles both the temporal act of reading and the sense of narrative chronology, an unsettling only furthered by "Cabiya's" assertion that trying to create any kind of order in the scrapbook "ingresa al caos de todas formas" (9) ["you will wind up in chaos" (v)]. In the "chaos" of the documents collected in Isadore's scrapbook, two dominant storylines emerge: the first-person narrative of a privileged, sentient zombie and the tale of the making and contemporary exploitation of a more traditional unconscious Haitian zombie, threads that, it slowly becomes clear, are connected through Isadore herself.

In contradistinction to Gerry Canavan's observation that "the audience for the zombie narrative never imagines itself to be zombified" (432), Cabiya's text introduces a new kind of undead "remake": the zombie as sentient protagonist, aware of his liminal state and anxious to return to his human condition. Although it is not clear just exactly how he became a zombie, *Malas hierbas'* undead narrator is neither an unconscious cannibal nor a mindless servant; as he narrates the sections of the novel that encompass his story, he is an effete urban sophisticate, scornful of those more decrepit zombies "que llevan años vestidos con los ajados gabanes que tenían puestos el espantoso día en que se despertaron en el interior de un féretro" (20) ["who spend years dressed in the rumpled overcoats they had on the terrifying day when they awoke inside a coffin" (3)]. Before his untimely demise, he was the scion of a wealthy Santo Domingo family. "Reborn" as a member of the undead, aware of the fragile nature of his decomposing carcass, he uses his money and privileged position to fashion the "perfect simulacrum" of a normal life (*Wicked Weeds* 3). In the hope that he may someday return to humanity, he obtains a job as the executive vice president of the Research and Development Division of a large pharmaceutical corporation, under whose auspices he can carry out research into the condition of zombiehood and search for a cure to his condition. He is convinced that he can find a solution to his zombie state through scientific means, by understanding both the chemical compounds that trigger zombification and the mechanism in the brain that allows for the perpetuation of the undead state. Despite the freedom that his social position, education, and wealth afford him, his position as one of the undead keeps him laboring for his "freedom," even if he does this from within the confines of a modern laboratory.

As a sentient zombie scientist, the narrator is simultaneously the subject and the object of his research. He lives in constant fear that his identity as a member of the undead will be discovered and his "monstrousness" revealed. Belisle argues compellingly that in disguising himself as a living human the zombie narrator is "passing life," in the same way that someone identified as Black might "pass" for white. Yet racial passing is a transitory state, one that "begets an interminable movement without fixity of form or definition because one can never become the person for whom one passes" (Belisle 32). Although he is successful in camouflaging his physical person, the zombie scientist's act of disguise results in "a fictive form of life called 'citizenship' that grants him neither specificity nor completeness enough to liberate him from a living death" (32). He may have economic and even intellectual capital, but his undead identity keeps him perpetually in a state of social marginalization, as much a limbo as his biological suspension between life and death.

Although he has an intellectual consciousness, the zombie narrator is keenly aware of what he lacks: the ability to feel, to form emotional relationships with living human beings. This lack of affective connection means that he leads a solitary life, one almost completely devoid of human contact, another ironic way in which Cabiya's zombie differs from Romero's crazed zombie hordes. Dionisio, one of the oldest zombies in Santo Domingo and the narrator's confidant and adviser, diagnoses the narrator as lacking qualia, a sense of self that is connected to the world. Dionisio explains: "Un vivo puede comprender que las cosas que *le* suceden, le suceden a algo que *es* él, su yo, la consciencia de ser uno mismo. Si siente alegría o pena, si lo sobrecoge la belleza o el peligro, sabe que todas esas cosas las está sintiendo él, de tal modo que percibe las *cualidades* de las cosas" (24, italics in original) ["A living person can understand that the things that happen *to him*, happen to something that *is* him, his self, the consciousness of being oneself. If he feels joy or sorrow, if he's overwhelmed by beauty or by danger, he knows that he himself is feeling all of these these things in such a way that he perceives the *attributes* of each" (6)]. As Dionisio makes clear, both he and the narrator have consciousness: they can reason, think, and use evidence to arrive at logical conclusions. What they lack is the affective connection that provides depth and context to basic perception. Although the narrator has managed to replicate humanity with makeup and clothes, he is unable to truly connect to his sensorial experiences.

Despite seeming to make little progress to understand zombification from a scientific perspective, the narrator's social isolation and zombified interpersonal interactions begin to change as he experiences a gradual awakening to human sensation and emotion through an unexpected source: his interactions with the three female scientists with whom he shares his lab. Mathilde, Patricia Julia, and Isadore (the same Isadore whose scrapbook we are reading) are friends who have known one another since college. The three women begin to behave in what can only be described as an increasingly flirtatious manner. They compete among themselves to assist him with laboratory tasks, they begin to wear perfume, and they use more makeup than before. When they find themselves alone with the narrator, they arrange themselves in poses that seem designed to serve as potential seduction scenes. The zombie scientist chronicles these activities as though he does not understand what is going on, reacting awkwardly to what seem to be obvious provocations. Yet while he purports not to understand that these encounters are meant to be flirtatious, he does notice clear physical responses to the women in himself. He remarks to Dionisio, "A mí todo esto me provoca una desazón extraña, un vacío en la boca del estómago, como de vértigo" (55) ["It all puts me ill at ease, gives me a pit in my stomach, like vertigo" (27)]. The narrator perceives that his interaction with these women inspires a strong reaction in him; his struggles have to do with how to assimilate and respond to that provocation. Some kind of emotional shift is clearly under way. It is as if he is being controlled—pulled to react physically and emotionally in ways he does not consciously understand.

The narrator's growing emotional response to his laboratory companions comes to a head when the women finally persuade him to come out dancing with them. At a club in Santo Domingo's Zona Colonial, Mathilde steals him away from the dance floor, shepherding him upstairs to a lounge area for a kiss. When they finally do kiss, the narrator discovers that Mathilde is crying. As the tears fall on his cheek, he experiences both a sudden realization of the simultaneous closeness and separation of their cheeks and a sudden rush of empathy for Mathilde: "De pronto *imaginé* por qué lloraba. Por un mágico instante *fui* Mathilde y *supe* por qué lloraba. Pude ponerme en su lugar" (181, italics in the original) ["Suddenly, *I imagined* why she was crying. For a magical instant, *I was* Mathilde and *I knew* why she was crying. I could put myself in her place" (115)]. One might say that in this sudden sense of both separation and connectedness the narrator begins to perceive his own qualia. In other words, he begins, from the standpoint of an emotional consciousness, to sense what it is like to be human.

The narrator's growing qualia may have been awakened with the kiss from Mathilde, but the object of its awakening is clearly Isadore. On his night out with the three women, the zombie returns to the dance floor to find Isadore engaged in conversation with a group of three men. One of the men wants Isadore to dance, but she rebuffs his advances, first verbally and finally by taking the zombie's hand and introducing him as her boyfriend. Although Isadore appears to make this gesture as part of an act, the two continue to hold hands even after the rejected suitor and his companions have departed. This voluntary connection, which is both physical and emotional, is the watershed moment in the zombie's coming to consciousness, what he identifies as a "return to life." As he tells Dionisio, "Era como si ninguno de los dos quisiera tomar la decisión de soltarse, pero también había otra cosa, una extraña sensación de que habíamos perdido nuestras manos para siempre, de que nuestras manos, en adelante, no podrían existir de otra manera que no fuera enlazadas" (216) ["It was as if neither of us wanted to make the decision to let go, but there was also something else, a strange sensation that we had lost our hands forever, that our hands, from that moment forward, could not exist unless they were intertwined" (142)]. For the reader, this moment signals the realization of the attraction between Isadore and her boss. It is also the moment when the zombie fully perceives a simultaneous interconnectedness with another being and his own integrity. This very human connection also allows him to imagine a future with Isadore, a future full of continued human interactions. The process of zombie-human transformation is seemingly carried out by emotional connection rather than scientific labor.

The Laboring Undead

It is no coincidence that the zombie narrator's experience of human connectedness occurs with his colleague Isadore. As the novel gradually reveals, Isadore, the daughter of Haitian immigrants, is engaged in an investigation into the nature and origins of the undead that parallels that of her scientist supervisor. However, Isadore's search for the secret to making and unmaking zombies will not remain confined to the laboratory. It is also an investigation into the permeable, complicated border between Haiti and the Dominican Republic. The zombie narrator's quest to recover his humanity provides a counterpoint to Isadore's exploration as a search focused on the history of the enslavement of Haitian zombie workers and their transnational journey to further exploitation in the Dominican capital.

Isadore's interest in zombies is awakened by a key experience from her youth that also proves to be one of the novel's most significant scenes. Dark-skinned, intelligent, and industrious, young Isadore is friends with Valérie, the lighter-skinned, less-academically-inclined daughter of wealthy Haitian émigrés. One night at Valérie's house, Isadore is witness to a kind of "macabro *Tupperware Party*" (50): Adeline, Valérie's mother, invites a number of her socially privileged friends over for drinks and hors d'oeuvres. At the end of the evening, she reveals the ultimate purpose of the gathering when she introduces them to Gracieusse, a zombie servant who works in her kitchen. Gracieusse makes a distinct impression on both Isadore and Adeline's guests:

> Era una congo tan negra que arrojaba destellos azules. Su cabello era un desastre, erizado y descuidado, como si recién hubieran desatado las correas que la sujetaban a una sesión de electroshocks. Era bajita, de brazos largos y cara ruin. Estaba descalza y cubría su desnudez con una miserable faldita amarilla y una vieja blusa rosada. Ambas prendas le quedaban muy pequeñas, como si la niña se hubiera convertido en mujer de un día para otro . . . como si nunca se hubiera quitado la ropa que le pusieran alguna vez durante su infancia. Pero lo más terrible de su aspecto eran los ojos: orbes blanqueados que no dejaban de dar vueltas en cuencas desprovistas de párpados. (47)

[It was a Congo so dark that her skin glinted bluely. Her hair was a disaster, unkempt and standing on end, as if she'd just had the restraints from an electroshock session removed. She was very short, with long arms and an abject face. She was barefoot, and covered her nakedness with a scant yellow skirt and an old pink blouse. Both were too small for her, as if the girl had transformed into a woman overnight—as though she had never taken off the outfit someone had once dressed her in as a child. But the most terrible thing about her appearance was her eyes: blanched orbs that rolled in perpetual circles inside lidless sockets. (22)]

Gracieusse, in this case, is the "Tupperware" for sale; Adeline hopes that her guests will want to order zombie servants for themselves from her provider in Haiti. The women are initially repulsed by the zombie's disheveled appearance and the uncanny aspect communicated by her lidless eyes. However, when Adeline explains the social and economic advantages of having a zombie maid—Gracieusse neither sleeps nor eats, has no wants or desires, and exists purely to serve—the women fall all over themselves to pay the deposit to order their own zombie "chacha."

The episode with Gracieuesse lays bare in the clearest way possible the social divisions in Dominican and Haitian society. Gracieusse's physical appearance carries all the signs of social marginality for the cultural environment of urban Santo Domingo: dark skin, unkempt hair (that in its natural state further emphasizes her Blackness), and ragged, ill-fitting clothes. What initially upsets the women at the party is not that Gracieusse should be allowed to exist in this state—indeed, she is a stand-in for the many others, living and undead, who exist in something close to this situation—but that she has appeared in their midst, that her abjection has been made temporarily visible. When they discover the advantages that her labor can provide to them, they are only too happy to benefit from—and, indeed, exploit—a similarly abject being. As Adeline explains, the zombies the women purchase will arrive blindfolded, their ears sealed with wax. When "awakened" they will serve unquestioningly the first person they see and hear. Gracieusse is a zombie along the lines of the classic Haitian model; unlike the zombie hordes who, according to Canavan, are seen as both a threat and as expendable others, the compliant Gracieusse and those like her present no threat. Instead, they function as visible symbols for the kind of labor exploitation that allows capitalist society to operate and for the race and class hierarchies that legitimate this kind of social marginalization. Nor do the bonds of national identity serve to mitigate this system; even though the Dominican housewives view Adeline as too exotic—"negra, exquisita, francesa" (41) ["black, exquisite, French" (16)]— to be one of them, in the end it is Adeline who propagates the exploitation of her fellow Haitians, as she and her wealthy Dominican peers are united by being the consumers of the enslaved zombies.[30]

Isadore is the only one at the gathering to find herself moved by the scene. As she notes in her account of the incident, "Necesitaba compartirlo" (50) ["I needed to share it" (24)]. Although she is initially unable to share her feelings, her encounter with Gracieusse is the seed that sets her off on a search to understand zombies. Isadore's investigation is two-pronged: she hopes to discover where zombies like Gracieusse come from and how they end up in Santo Domingo, to understand the pathways of labor exploitation. But she also wants to understand the biological processes that make zombies possible, a desire that has motivated her studies in pharmacology and ethnobotany.[31] Both of these searches require her to "enfrentar[se] a [sus] orígenes" (72) ["confront [her] origins" (39)]. They will take her back across the border to Haiti, to her father's hometown, and into Haitian history.

When she returns to her father's village in Haiti, Isadore uncovers a zombie origin story that connects to both labor and politics. The story comes courtesy of the testimony of Isadore's cousin Sandrine, who has become a kind of matriarch of the village. During the dictatorship of "Papa Doc" Duvalier, two men with magical training meet in Port-au-Prince's infamous Citadelle prison: Papá Vincent, future patriarch of Isadore's father's village, and a talented young man named Placide. Determined to escape from the prison, they use their magical gifts to fake their own deaths, entering a deathlike state—another kind of temporary undeadness—so that the jailers will have their bodies carted out of the prison. Once outside the jail, however, they are set upon by two "devils" who, believing them dead, come to steal their clothes. When Placide reveals that he is actually alive, one of the devils steals Placide's life force. But at the other devil's insistence, he leaves him with four things: a cashew seed, a peanut seed, his recipe for making "black sand" (i.e., zombification), and some "white sand," the antidote. Once the devils have gone, Papá Vincent brings Placide back to life. But Placide is a changed man. He and Papá Vincent divide up what the devil has left them, Papá Vincent taking the white sand and the peanut, "alegando que el cájuil es una planta malévola que saca ronchas" (204) ["arguing that the cashew is an evil plant that produces welts"], and Placide taking the recipe for black sand and the cashew seed, because he views peanuts as a less valuable crop. The two men go on to found adjoining but completely separate communities, one a poor but harmonious small town, the other a spectral place whose wealth is built on the fabrication and exploitation of zombie labor.

In Sandrine's childhood memory, Placide's zombie town functions as a kind of bogeyman, a cautionary tale for those foolish enough to venture over the fence dividing Placide's land from Papá Vincent's community. Sandrine shares that as a child she, Isadore's father Pascal, and their friend Gracieusse crossed over into the town of the zombies on a dare and discovered the dark transformations that take place there. Sandrine and Pascal are eventually rescued by Papá Vincent, but Gracieusse—as the reader knows—was not so lucky.

The tale of Papá Vincent and Placide establishes a Manichean contrast between the humans and the zombies, between the close-knit community of Isadore's family's town and the economic exploitation and devaluation of human life that happens on Placide's side of the fence. As Melanie Pérez Ortiz observes of Placide's side, "Se trata de una comunidad muerta, sacrificada a favor de la máquina de sentido y el capital" (206) [This is a dead community, sacrificed in favor of capital and the machine of sense]. Yet the division of good and evil is not so clear as it might be, for the border between the two communities to a certain extent separates and fortifies the identities of each. Papa Vincent and, implicitly, other adults in the community are aware of the zombies on the other side of the wall, yet they allow Placide's exploitation of them to continue, just as a city like Santo Domingo can contain both the exploited undead like Gracieusse and sentient, self-seeking zombies like the scientist narrator. The existence of the zombies on the other side of the wall also contributes to the isolation of Isadore's village. As her cousin Sandrine observes, thanks to the activities taking place in Placide's village, "[Ningún forastero] dura entre nosotros más de una noche, acaso dos" (82) ["(No outsider) lasts more than one night with us, maybe two" (44)]. Even if the inhabitants of Papá Vincent and Sandrine's village are not actively involved in creating or exploiting zombies, the darkness of what takes place in Placide's village casts a long shadow.

The story of Placide, Papá Vincent, and the tale of the two Haitian towns also reveals the pliable nature of time in Cabiya's novel. In its structure, the zombie-origin story that Sandrine relates is a myth, a category of narrative that Martinican writer Édouard Glissant characterizes as "the first state of a still-naïve historical consciousness" (71). Glissant asserts that myth "explores the known-unknown" (71), introducing mysterious or unexplained elements even as it provides explanations of others. Placide and Papá Vincent's story explains how the two communities came to exist side by side, even as it takes the existence of white and black magic and their powers as givens. Interestingly, however, this mythic origin story is also one of the moments in the novel that is most concretely anchored in a historical temporality: the Duvalier dictatorship in Haiti. By contrast, some of the other documents in Isadore's scrapbook, in particular the zombie scientist's narrative, take place in a hazy "present-day Santo Domingo" unanchored to specific dates or chronology. This temporal fog will become particularly important as the novel moves toward its conclusion.

The Zombie Histories

Lauro argues that "the zombie's history is one that can be reconstituted only by sifting through the literary fragments of empire" (8). Isadore's album, literally made up of pieces of text, anecdotes, twice-told tales, and rediscovered recipes, is a collection of these fragments. When the zombie scientist finds the scrapbook during a visit to Isadore's apartment, he provides this description of it:

> Era un *scrapbook* caótico y enrevesado que no obedecía los dictámenes de ninguna progresión lineal. Era obvio que Isadore lo había confeccionado sobre la marcha, abriéndolo al azar y utilizando la primera página en blanco sobre la que recaía su mirada. Se echaba de ver que Isadore era esclava del hemisferio derecho de su cerebro. De este tipo de cosas, por supuesto, nos damos cuenta solo quienes somos esclavos del izquierdo. Pero, ¿qué zombi no lo es? (*Malas hierbas* 99)

> [It was an intricate and chaotic scrapbook that did not obey any of the dictates of linear progression. It was obvious that Isadore had created it on the go, opening it at random and using the first blank page her eye fell upon. Clearly, Isadore was a slave to the right hemisphere of her brain. Of course, this is the sort of thing that only those of us who are slaves to the left side would notice. But what zombie isn't? (56)]

As revealed through the texts in her scrapbook, Isadore's search is an attempt to understand the border between life and death (or life and unlife), a search that in some ways is as philosophical and social as it is scientific. The zombie's description of Isadore as "enslaved to the right side of her brain" recognizes the personal, emotional stake that Isadore has in the project, despite her background as a scientist. Yet the scrapbook is also a textual compendium, an archive that reflects zombie mythology as much as it does the "real" zombie stories that Isadore uncovers. It includes not only the narratives that Isadore gathers on her own but also the many literary and cinematic references that she collects and analyzes. These constitute what Cabiya himself has called a "prehistory of zombies" [Oloff, "Lo humano es una historia"]. Together, these stories also illustrate Lauro's argument that "all zombies are inherently remakes" (148). If Isadore's documentation of her investigations is a compilation of multiple kinds of documents, Cabiya's multidimensional text is a self-conscious refashioning of the zombie narrative that places old narratives in new, revealing contexts.

"Cabiya" the scrapbook curator begins the novel by warning the reader of the difficulties of constructing a coherent narrative, and a final set of documents twists these narratives together in new ways. The transcripts of a series of police interviews, which bookend the scrapbook if read in order, inform us that the zombie scientist was shot shortly after the events he records in the nightclub. In their interviews with Mathilde, Patricia, and Isadore, the police detectives suggest that the zombie narrator may not have been a zombie at all. Rather, the detectives assert, he was a young man, actually named Dionisio, afflicted with Cotard's Syndrome, a mental disorder that results in an individual believing they are dead or do not exist. Was the zombie scientist never actually a zombie? Belisle reads these reports as the key to Cabiya's novel, arguing that "by introducing Dionisio's madness at the end of the novel as a clear-cut condition of possibility, Cabiya seems to foreclose the very speculative nature of *Malas hierbas*" (33). If the narrator's "undeadness" is merely a question of psychological (mis)perception, then much of his story is also a fiction, and his "passing" has been multilayered: he has been a sick human who, thinking he is undead, "disguises" himself as one of the living. Although it still would not explain the existence of Gracieusse, this explanation for the zombie scientist's existence creates an even bigger divide between the wealthy sentient zombie, whose zombification is only psychologically enforced, and the unconscious Haitian zombie woman, whose exploited limbo state seems indefinite.

The last chapter of the zombie scientist's own narrative, however, suggests another possible end to his story. The zombie describes a kind of awakening: a blindfold he has been wearing is removed, and he finds himself in the presence of three women (implicitly Isadore, Mathilde, and Patricia Julia): "Me toman de la mano, me conducen, y yo las sigo. Sé que estaré bien a donde quiera que me lleven. Me invade una sensación de sumo bienestar" (216) ["They take me by the hand, they lead me, and I follow them. I know that I will be fine, wherever it is they take me. I'm overcome by a sensation of supreme well-being" (155)]. Whether or not he was a zombie to begin with, the scientist narrator's description suggests that he has been "remade" into a zombie by Isadore. If this is the result, the "album" that we have been reading is in fact a lab notebook, the documentation of an experiment recorded in this last chapter in the first person, the culmination of another kind of labor.

If we understand Dionisio's last journal entry to be a description of his awakening into "zombieness," then Isadore has ultimately chosen to make her own zombie, despite the exploitation and suffering she has witnessed. As a woman of Haitian descent, her choice to zombify a wealthy Dominican man can be seen a kind of overwriting of historical patterns of domination, a reversal of the previous narratives. But it also means that Isadore has "crossed over" to Placide's side, even if her motivation appears to be—at least partly—emotional connection rather than financial gain. The zombie's last narrative, with its description of a feeling of "supreme well-being," suggests that upon his reawakening he achieves a state that is both sentient and zombified; he is fully connected to his sensual experience of the moment, even as he is clearly under the control of a master or masters. If this is the case, it would appear that Isadore has achieved a new fusion of the two kinds of zombie. The zombification of an elite white male by a brown-skinned woman of Haitian descent is clearly a turning of the tables. For both the zombie scientist and Isadore, this new stage in undead evolution may be the opening to a new reality and a new way of being in relation. Yet it is unclear what it will change for those undead workers, like Gracieusse, who continue to labor unseen.

Human Transformations

Malas hierbas reveals itself to be a text steeped in both zombie history and Caribbean history; drawing on zombie history only to "remake" it, Cabiya's novel highlights parts of Hispaniola's complex racial and social past that have continued into the present. In contrast, Pabsi Livmar's short story "Golpe de agua," from her collection *Teoremas turbios* (2018), mines present economic and environmental crises as material for envisioning future traumas. Livmar's narrative strips the zombie figure of its heritage and social signification, reducing it to its most minimal elements in order to produce a new, powerful scenario based on particulars of the Puerto Rican context. In a sense, she makes literal Melanie Pérez Ortiz's observation that the islands' series of economic and environmental crises has rendered Puerto Ricans "como muertos-vivos, sobrevivientes de una sucesión de finales de mundos" (16) [like the living-dead, survivors of a succession of world endings]. Livmar's "remake" of the zombie focuses on its connections to both labor and capital. Indeed, she uses the figure's abjection to highlight the tenuous nature of the borders separating the human and the undead.

"Golpe de agua" begins in a near-future, postapocalyptic Puerto Rico, at least as experienced by some of its residents. As in many postapocalyptic narratives, the story of the formation of this near-future island is anchored in the reality of the recent history of the island's debt crisis: "En el 2015 comenzó propiamente la debacle. El gobernador de entonces anunció que la deuda era impagable y, como efecto dominó, las acciones de los bancos puertorriqueños dieron una caída bochornosa en Wall Street" (16) [The debacle actually began in 2015. The governor at the time declared that the debt was unpayable and, like the domino effect, shares of Puerto Rican banks fell precipitously on Wall Street]. These statements refer clearly to what happened in 2015, when then-governor Alejandro García Padilla informed the US government that Puerto Rico was unable to pay its debt, valued at US$ 72 billion, nor its US$ 49 billion in public pension obligations (Lloréns and Stanchich 86). In Livmar's narrative, the resulting financial crisis leads—as it did in real life—to an exodus of Puerto Ricans from the islands, at the same time that rich Americans are encouraged to purchase property in Puerto Rico. Livmar's text also re-creates the drought conditions that the islands suffered in 2015, as much a reflection of climate change as Hurricane María, which would hit the island two years later. In her story, however, the government's desire to cater to wealthy property buyers and solve the drought problem for these moneyed clients has disastrous results: the government seeds the clouds, and the seeding chemicals combine with two separate virus strains to produce a toxic and deadly combination. Humans exposed to the toxic rain and infected by the viruses undergo a two-stage viral infection; the first virus attacks and destroys their vital organs, while the second virus, which essentially "no es otra cosa que un reanimador de cadáveres" [is nothing but a reanimator of dead bodies], turns the infected into zombies. Identified solely as *trabajadores* (workers), these zombies become the labor force that "hasta que sus cuerpos se quebrantan, mantienen la isla funcionando . . . para el uso y deleite de quienes reciben el agua purificada del ciclo hidrológico" (22) [until their bodies break down, keep the island functioning . . . for the use and delight of those who receive the water from the hydrological cycle]. In an echo of other historical crises, such as Hurricane María, the islands' native population bears the physical evidence of the cost of this strategy. As the story's narrator notes, the contaminated rains are carefully steered away from wealthy areas: "Las aguas infectadas cayeron solo en zonas poblacionales específicas" (17) [The infected waters fell only on specific population zones]. Although never explicitly stated, the "golpe de agua" (water strike) of the story's title would seem to refer to the devastating effects of the contaminated water. Those most affected, largely working-class Puerto Ricans, become expendable lives, willingly sacrificed by the government in exchange for the necessary capital from wealthier (whiter) residents.

The existence of the trabajadores and the full scale of the island's degradation are not immediately apparent to the reader. Livmar's narrative begins in a kind of refugee camp populated by people who have managed to avoid being completely infected by the toxic rain. In their water-tight shelter (including a greenhouse), the group survives by repeatedly boiling their water and avoiding being outside when any rain falls. Yet even with all their precautions, mistakes are made, for which people pay with their lives. As the story begins, the narrator and her brother are assisting with a terrible process, preparing to kill a sick child before he becomes a zombie. The death is carried out in a violent yet ritual fashion: the boy's mother stabs him, after which the narrator's brother cuts off his head and right foot with a sword. The narrator's observation, "Había ayudado a matar otro niño" (13) [I had helped to kill another child], indicates that the ritual quality of the death is due to practice; this is not the first time they have had to sacrifice a member of the community, nor will it be the last.

The emotionally chilling nature of the story's opening scene gestures toward the deep irony of the refugees' situation; though banding together has allowed the community to avoid becoming zombies, their own survival strategies have begun to erase the characteristics that separate the humans from the undead. Community members are nameless; most characters are identified only by their initials, and the narrator-protagonist never identifies herself in any way. In the one scene in which she asks the name of an adolescent girl that they have rescued, the narrator tells the girl, "Lo que no se nombra, no existe" (38) [What is not named doesn't exist]. Yet the girl does not give her full name, only an initial, K., and the narrator does not reciprocate by naming herself in the text. This seemingly intentional anonymity implies a kind of half existence; the refugees have not completely ceased to form ties, but neither do they exist for one another as fully realized individuals with personal histories. Indeed, before we can learn anything about K., she reveals to the narrator that she is already infected with the virus, and the narrator is forced to kill the girl before she completely transforms into a zombie. The relationship that we see forming between K. and the narrator ends before it can truly blossom.

As they attempt to survive in a situation that allows them limited movement, the members of the refugee community resort to feeding themselves in ways that also begin to blur their relationship to the zombies. Although they attempt to grow as much food as they can in their greenhouse, they survive in part thanks to eating the human flesh that they "rescue" from infected human companions after they are sacrificed. The reader's first glimpse of this cannibalism occurs in the opening scene; as they are preparing to kill the child T., the narrator's brother C. warns them, "Apúrense, o no queda nada" (10) [Hurry, or there will be nothing left]. The reader does not initially understand this statement; it is only later, when the narrator sacrifices K. and spends most of the night "separando la carne y los órganos servibles de los inservibles" (40) [separating the edible flesh and organs from the inedible ones] that we understand the purpose this flesh is destined to serve.

In making the human survivors the flesh-eaters, Livmar "cannibalizes" both the Romero zombie and the Haitian original. Dalton argues for understanding the post-Romero zombie itself as a figure that "cannibalizes" the Haitian zombie. Indeed, he observes that the desire to eat human brains is a strong marker of this creative variation (3). Yet like the zombie, the cannibal is also a liminal figure; Carlos Jáuregui observes that the ingestion of another human calls into question the division between self and other, such that cannibalism functions as "un tropo que comporta el miedo de la disolución de la identidad, e inversamente, un modelo de apropiación de la diferencia" (13) [a trope that conveys the fear of the dissolution of identity and, conversely, a model of the appropriation of difference]. In "Golpe de agua," there is no sense that cannibalism is in any way a liberatory practice. Indeed, in Livmar's story the barrier between those consuming and those consumed is particularly fragile; anyone infected will quickly become the consumed rather than the consumer. This gives a chilling tone to the scene in which the community sits together to eat "como si fuésemos una gran familia" (37) [as if we were one big family]. The phrase calls to mind the description of Puerto Ricans as "la gran familia puertorriqueña," yet the coming together of this ragtag group of cannibalistic survivors is literally, rather than metaphorically, tenuous. This may account for the characters' relative anonymity; only chance can say when someone will find themselves on the other side of the boundary between those eating and those being eaten.

In contrast to the cannibalistic human survivors, the trabajadores, unlike the classic post-Romero zombies, have no insatiable desires. They exist exclusively as a slowly expendable labor force: "Eran todos hombres, de cuerpos fornidos pero ya débiles y visiblemente deformes . . . Esas son algunas de las características más comunes de los *trabajadores:* sus cuerpos expiden los abusos, las largas horas de trabajo, la falta de cuidado y aseo, de atención médica debida, de calor humano" (25) [They were all men, with muscular bodies that were now weak and visibly deformed . . . These are some of the *workers'* most common characteristics; their bodies radiate the abuse, the long work hours, the lack of care and hygiene, of medical attention, of human touch]. The bodies of the zombie workers are the physical expression of their exploitation. They are literally worked until they can work no more. Although they do pose a threat to the human survivors, they exist largely as examples of an even-more-abject, less-than-human existence. When the narrator and her brother C. see two caged trabajadores on one of their rare excursions outside the refuge, C. asks the narrator, "¿Qué te agobia tanto? ¿Qué estén allí encerrados, o que nosotros estemos acá afuera, sin poder hacer nada?" (19) [What weighs on you the most? That they're locked up there, or that we're out here, unable to do anything about it?]. The trabajadores are the physical symbol that reflects the humans' own vulnerability back at them.

Indeed, while texts such as *Juan de los muertos* still cast the zombie in the role of the monster, Livmar's text, applying "monstrous" characteristics to both humans and trabajadores, makes it clear that both zombies and humans are at the mercy of the more monstrous forces of politics and capital. As the narrator observes at one point, "El gobierno es nuestro depredador común y la selección natural moldea tanto a la presa como al depredador" (35) [The government is our common predator and natural selection shapes the prey as well as the predator]. Zombies and humans are jointly deformed by the exploitative and literally toxic situation on the island. Even as the virus enslaves the trabajadores, the threat of the virus keeps the human refugees stuck in their own kind of prison, where they survive by killing and eating those they must kill. The oblique references to deceased family members—C.'s husband; the siblings' mother—hint at the full lives they lived before the government-created apocalypse. Laboring to survive as killers and cannibals, Livmar's Puerto Rican refugees are themselves "undead," caught between their previous lives and their oncoming but almost certain destruction.

There is no tongue-in-cheek rewriting of the zombie narrative to be had for Livmar's characters. Although the text is full of intertextual references to classic fantasy, sci-fi, and horror texts and creators—H. P. Lovecraft, Steven Spielberg, J.R.R. Tolkien's *The Lord of the Rings*—it significantly does not include any references to zombie texts or history. Indeed, the literary worlds these references call up serve mostly to emphasize that the narrator's life does *not* take place in a fantasy world where anything is possible. Instead, by resituating the zombie within a contemporary Caribbean landscape of crisis, exploitation, and collapse, "Golpe de agua" returns the zombie narrative full circle to its beginnings as a symbol of racialized labor exploitation and capitalist extractivism. "En otra vida" [In another life], the narrator states, "C. y yo hubiésemos sido escritores, historiadores, narradores de la vida cotidiana, más en esta vida nos faltaban papel y tinta y nos sobraban los muertos" (34) [C. and I would have been writers, historians, narrators of daily life, but in this life we had no paper or ink, and too many dead people]. The narrator, her brother, and their refugee companions maintain their humanity through their consciousness and their human contact; we see the narrator and her brother share various moments of tenderness throughout the story. Yet as the narrator states at the end of the story, "El fin del mundo es ahora, todos los días, porque sucede cuando todo lo que conoces se derrumba y no puedes hacer nada para evitar la destrucción" (42) [The end of the world is now, every day, because it happens when everything you know falls apart and you can do nothing to avoid the destruction]. The conditions of marginal survival keep them trapped in an ever-narrowing range of narratives and a shrinking field of possibilities.

The Limits of the Remake

If the zombie as an internationally popular figure explores the borders between human and undead, the recent Caribbean texts I examine here focus on how humanity has established and maintained those borders in the first place. Their narratives "remake" the figure only to reinstate some of its original meaning; using gradations of zombie consciousness and sentience, they show how systems of privilege in the Caribbean—and, in the case of *Malas hierbas,* modern-day affective sensibility—are both bolstered by and connected to historical forms of racialized exploitation. Kerstin Oloff argues that *Malas hierbas* represents an attempt to "'world' the zombie," to "insert [a critique of Dominican-Haitian relations] within a larger, global framework" ("Towards the World-Zombie" 190), and a critique of global structures of exploitation can certainly be found in both Cabiya's and Livmar's texts. Yet their critique of local, Caribbean conditions is particularly resonant.

It is worth noting, however, that all four texts this chapter examines end on an ambivalent, unresolved note. Turning away from the reinstatement of social order we might expect to find at the end of a zombie narrative in the horror genre, *Juan de los muertos*, "That Zombie Belongs to Fidel!" and "Golpe de agua" all leave the reader in a state of dystopian suspension. In the case of the two Cuban texts, Juan and Mota's narrator are both "freed" from the previous status quo, but it is unclear what spaces of possibility are left open to them. Even if the zombies' arrival highlights the Revolution's own stagnation, the ongoing apocalypse seems to offer only nihilist alterity as a space of futurity. Livmar's story might be understood as even darker, as it finds no liberating potential in this gradual human sacrifice.

Cabiya's novel may come the closest to highlighting the expanded potential of a radically remade zombie, as well as a possible alternative, however radical or dystopian, to these (neo)colonial, patriarchal systems. Neither exploited slave nor mindless cannibal, the sentient zombie that Isadore awakens at the end of *Malas hierbas* is a new model, one whose creation undoes the established gendering of power and proposes a new reality. Yet if the zombie narrator's transformation in *Malas hierbas* allows him to paradoxically to achieve a more intense level of feeling than he had experienced as a "human," what the future holds for this remade zombie remains unclear. What does Isadore intend to do with her new creation? The witnessing of a life beyond humanity provides the zombie—and the reader—with an altered perspective, but a final transformation may be far from complete.

5

After World's End

Caribbean Postapocalyptic Narratives

"The Caribbean is not an apocalyptic world," declares Antonio Benítez Rojo in the introduction to his now-classic *La isla que se repite: el Caribe y la perspectiva postmoderna* (1989; *The Repeating Island: The Caribbean and the Postmodern Perspective*, 1996), adding, "The notion of the apocalypse is not important within the culture of the Caribbean" (xiii). Benítez Rojo makes this observation as part of his attempt to understand—and categorize—the conditions that make the Caribbean a distinct region, something more than a collection of islands. By way of illustrating the Caribbean's rejection of apocalypse, he offers up a personal narrative from the time of the Cuban Missile Crisis, specifically, the moment when he knew that the crisis would not develop into a full-fledged nuclear conflict. In the scene he conjures from memory, Havana's children have been evacuated and the city is at a standstill. As Benítez Rojo observes from his balcony, two Black women pass by "de cierta manera" [in a certain kind of way]:

> Me es imposible describir esta "cierta manera." Sólo diré que había un polvillo dorado y antiguo entre sus piernas nudosas, un olor de albahaca y hierbabuena en sus vestidos, una sabiduría simbólica, ritual, en sus gestos y en su chachareo. Entonces supe de golpe que no ocurriría el apocalípsis. Esto es: las espadas y los arcángeles y las trompetas y las bestias y las estrellas caídas y la ruptura del último sello no iban a ocurrir. Nada de eso iba a ocurrir por la sencilla razón de que el Caribe no es un mundo apocalíptico. La noción de apocalipsis no ocupa un espacio importante de su cultura. (xiii)

> [I cannot describe this "certain kind of way"; I will say only that there was a kind of ancient and golden powder between their gnarled legs, a scent of basil and mint in their dress, a symbolic, ritual wisdom in their gesture and gay chatter. I knew then at once there would be no apocalypse. The swords and the archangels and the beasts and the

trumpets and the breaking of the last seal were not going to come, for the simple reason that the Caribbean is not an apocalyptic world. The notion of the apocalypse is not important within the culture of the Caribbean. (10)]

As his reference to "swords and archangels and the beasts and the trumpets and the breaking of the last seal" indicates, Benítez Rojo clearly understands the idea of apocalypse in a biblical sense. Frank Kermode observes that apocalypse, from its scriptural beginnings, carries with it a sense of linear time.[1] By arguing that the concept of an apocalypse "is not important within the culture of the Caribbean," Benítez Rojo implies that the region is not involved in a conceptualization of history that could yield an apocalyptic crisis. In the case of the Cuban Missile Crisis, Cuba (and by extension the greater Caribbean) is not one of the large foreign powers struggling over the fate of the world; it lies outside the decisions shaping this history. For him, the "certain way" in which the two Afro-Cuban women walk is thus outside this idea of Western linearity. Numerous critics have commented on this passage, with many of them highlighting the exoticizing or essentializing nature of the portrayal of the two women.[2] Cultural essentialism aside, however, Benítez Rojo uses the women's movement to make a temporal observation. In a larger sense, he implies that Caribbean time is other.

The creators of more recent Caribbean fiction and film would appear to disagree. Ironically, thirty years after Benítez Rojo looked out of his balcony at the women whose way of moving calmed his fears, apocalyptic and postapocalyptic narratives have become a frequent feature of Caribbean literature and film. Indeed, Ángel Rivera observes that Puerto Rican science fiction displays a "clear tendency" for catastrophic narratives (19). Although they may not imagine events that constitute the absolute "end of everything," numerous novels, stories, and even films that have appeared in the last two decades explore what happens when a major catastrophe (political, social, or environmental) creates a seismic shift in world or worldview. Texts that feature apocalyptic shifts include dystopian allegories, parables set in the wake of environmental disasters, and speculative amplifications of current political and economic crises. Postapocalyptic scenarios also, notably, appear in texts that posit new futures by exploring alternate histories.[3]

These Caribbean narratives take their place in a literary-world marketplace currently flooded with novels, short fiction, films, and TV series that play with apocalyptic and postapocalyptic scenarios.[4] Although explanations for this thematic vogue differ, many critics see the preference for narratives that play with world-ending as a reflection of widely shared systemic anxieties. Slavoj Žižek has characterized this as a crisis of global capital; Mariano Siskind sees it as a reaction to an "unworlding," or a recognition that "[t]he world, as the signifier that names the desire for an impossible but operative universal reconciliation, no longer exists" (208). Heather Hicks, writing about the postapocalyptic novel in English, observes that the texts she examines "use the conventions of post-apocalyptic genre fiction to interrogate the category of modernity" (2). Brazilian theorists Déborah Danowski and Eduardo Viveiros de Castro argue that world-ending scenarios became more prevalent beginning in the 1990s, as a scientific consensus began to emerge about the effects of climate change on life on Earth (4). Seemingly in agreement with Danowski and Viveiros de Castro, Ursula Heise argues that apocalyptic narrative "has been one of the most influential forms of risk communication in the modern environmental movement" (122), a way of urging people to take action. Despite shared fears related to the current moment, however, (post)apocalyptic narratives in the Caribbean stand out from these general trends.

The Caribbean maintains an intimate and long-standing relationship with catastrophe that makes these new fictions less than novel. It could be argued that the Caribbean "is not an apocalyptic world" not because of its separation from apocalyptic experience but rather because it is always already *postapocalyptic*. In his study of apocalypse(s) in Haitian cultural production Martin Munro observes that European colonization, Indigenous genocide, and the African slave trade, which served as some of the founding elements of modern Caribbean societies, were in themselves cataclysmic, world-ending events for those individuals that experienced them, and the traumas produced by those experiences have lingered (5). As numerous critics have shown, "modernity" has been a fundamentally uneven and unstable category in a Caribbean context, even as those institutions that underwrote Caribbean traumas—slavery and the plantation system—have also been shown to have been constitutional components of the modern era in the Western Hemisphere.[5]

This chapter explores the ways in which recent Caribbean postapocalyptic narratives deviate in both form and function from similar fictions written and set elsewhere. As both Ditella de Cristofaro and Monika Kaup argue, apocalyptic narratives are, fundamentally, "narratives about time" (Kaup 55). James Berger, in his study of postapocalyptic literature of the

1990s, observes that apocalypse has been understood more broadly as a cataclysmic event that "resembles the end" or "explains the end" (5). Yet what does the performance of an ending mean in a place in which apocalypse is foundational? If we understand the Caribbean as a region founded on trauma and beset by historical memories of catastrophe as well as contemporary crises that continue to produce it, it is easy to see how postapocalyptic narratives carry a different weight and serve a different function beyond expressing fears of the end. They are not about the/a final, definitive end itself—in this, I think Benítez Rojo was correct. Rather, in line with Berger's observation, Caribbean postapocalyptic narratives are fictions of "something that resembles the end," the rehearsal of a particular kind of ending. In this performance, it is not the ending itself that matters, but rather the potential for revelation that its enactment holds. These performances illuminate and interrogate the contemporary Caribbean's intimate relationship with catastrophe even as they posit different ways in which that relationship might be revised or reframed.

Always Already Postapocalyptic: The Caribbean as a Space of Catastrophe

Caribbean catastrophes are very much man-made, the product of historical, political, and economic processes; Yarimar Bonilla argues that colonialism itself might be "best understood as a kind of disaster" (1). Sonya Posmentier observes that in modern African American and Caribbean literature, "cultivation" and "catastrophe" appear as intersectional rather than oppositional events or experiences: "[I]n the United States and the Caribbean, cultivation in the form of agricultural labor has been a social catastrophe in and of itself" (3). Indeed, Martinican philosopher Édouard Glissant begins his *Poetics of Relation* with an evocative vision of the Middle Passage that describes the violent journey of enslaved Africans from their homeland to the New World as an "abyss" or a series of "abysses": "Experience of the abyss lies inside and outside of the abyss. The torment of those who never escaped it: straight from the belly of the slave ship into the violet belly of the ocean depths they went. But their ordeal did not die: it quickened into this continuous/discontinuous thing: the panic of the new land, the haunting of the former land, finally the alliance with the imposed land, suffered and redeemed. The unconscious memory of the abyss served as the alluvium for these metamorphoses" (7). For Glissant, the cataclysmic experience of the slave ship marks a traumatic rupture even as it constitutes a formative element of Caribbean culture, an experience whose imprint will continue to mark Caribbean cultural practices and production for generations to come.[6] Following Glissant's observation, Munro notes that "images of apocalyptic endings" appear in quite a literal way in many of the major works of Caribbean literature (15). Produced by those who have been shaped by "the unconscious memory of the abyss," Caribbean creative expressions are also, by extension, always already postapocalyptic, even when the founding apocalypse has not been directly experienced by anyone currently alive.

In addition to the role of apocalyptic events and processes in the historical formation of the Caribbean, modern events, particularly those related to climate change, have given Caribbean societies many contemporary experiences of catastrophe. The last decade alone brought a devastating earthquake in Haiti (2010), as well as some of the worst hurricanes the region has seen: Hurricane Irma (2017), which destroyed 95 percent of the island of Barbuda, in addition to inflicting serious damage to Cuba and Puerto Rico; and Hurricane María (2017), which leveled Puerto Rico, the US Virgin Islands, and Dominica (among others). Of course, the catastrophic nature of these events is not limited to the damage wrought by the hurricanes themselves; as Yarimar Bonilla and others have shown (and as I detail in chapter 1), the true catastrophe related to weather events is "socially produced" and its effects are unevenly distributed (Bonilla 1).

These recent environmental disasters, in addition to ongoing environmental degradation and diverse political and economic crises, have added to or amplified various states of regional crisis, whether they have taken the form of Cuba's post-Soviet Special Period or Puerto Rico's debt restructuring. Lauren Berlant's idea of "crisis ordinariness" and Rob Nixon's work on what he has termed "slow violence" suggest that the experience of poverty and environmental degradation produces its own kind of crisis state.[7] As I discuss in this study's first chapter—and as Bonilla has so clearly detailed—stagnant responses to a single catastrophic event like Hurricane María can also be experienced as a kind of slow violence themselves. Although, as Rosalind Williams notes, the idea of "crisis" has come to be used to refer to "a generalized, encompassing condition rather than an event" (522), both these ongoing conditions of "crisis" and single catastrophic events such as hurricanes result in a sense that the world as it was previously experienced or understood has ended. These crises are augmented to some extent by the closing of what David Scott has identified as the horizon of "the seemingly progressive rhythm" of time (13), what Paloma Duong has identified as our current "post-socialist condition" (7). In thinking about these conditions, given the region's relationship with cataclysmic or traumatic events, we might read Benítez Rojo's memory of the two women passing by very differently—as a particular kind of survival strategy in the face of an apocalypse that not only has not yet ended but is in some ways always ongoing.

Tangling the Postapocalyptic Time Loop

As it has come to be defined by its appearance in the Bible's Book of Revelation, apocalypse is both ending and revelation. As Kaup observes, "By destroying the world, apocalyptic thinking reveals the core essence of the order of the world" (52). It is this capacity for revealing what would normally remain hidden that Junot Díaz highlights in his essay on the 2010 Haitian earthquake, fittingly titled "Apocalypse." For Díaz, modern-day apocalypses are important precisely for how they let us to see what might not otherwise be visible: "Apocalyptic catastrophes don't just raze cities and drown coastlines. . . . [T]hey allow us insight into the conditions that led to the catastrophe" (2). A cataclysmic event tears aside the veil of the status quo, forcing us to confront the many conditions and events that contributed to it, makes visible situations that some have wanted to hide—or to which we have not wanted to bear witness.[8] In the case of Hurricane María, for example, Bonilla argues that it revealed "the forms of structural violence and racial-colonial governance that had been operating in Puerto Rico for centuries" (2). If an apocalypse is, as Díaz lyrically observes, "a darkness that gives us light" (25), that light illuminates not the future but rather the present and, more specifically, the ways in which the past, with its errors and injustices, has made the present possible. Catastrophe has the power to clarify the causality and connections between these different temporal moments.

In narrative terms, scholars generally distinguish between apocalyptic and postapocalyptic narratives. As Kaup explains, "Whereas apocalyptic narrative is about getting ready for the coming end of the world, postapocalyptic narrative is about crawling out of the rubble and remaking the world from within the wasteland of ruins" (52). In the postapocalyptic narrative, revelation is brought about through the juxtaposition of two temporal moments: before and after the catastrophe. Berger remarks on the fact that apocalyptic writing often takes place in—and also centers on—the time *after* the apocalyptic event, rather than the present of the event itself: "Something is left over, and that world after the world, the *postapocalypse,* is usually the true object of the apocalyptic writer's concern" (6). This concern for revealing the pre- while simultaneously exploring (or conjuring) the post- gives apocalyptic fiction a temporally uncertain condition of expansion and contraction, what Berger has called a "time loop": "Apocalyptic writing takes us after the end, shows the signs prefiguring the end, the moment of obliteration, and the aftermath. The writer and reader must be both places at once, imagining the postapocalyptic world and then paradoxically 'remembering' the world as it was, as it is" (6). In this way, postapocalyptic writing not only reveals the past that led up to the (postapocalyptic) present; it also creates a strong causal relationship between the two temporal spaces. If, as Carl Freedman asserts, science fiction offers the ability of historical fiction to "engage historicity"—i.e., reflect on the past—from the future's ideologically "baggage-free" position, postapocalyptic science fiction tightens that relationship, intensifying the temporal space of the future possible that science fiction offers.[9] This is, in part, what Diletta de Cristofaro refers to as the "critical temporality" of the contemporary postapocalyptic form.[10] It forces the reader to be simultaneously and acutely aware of both temporal moments, as well as the relationship between them.

The tension maintained by the postapocalyptic loop is what seemingly prevents narratives in this genre from becoming nihilist fictions. In narrating a scenario "after the end," postapocalyptic fiction works in a kind of reverse fashion, moving past our worst nightmares to "speculat[e] about new tomorrows after the end" (Kaup 52). This positioning reminds us that life has not, in fact, ended, and even offers us a kind of hope beyond the end. Philosopher Ernst Bloch contends that the utopian impulse can be seen as a kind of hope, but he distinguishes between hope and certainty: "Hope is not confidence. Hope is surrounded by dangers, and it is the consciousness of danger and at the same time the determined negation of that which continually makes the opposite of the hoped-for object possible" ("Something's Missing" 17). If dystopias give us a vision of the worst of society, postapocalyptic fiction has the capacity to reveal the negative causalities relating to dystopia, without forcing us to relinquish that utopian impulse.

In recent Caribbean postapocalyptic fictions, the reveal remains the function of the postapocalyptic form; narratives set in a postapocalyptic moment highlight some of the issues that led to the catastrophe, whether these are social, political, or class-based. Yet by dwelling, as they do, in and on time "after the end," these narratives are about more than simply critiquing the problematic conditions of the present. They also offer an opportunity for their creators to imagine possible futures, and these futures are themselves revealing of the ways in which factors such as race, gender, and social class affect our view of the world. For this reason, I think it's no coincidence that some of the texts I examine that most clearly deal with questions of race are narratives that play with the postapocalyptic form.

Yet as narratives describing the postcatastrophe of a region in which catastrophe is neither novel nor singular, these Caribbean postapocalyptic fictions lack the straight line between pre- and post-temporal moments. What is often revealed is not so much linear causality as it is palimpsestic relation: future imagined catastrophes are, in fact, remarkably similar to current crises and bear the imprint of foundational devastations. The unfinished, ongoing nature of the Caribbean's relationship to catastrophe disrupts the binary nature of this time loop and complicates the conditions for utopian hope. Instead, the region's particular relationship to apocalypse inevitably creates a temporal loop where space and time blend into each other. It is no coincidence that Berger's postapocalyptic time loop echoes the "loop" that structures Timothy Morton's idea of dark ecology. For Morton, both ecological awareness and human interference in ecology have a twisted, looping form; the Anthropocene has made human beings both the perpetrators (as a species) of massive changes to the Earth's ecosystems, even as we are also (as individuals) the recipients of the effects of those changes. As Morton observes, in this "weird," relationship, "Place has a strange loop because place deeply involves time. Place doesn't stay still, but bends and twists: place is a twist you can't iron out of the fabric of things" (11). In both cases, the loops' tension is structured and maintained through a causality of relationship, yet Morton's loop suggests the twists and turns that the postapocalyptic form acquires in the Caribbean. The end result of this loop can be a kind of stasis. (We are aware, on some level, that we are the perpetrators, but we are reluctant or unable to alter our behavior, even as we are also the victims of potential disaster.) As much as postapocalyptic narratives involve events that result in radical change, they can also highlight a resistance to change. This resistance can be seen at a systematic level, from the perspective of narrative structure (closure or resolution), or in the attitudes and actions of individual protagonists.

To show how Caribbean postapocalyptic narratives disrupt the apocalyptic temporal loop—and to explore what this innovation means for both narrative form and the broader Caribbean narrative in terms of attitudes toward and understandings of catastrophe, this chapter examines three recent postapocalyptic texts: Cuban writer Erick J. Mota's novel *Habana Underguater* (2010), Dominican director José María Cabral's film *Arrobá*

(Enraptured, 2013), and Dominican writer Rita Indiana's novel *La mucama de Omicunlé* (2015; *Tentacle*, 2018). Set in a permanently flooded Havana, *Habana Underguater* (2008) imagines what would have happened if the Soviet Union had "won" the Cold War and the United States had collapsed. Yet the militarized, politically fragmented city revealed in Mota's novel recalls current social and political divisions as much as it explores future ones. Less a strict postapocalyptic narrative than a tale of time travel, Cabral's film focuses on three aspiring bank robbers who use a time machine to get a second chance at completing a job that has gone awry. Although a visit to a postapocalyptic future stops their time-hopping, it seems less likely to provoke more radical epiphanies. Moving through multiple temporal moments from the recent past as well as Dominican colonial history, Indiana's novel situates the reader "after the end," using the heightened tension provided by postapocalyptic dystopia to both highlight dysfunctional elements of the contemporary Dominican present and reveal what stands in the way of radical change (both good and bad). All three texts complicate the tension suggested by Berger's "time loop" by creating an expanded sense of temporal possibility and allowing the reader to explore what it means to imagine a Caribbean apocalypse as something beyond the crisis of the status quo in this moment. Yet while these twisted Caribbean time loops create the space for considering alternative pathways to our future, they do not, as in Benítez Rojo's vision, avoid, bypass, or otherwise offer a way out of catastrophe. Complicating the idea that postapocalyptic fictions are "premised on catastrophe as the formative break that wipes the slate clean" (Kaup 52), they show us how completely Caribbean catastrophes are embedded in the broader world and how difficult it is to "wipe the slate clean," to set that world aside.

After the Flood: The Adventure-Game World of *Habana Underguater*

The first paragraph of Mota's *Habana Underguater* is very much solely concerned with the uncomfortable present of its first-person narrator: "Primero fue el dolor de muelas. Y luego. Y luego también. El dolor de muelas persiste en todo momento y carece de posición de alivio . . . No existe sentencia ni castigo en el mundo que supere a un dolor de muelas" (9) [First came the toothache. And again. And again. The toothache is a constant presence, and no position offers any relief . . . There's no sentence or punishment in the world worse than a toothache]. The gnawing, ever-present physical pain that the paragraph chronicles is centered in the body of Pablo, an ex-soldier-cum-contract killer and one of the novel's protagonists. The toothache in question is a leitmotif in the text; Pablo will continue to experience this very present pain throughout the course of events that the novel chronicles. Yet in retrospect, what stands out about this first description is the slippage between present and past tenses: as it turns out, temporal slippages—and the weight of the past on the present—are fundamental to the novel as a whole.

Pablo's toothache offers the reader a relatable embodied experience to hang on to in the present of Mota's novel, for it soon becomes clear that the rest of the "present" is a complicated new landscape shaped by a radically different past. *Habana Underguater* (2010) can be categorized as an alternate history or "uchronia," a narrative that conjures an alternative present by positing a different outcome for major historical events. Mota's uchronia imagines a dramatically different narrative for the denouement of the Cold War, with significant implications for Cuba. In the novel's reimagining of history, it is the Soviets who emerge from the decades-long rivalry as the stronger union; the United States is in ruins after a series of armed conflicts, both internal and with Mexico, and the refugees crossing the Florida Straight now head south toward Cuba. In 2016, when the novel opens, the Soviet Union has only recently severed ties with the island, meaning that the Soviet influence over Cuba—both cultural and political—has been longer lasting. With the major players, the United States and the USSR, in radically different positions compared with the historical course of events, the reader is forced to rethink Cuba's own position in this new geopolitical landscape.

As Javier de la Torre Rodríguez observes, the uchronia was originally understood as the temporal equivalent of utopia: if a utopia, in its original conception, was a "no-space" (an ideal place existing in no actual location), then the uchronia is a "no-time," a corrected history that does not exist (339). Yet contemporary writers who have taken up the uchronia form have used it more to speculate about alternative historical outcomes— some of them very dark—than as a way to imagine more perfect historical trajectories.[11] In the case of *Habana Underguater,* there is nothing utopian about the alternative present that Mota conjures. The collapse of the United States and the resulting chaos have not led to greater prosperity for Cuba; indeed, the US wars provide a dystopian background to the island's own challenging reality. In addition to the chaos of the broader geopolitical landscape, Mota's Havana has also fallen victim to an environmental catastrophe; a massive hurricane has resulted in the permanent flooding of the city and a complete rearrangement—and fragmentation—of both economic and political power structures. In its new, post-hurricane, "underwater" configuration, the city exists less as a single unit and more as a loose confederation of micro city-states, each run by its own organizational entity. Some of these are governmental; some, like the Corporación Unión Católica (or CUC, a play on the nickname for the Cuban convertible peso), are religious, corporate, or a complicated fusion of the two. The Afro-Cuban Abakuá religion has acquired significant political power, while the Orishas, the religious deities of the Regla de Ocha (Santería) religious tradition, have gone into cyberspace, so that power and control are exercised as much within the virtual world as in the material one.[12] "Habana Underguater" (Havana Underwater) thus displays many classic characteristics of a cyberpunk environment (which I discuss in greater detail in chapter 2): it is a technologically sophisticated, highly computerized world, in which human beings coexist with AIs and life in the Matrix blends into the flesh-and-blood reality beyond. It is also a place dominated by power struggles enacted both through physical violence and through attacks on the virtual plane.

Pablo has returned to Cuba after being trained by the Soviet special forces and serving in various combat regions of the United States. In Havana, he is hired to recover an *ebbó*, or ritual offering, that has been stolen from the Orishas. When it turns out that the thief, Rama, is not only a video game-playing teenager who has stolen the artifact to fund his adventures in virtual reality but also his girlfriend Diana's cousin, Pablo refuses to complete the job and in fact arranges for the boy to go into hiding. The Orishas, seeking revenge for breach of contract, hire Pedro, another ex-soldier and former associate of Pablo's, to take out Pablo and finish the job. Pedro and Pablo soon discover the setup and team up, after a fashion, in an attempt both to protect Rama and to find a way to either satisfy or stay clear of the Orishas, the Abakuá, and the various hit men that each organization sends after them for contracts not honored. In the end, the ebbó that Rama has stolen turns out to be a kind of digital map, a key for how to hack into a Soviet space station, and he and his friends must go into cyberspace to make use of this key and return it to the Orishas.

Habana Underguater's plot is clearly somewhat byzantine, yet as Rachel Price points out, the twists and turns of this adventure narrative serve as a method for "knitting together histories" (*Planet/Cuba* 81). The central protagonist of *Habana Underguater* is really the city of Havana itself. Like the initial description of Pablo's toothache, Mota's novel seems insistently focused on the Cuban capital's altered yet still-recognizable physical present. More specifically, it uses the plot, with its rapid-fire action and shifting, unstable loyalties, as a way to explore how this alternative Havana's physical form is representative of inventive Cuban adaptations to politico-religious power struggles, new neocolonial interventions, and environmental catastrophe. The title of each of the book's chapters is drawn from the topography of this new Havana, both terrestrial and digital: "Capítulo 1: Ciudad Reggae"; "Capítulo 4: Red Neural Global" (212) ["chapter 1: Reggae City"; "chapter 4: Global Neural Network"]. In the same way that Michel de Certeau suggests that the urban walker creates his own geography via his passage through the city, the novel's plot contrives to limn Havana's new urban geography, shaping the city for the reader as the protagonists pass through each different neighborhood.[13] When the book opens, Pablo is ambushed by the "Aseres," the Regla de Ocha's security agents, in Centro Habana. The nineteenth-century core of the Cuban capital—today home to the city's greatest population density—still functions in Mota's text as a kind of Ur-landscape for urban popular life. Pablo and Pedro, having discovered their contractual adversarial relationship, then flee to Viejo Alamar—set on the site of the current Alamar housing project east of Havana—to think.[14] A visit to where Rama is hiding takes them to *Underguater,* the flooded portion of the city and a kind of postwar-Berlin no-man's land formed by coastal sections of Centro Habana. The search for a safe way to get on to the web sends them out to the outlying neighborhoods of La Víbora and Lawton, moving outward (south and west) in ever-widening concentric circles.

The uchronic aspect of Mota's text adds another twist to the temporal loop between pre- and postapocalypse: the novel's version of Havana, like Mota's narrative, is a palimpsest. We understand the new urban geography that the novel lays out not on its own but via a comparison with the present-day Havana's current urban landscape. Take, for example, the opening description of the novel's second chapter, which describes Ciudad Reggae (a flooded section of what once was the Centro Habana neighborhood of Cayo Hueso):

> Un ejército de niños en short y sin camisa se lanzaba desde los balcones superiores y bajaban por las ventanas sin cristales hasta el mar. Pero la mayoría se mantenía lejos del agua, en los pisos abandonados, uno o dos niveles por encima de la línea de marea. Las parejas buscaban los balcones con vista al horizonte, al tiempo que las pandillas de principiantes merodeaban por los pasillos deshabitados, destruyendo

muebles y equipos electrodomésticos olvidados. Por encima del quinto piso, las familias ya establecidas, tendían innumerables prendas de vestir que, colgando de los balcones, se agitaban al compás de la brisa matutina y del reggae. (19)

[An army of shirtless boys in shorts launched themselves from the upper balconies and descended past the empty window frames toward the sea. But most of them stayed far away from the water, on the abandoned floors one or two levels above the tide line. Couples searched for balconies with a view of the horizon, while novice gang members circulated through the uninhabited passageways, destroying forgotten furniture and appliances. From the fifth floor upwards, the established families lay numerous pieces of clothing out to dry. Hung from the balconies, they fluttered to the rhythm of reggae and the morning breeze.]

As the above description reveals, and as Price observes, "Mota's city both is and is not Havana" (82). In this description, normality and the aftermath of destruction coexist. Small boys in shorts swimming off the Malecón are a feature of the visual landscape of our contemporary Havana (as well as a leitmotif of numerous photographic and cinematographic documentations of Havana's coastline). The laundry hanging out to dry is, similarly, a visual marker of the urban landscape in older parts of the city, particularly those such as Centro Habana with dilapidated housing and pronounced overcrowding. But these elements of recognizable domesticity underlay the markers of the flood: abandoned buildings with several floors underwater, and the decaying remains of the possessions of tenants who have long ago fled. The mention of roving gangs hints at a social order only tenuously preserved.

As José Quiroga explains, the palimpsest, like apocalypse, is a form engaged with both destroying and revealing: "The palimpsest does not reproduce the original, but it dismantles it, writes on top of it, allows it to be seen. It is a queer form of reproduction, one where two texts, two sites, two lives, blend into one continuous present" (ix). In its layering, the palimpsest is both spatial and temporal. Mota's text takes palimpsestic representation to the realm of architecture and public space; as the above description of Ciudad Reggae indicates, the large-scale flooding of Havana has resulted in a new city, but the ruins created by this uchronic storm gesture back to and exist in tandem with currently circulating images of Havana (and, implicitly, of Cuba more broadly) as a ruin, a characterization that became particularly pronounced following the economic crisis and the material shortages of the post-Soviet Special Period.[15] In this sense, Juan Carlos Toledano Redondo is not wrong when he identifies Florinda, the hurricane that floods Havana in the novel, as "una alegoría de la propia historia cubana" ("Lo que se llevó el Ciclón de 16" 83) [an allegory of Cuba's own history]. Havana's geographic footprint has changed very little since 1959 (with the exception of some new hotel and service areas); Anke Birkenmaier and Esther Whitfield observe that the city remains essentially "the same text that architects, writers, and artists are debating in the 1950s through the 2000s" (6). Even as he introduces a new post-hurricane geography, Mota assumes a reader familiar with post-1959 Havana; despite how much traveling his characters do through the city's various neighborhoods and city-state spaces, the text significantly never provides us with a map. The palimpsestic juxtaposition of current and imagined ruins has the effect of flattening the newness of this uchronic space. This is "crisis ordinary." The ruins may be different, but *habaneros'* survival in their midst seems to be very much the same.

As Habana Underguater's geography indicates, the specter of crisis that haunts the novel is not so much—or not only—the environmental catastrophe brought on by a (future) hurricane. By devising a different outcome for the Cold War, Mota's novel ponders what might have happened to Cuba had the dissolution of the Soviet Union—the main cause of Cuba's economic collapse during the Special Period—not taken place. Its conclusion seems to be that a reversal of the global power dynamic does not necessarily result in an improved situation for Cuba. In *Habana Underguater,* the Soviet influence is, naturally, stronger; both Pedro and Pablo were trained by elite Soviet combat units, and the weapons and hard technology circulating in the novel are largely Soviet in origin. Yet despite having been spared economic collapse, Cuba operates in a state of political fragmentation. The central government of the Fuerza Unida de la Habana Autónoma (FULHA, a play on "fula," Cuban slang for a US dollar), the Abakuá, the Orishas, and the CUC all exist in an uneasy truce, as their military fortifications turn the city into a series of police states. What Mota borrows from cyberpunk's dystopian framework is a world in which late capitalism has diminished the influence of the state. In this case, however, the result has not been the dominance of corporations but a carefully choreographed power struggle, a division of the spoils between private, state, and religious actors.

The Place of the Orishas: Orishapunk as Patakí

Within the militarized environment of Mota's alternative Havana, Afro-Cuban religious elements occupy a central—and significant—position. Although Mota's novel does not position Regla de Ocha (the Cuban name for Santería) as a temporal or ontological solution to his dystopian alternative Havana, there are many aspects of the novel that indicate that his incorporation of Ocha elements has not been casual or unconscious. Indeed, with his very deliberate use of Ocha terminology, Mota is evoking *cubanía* (Cubanness) in a certain way ("de cierta manera," if I may be allowed to reference Antonio Benítez Rojo). In a technologically dominated society, the Orishas, as AIs, manage and navigate the virtual plane much as the actual Afro-Cuban deities occupy the spiritual one. In the same way that an actual Regla de Ocha initiate establishes a particular spiritual relationship with the orisha who is his or her "parent," the Orisha AIs maintain a special connection with their hackers. When Pablo kills Daniel, a *babalawo* (Santero priest), he observes, "Siempre que se choca con un santero hay que dejarlo bien muerto o el Oricha que lo protege te matará desde la Red" (37) [When you get into a conflict with a Santero you have to leave him really dead or the Orisha that protects him will kill you from within the Matrix]. Just as the Orishas in the Regla de Ocha worldview have power over human life, so the Orisha AIs can choose to protect or kill human beings who become involved with them.

Beyond the creative adaptation of Ocha mechanics to the technological dystopia of Habana Underguater, parts of Mota's novel can be seen as operating according to more symbolic levels of religious meaning. Ochosi, the Orisha whose altar has been robbed, is the hunter, a fitting deity to represent (or come into contact with) a paid assassin. Ochosi also happens to be the Orisha most closely connected to ideas of justice, and justice is a central preoccupation of several of Mota's protagonists. Daniel and the Aseres want justice (i.e., compensation) for the job they've asked Pablo to do that he has not done; Pablo wants to practice justice ("tengo mi ética"), and once he finds out that he was betrayed by Diana, he ends the novel almost ready to "carry out justice" and kill her in revenge, until his toothache stops him. Pedro, as an Abakuá initiate, must abide by certain ethical codes of masculine conduct, killing only when a just punishment is mandated. Pedro will also privilege justice over blood, when he kills Miguel, his half brother and fellow Abakuá initiate who has been trying to collect a bounty on his head. Despite their current calling as contract killers, ex-soldiers Pedro and Pablo operate via a code of ethics; yet in staying faithful to those codes, the pair find themselves outside any kind of state or official control, meaning they must ironically resort to violence both to achieve their aims and in self-defense.

As the choice of Ochosi indicates, the aspects of Afro-Cuban culture that are highlighted in the novel seem to be masculine ones. One of the three *Guerreros* (Warriors), along with Eleguá and Ogún, Ochosi is one of the Orishas concerned with people's dealings *en la calle* (on the street), as opposed to activities or relationships associated with interior, domestic space. David Brown, in a discussion of Ocha religious attire, observes that in the move from Africa to the Caribbean, specific aspects of the Guerreros became more pronounced during their time in Cuba: "If the Lucumí Warriors, Eleguá, Ogún and Ochosi, owe their forest occupations and iconography to the itinerant Yoruba hunter-herbalist prototype, they were remodeled in the historical experiences of conquest, slavery, revolution, and urbanization as fierce, path-clearing paramilitary *cimarrones* and combatants who wear *sombreros* and wield hooked branches, machetes, and bows and arrows. . . . Obatalá's house of order and hierarchy can be subverted by the ethos of the forest and the street" (274). One could argue that the violent conflicts that take place in the dystopian environment of Habana Underguater are a kind of exaggerated version of this warrior aesthetic. Significantly, the teenage hackers who steal the ebbó also take on the names of masculine deities, but from Hindu mythology—Rama, Shiva, etc.—as if to signal both their separation from the Orisha enterprise and their participation in a space of masculine conflict.

In borrowing from Regla de Ocha, Mota's narrative and his characters operate within a racialized religious symbology that, as Price observes, gestures to Cuba's colonial history as well as to the historical connection between science fiction and colonialism (86). Yet the novel does not engage directly with the Afro-Cubanness of Ocha. Afro-Cuban folklore—and Regla de Ocha in particular—has occupied a very particular place in Cuba since the beginning of the Special Period. Although, as Robin Moore argues, Afro-Cuban folkloric performance "served for decades as one of the few means Cubans of color had to promote markers of blackness in a context that did not allow for a frank discussion of racial concerns" (196), it has also become a commodity packaged for consumption by tourists who eagerly attend Santería rituals and the Sunday afternoon rumba sessions in the Callejón de Hamel.[16] Mota calls attention to the centrality of Afro-

Cuban religious practices in contemporary Cuban society, only to make them, in a potentially ironic gesture, a site not of folkloric or religious authenticity but of high technology. The Orishas and the Abakuá are racialized—in that anyone with some knowledge of their origins will trace their presence in Cuba to the island's importation of enslaved Africans. But they appear in Mota's narrative as two more sets of players in the flooded city's new power dynamics.

Even as it pays close attention to the construction of this diverse urban fabric, Mota's fable diverges from the postapocalyptic form in that it does not really engage with the conditions that produced the postcatastrophe world in the first place or with possible solutions on a wider level. The battles, car chases, and shoot-outs in the text give the novel the rhythm of a video game, as Price has noted, but they feel incidental to the wider circumstances of the novel's world (81). Despite the text's interest in exploring this new, alternative Havana, its dystopian nature seems to be taken as a given; whether the United States wins the Cold War or the USSR emerges triumphant, the question of how Cuba might avoid crisis is never really addressed. Pedro's and Pablo's actions may save Rama and his friends and remove some corrupt leaders, but the two ex-soldiers are seldom concerned with "the bigger picture." As in an adventure game, they deal with the cards they have been dealt, whether that be a head-splitting toothache or an AI-connected assassin. Survival depends—as it does for many—on their social networks and their own skill and ingenuity.

Better Next Time Around: *Arrobá's* Alternate Histories

A film that centers on personal skill and ingenuity, José María Cabral's *Arrobá* (2013) is not, at first glance, a postapocalyptic narrative. Cabral's second feature-length film after the thriller *Jaque Mate* (Check mate, 2011), *Arrobá* might best be described as a time-traveling buddy comedy.[17] In the film's first scene, three friends—high school teacher-cum-aspiring scientist Pedro (Kenny Grullón), down-on-his luck father Samuel (Irvin Alberti), and hapless goofball Pilón (Alexis Valdés)—rob a bank. Poorly planned and haphazardly executed, the robbery soon goes wrong; shots are fired; Samuel, a security guard, and the bank's manager are all wounded, and Pedro accidentally calls Pilón by his name, a mistake that makes their discovery and arrest almost certain. Desperate to escape their predicament, Pedro proposes a novel solution: that they use the time machine he has been building in his workshop to travel back in time to just before the robbery and in so doing correct the mistakes made in their first attempt. Pedro's idea—and the time machine itself—both work, and the trio successfully travel back to just a few hours before the initial event. However, their second attempt proves only slightly better than their first, as this trip causes them to make other mistakes, including taking the attractive bank manager, Candy, hostage. Undeterred, the would-be robbers (with Candy now in tow) decide that the solution to a successful robbery lies in going back even further into the past to commit the crime. It is at this point that Pedro's time machine begins to go haywire. The result, as Samuel Ginsburg notes, is that "the group accidentally travels through Dominican history" ("Future Visions" 12). These travels, which send the would-be robbers not only further backward but also forward in time, allow the film to both reflect on the errors of the past and contemplate alternative futures, some of them very bleak indeed, thus elaborating a kind of hypothetical postapocalyptic time loop.

In his study of time travel in Latin American literature, Rudyard Alcocer argues that the time-travel narrative cannot fully be considered science fiction, since certain literary examples "seem more closely related to activities that could be variously categorized under spiritism, sorcery, magic, religion, and the fantastic than to either the uncanny or science fiction" (12). Although I concur with Alcocer's characterization that time travel can often appear more speculative than scientific, I find it significant that Cabral's film goes to some trouble to elaborate the scientific nature of his protagonists' temporal wanderings. Faced with Samuel and Pilón's confusion and skepticism, Pedro explains that his time machine, "Cronos," operates by traveling through wormholes in the space-time continuum. To convince his friends of the validity of this rationale, he even goes so far as to put on a kind of promotional video prepared by another scientist, who elaborates on Pedro's explanation. Cronos appears as a small booth covered in corrugated iron, its homemade appearance lending it a kind of scruffy authenticity, what Peruvian American filmmaker Alex Rivera has called a "*rasquache* aesthetic."[18] Through both the time machine as material artifact and the explanation of its operation, *Arrobá* seems to be arguing for seeing this particular mode of time travel as an autochthonous creation. The scientific concepts powering Cronos may be universal, but this is a Dominican time machine traveling through a particularly Dominican timescape.

Karen Hellekson observes that alternate histories, of which *Arrobá* is one, seek to "redirect the arrow of time, to cause a change and therefore change an effect" (36). Pedro, Samuel, and Pilón begin their time machine travels wanting to change only one event: the outcome of their bank robbery. Yet with each successive jump in time, their journeys create new alterations in time's arrow, some of which require subsequent travels in time to correct. Although the narrative limits imposed by the medium of the feature-length film prevent *Arrobá* from extensively exploring the potential changes that might be caused by the trio's jumps in time, the trajectory of their journeys highlights for the viewer the role that catastrophes both environmental and sociopolitical have played in shaping Dominican history. The futures that they witness trace a significant line between these catastrophes and the national anxieties they generate.

Each of Pedro, Samuel, and Pilón's temporal jumps takes them to a historic moment marked by some kind of national crisis. When their first attempt to "re-do" the robbery goes wrong, their second jump takes the trio and Candy to the same bank in 1991, when Candy's father, not Candy, is the bank manager. This lands them in the second year of the sixth presidency of Joaquín Balaguer, a period of economic crisis characterized by runaway inflation due in part to outstanding IMF loans and by the emigration—much of it illegal—of thousands of Dominicans as a result of these economic pressures (Moya Pons 443). Balaguer addressed this crisis in two ways; first, by forcibly deporting thousands of Haitian workers (and Dominican-born workers of Haitian descent), and second, by refusing to print additional money. Although little of this economic and political backdrop is visible on-screen, the conditions of this economic austerity may be what allow them to escape. When cornered by the police, Pilón, who grew up in Cuba (and is played by Cuban comedian Alexis Valdés), launches into an apparently heartfelt defense of the "oppressed proletariat." Asserting that they have robbed the bank to give back to the country, he divides their money into piles dedicated to various national needs—health care, education, infrastructure, and so on. Although they are forced to leave the money, the solidarity Pilón demonstrates for the officers as "fellow workers" not only persuades the police to let them leave but also, humorously, moves them to escort the would-be robbers to their getaway vehicle.

When Pedro decides that the 1990s "is not their decade," the friends' third trip into the past takes them to 1979, during the four-year presidency of Antonio Guzmán (1978–82) (Moya Pons 407). Although this is technically the most successful robbery the three friends carry out (with Candy's help), their triumph is cut short by two realizations: first, the currency they have stolen will be unusable in 2013 as the bills will have been pulled from circulation, and second, their visit has coincided with the arrival of Hurricane David, one of the strongest tropical storms ever to hit the Dominican Republic, which as they finish the job is about to make landfall.

Although the friends get away, their encounter with the hurricane damages the time machine, causing it to malfunction. Their next jump sends them "back to the beginning," as it were, for as they exit the time machine they encounter Christopher Columbus during what appears to be one of the admiral's early voyages to the island. Given that Columbus's "discovery" of the Caribbean opened the door for the founding cycle of Spanish colonization (with its accompanying genocide, exploitation, and importation of enslaved Africans), it is as if the machine has taken the travelers back to the origins not only of the country but also of Caribbean apocalypse more broadly. As both Dixa Ramírez and Néstor E. Rodríguez have shown, Columbus's connection to the Dominican Republic is central to certain long-standing nationalist narratives, in which he "came to symbolize Eurocentric visions of national identity" (Ramírez 111). In the brief moments in which the travelers interact with the Italian explorer, Columbus is unable to "assimilate" the visitors. He cannot place them—and with good reason; they literally don't belong in his world. Beyond the facile humor of this misrecognition, however, there is a deeper irony; the "founding father" of the Dominican Republic fails to recognize his supposed cultural progeny.

From the jump back to Columbus, the time machine appears to draw a direct line to the dictatorship of Rafael Leónidas Trujillo (1930–61), a crucial period in the Dominican Republic's history and, as Lauren Derby and others have shown, its own kind of dystopian *longue durée*.[19] Fleeing Columbus, the travelers find themselves transported again back to the National Bank, this time on the day of its inauguration in 1960, at the very moment that Trujillo himself is on hand for a ribbon-cutting ceremony. The film visually communicates the repressive political atmosphere in Ciudad Trujillo (as Santo Domingo was known during the dictatorship); in 1960, the aluminum gates surrounding the time machine's location are painted with a large pair of eyes, as if the whole scene were under surveillance. When Pedro and Pilón are caught trespassing on the ceremony, Trujillo orders his guards to kill the pair, after Pilón's Cuban vocabulary makes him suspect they are spies.[20] Rescued by Samuel and Candy, who have been left behind with the time machine, they end up dragging Trujillo with them in their haste to escape. As it happens, Trujillo is the basis for the central temporal complication in the friends' time travel. The removal of Trujillo from his own time period shifts time's arrow in a way that none of the would-be robbers' previous actions has done. When the group spirits Trujillo away in the time machine, they make it impossible for him to be assassinated. This is not a case of eliminating Trujillo or of going back to a crucial moment to prevent his ascension. Instead, the two subsequent jumps that the time machine makes in its current state of malfunction are to futures that imagine the possible outcome of a Trujillo who vanishes rather than being assassinated, a Trujillo who disappears but does not die.

As they jump forward with Trujillo in tow, the time travelers find themselves in a nondescript anteroom. "You're finally here!" says a young female attendant. She has straight (or straightened) hair, very pale blue eyes, and is dressed in a shimmery, silvery dress. "Who's going first?" she asks. Pilón, concluding—correctly—that they are backstage at a TV show, encourages Pedro to be the first volunteer. It does turn out to be a TV game show, but not the kind they had anticipated. The name of the game show is *Genoma Eléctrica* [Electric Genome]. Led to the stage by a simpering male host in heavy makeup and a toupee, contestants are strapped into a chair that runs a scan of their DNA. The machine then evaluates the contestant's "racial purity," declaring what percentage of their blood is "Dominican" and what is from an "inferior race." In a deeply ironic moment, Pedro is judged to be "Dominican," but Trujillo, who the group puts forward as the next contestant, is revealed to be composed of 51 percent "sangre inferior" [inferior blood].

The outcome of the DNA scans on *Genoma Eléctrica* is, of course, deeply reflective of Trujillo's politics and his own history. Despite coming from a rural family with roots on both sides of the Dominican-Haitian border, Trujillo was notorious for celebrating his country's ties to Spain and denying the importance of its African heritage, as well as for supporting intellectuals, such as Joaquín Balaguer, who elaborated a racist national ideology in their literary production.[21] Trujillo was reported to use skin-lightening creams and makeup to alter the color of his skin. His regime is also remembered for the notorious "Parsley Massacre" of 1937, in which several thousand Haitians residing in the Dominican Republic were brutally murdered and hundreds more pushed back across the border by the Dominican army, aided by civilians.[22] Although one might ask just how the idea of a Dominican "race" could be defined and demonstrated *genetically* given the national population's extreme heterogeneity, a game show that reinforces an idea of a "national racial purity" seems like a logical extension of the policies of Trujillo's regime and the ideas of national identity that his dictatorship celebrated and endorsed. At the same time, as Ginsburg points out, "Trujillo's failure to pass the purity test highlights the hypocrisy in his anti-Haitian policies" (4). The assertion of *Genoma Eléctrica's* host that the show, "ha cambiado el color del país" [has changed the color of the country] also suggests that this public genetic revealing may have devastating consequences for those judged to be "inferior." While policies instituted under Trujillo seemingly have brought Dominican society to this point, that contestants are still regularly judged to be of an "inferior race" suggests that these practices have not resolved the inconsistencies inherent in the nation's vision of itself.

If the visit to the set of *Genoma Eléctrica* were not sufficiently dystopian, the time travelers' final visit to the future allows them a glimpse of a true apocalypse. Jumping away from the game show, the travelers open the time machine to discover they have returned to the warehouse that in 2015 houses Pedro's workshop; this time, however, it is a dusty shambles, filled with piles of books and boxes. Panning right, the camera's gaze reveals two young men, clearly at home in a makeshift campsite, who stare at the travelers. A ticker tape on the television the men are watching tells us it is 2084. When Samuel opens the double doors, both the time travelers and the viewer are given a glimpse of a scene that might be something out of a Hieronymus Bosch painting: Santo Domingo's modern towers have been reduced to rubble, the smoke and flames of multiple fires obscure the view, and "Trujillo y Dios" is painted over the arched doorway of the warehouse's exit. "Dios y Trujillo" was the message on an electric sign erected in Santo Domingo during Trujillo's dictatorship.[23] The visual connection established between this hellish landscape and the gateway graffiti implies that the continued elevation of Trujillo and his policies is what has led the nation to this point; the reversal of the order—from "Dios y Trujillo" to "Trujillo y Dios"—suggests that this future incarnation of Dominican society now holds Trujillo to be higher than God. No other information is provided that indicates other possible causes of the Dominican capital's destruction. However, the brief glimpse of the apocalypse proves to be all the four travelers need to see of this future; they hop back into the time machine to eventually make their way back home, determining that they prefer to return to the present in one piece rather than continue to attempt to alter time—and history—to strike it rich.

As I have noted, these two glimpses of dystopian and implicitly apocalyptic futures are too brief to be truly explained or understood. Nor are they necessarily meant to be, as they are not a reality that any of the characters have a chance to experience; the film does not spend long enough in 2084 for the viewer to understand how this destruction may have come about. To quote Berger, these brief visions of alternative futures are fictions of "something that resembles the end." Indeed, while *Arrobá* is not, on the face of it, a film about reimagining Dominican history vis-à-vis Trujillo, the film nonetheless places him at the center of both a foundational moment in the past and two potential (dystopian) futures. Despite the superficiality with which the film treats both Dominican history and possible Dominican futures, the brief glimpses it offers seem to be urging its Dominican viewers to examine national narratives and attitudes about race.

The time-traveling friends are ostensibly ignorant of—or not interested in—politics. Indeed, when Pedro, who fancies himself the intellectual of the group, tells Pilón he wants to discuss his ideas after Pilón's speech to the workers in 1991, Pilón snaps back, "Ay, yo no sé nada de eso; ese discurso es algo que yo memoricé" [Oh, I know nothing about all that! That speech is just something I memorized]. Yet the moments they visit on their journeys turn out to be fundamentally enmeshed in national anxieties. Despite the film's lighthearted comedic framework, the centrality of Trujillo's dictatorship and questions of race and national identity stand out from the film's surface "buddy-comedy" narrative and contrast with the overall comedic tone of the film. Indeed, the friends' indifference to political consequences may be part of what allows them to undertake their subsequently devastating actions, by in effect prevent Trujillo from answering for his crimes.

Arrobá centers Dominican histories of catastrophe on Trujillo and his role in national discourse and the national imaginary. Yet while the film highlights the problematic racial discourse that Trujillo fortified, it remains largely oblivious to the ways in which, in the words of Maja Horn, "today's hegemonic notions of masculinity were consolidated during the dictatorship" (1). The film does nothing to question the gendered norms of the buddy caper. Candy, the attractive bank manager, seems to fulfill the function indicated by her name, serving as Samuel's (understated) love interest and eventually as a loyal assistant to her time-traveling companions, but as little more. The jumps in time are largely centered around male acts of (would-be) masculine bravado. Two older women who appear in the scenes at the national bank appear as caricatures: the stubborn office manager, the gullible grandmother. Indeed, if our brief glimpses into future apocalypse tell the viewer anything, it is how little the gendered makeup of Dominican society is questioned. Certainly nothing that the protagonists see in their travels causes them to shift. In the end, the three friends learn not to mess with a time machine—and that a life of crime doesn't pay. But it remains unclear whether their time travels have taught them anything more about Dominican society or about their own potential for effecting either positive or negative change.

Time Travel to Save the World

If *Arrobá* wears its postapocalyptic identity lightly, Rita Indiana's *La mucama de Omicunlé* offers us an apocalyptic future very much in line with the Caribbean's past and present conditions of crisis, both social and environmental. Set in the Dominican Republic in 2027, the narrative begins three years after a tsunami opened an underwater chemical weapons stash that the Dominicans were being paid to store for the Venezuelans, fatally poisoning the surrounding marine ecosystem and permanently flooding Santo Domingo.[24] All is not lost, however; a Santería prophesy identifies Acilde, maid to *santera* Esther Escudero, as holding the key to preventing the accident and subsequent ecological devastation. Acilde, a trans man, steals a valuable sea anemone from Esther's altar so that he can raise the money to buy Rainbow Bright, a pill that enables an innovative chemical female-to-male gender-confirmation process. After taking the pill and undergoing a successful physical transition, he awakens to find out that a parallel spiritual transformation has taken place; he has been reborn as an *omo Olókun*, a "child" of Olokun, the orisha of the ocean depths in the Regla de Ocha-Ifá (Santería), and he can now see into—and alter—other past times in which he is/has been alive. His task, he comes to understand, is thus to prevent the environmental disaster by altering prior events. His ability to do so seems to offer the only hope for turning back the environmental damage and its sociopolitical results.

Although the postapocalyptic moment in which Indiana sets the novel is not a distant future but one a mere decade away, the novel's epigraph grounds the reader in the history of Caribbean catastrophes. The quote is a verse—in English—from Shakespeare's *The Tempest*, specifically from the song Ariel sings to Fernando in Act I: "Full fathom five thy father lies, / Of his bones are coral made, / Those are pearls that were his eyes, / Nothing of him doth fade, / But doth suffer a sea change, / into something rich and strange" (9). Elements of the verse gesture toward the details of Indiana's narrative: "full fathom five" recalls the deep sea orisha Olokun, who will be Acilde's guiding orisha, and the "sea change" could be understood as a reference to Acilde himself, both as he undergoes a gender confirmation process and as he is transformed into the ocean being. But Shakespeare's play has long occupied a central position as a literary touchstone in Caribbean letters, given the ways in which it has been read as an allegory of colonization, particularly of the Caribbean.[25] From this perspective, "[F]ull fathom five thy father lies" could also be read as a reference to Glissant's "abyss," the ocean crossing of the Middle Passage during which so many enslaved Africans died and were thrown overboard. *La mucama's* epigraph thus reminds the informed reader that the novel's near-future disasters overlay this fraught history, "revealing the legacies of colonialism and imperialism as constitutive of ecological violence" (Decker and Oloff, 2). At the same time, the "rich and strange" hints at Indiana's interweaving of both Afro-Caribbean religious elements and speculative temporality, a hybrid form that Sharae Decker and Kersten Oloff have termed "the New Oceanic Weird" (2).

Perhaps the most notable aspect of the future that Indiana imagines for the Dominican Republic is not its radical difference from contemporary reality but its similarity with regard to both present and past sociopolitical issues. The novel's opening scene tells us everything we need to know about future systems of social exclusion. Acilde is cleaning Esther's Lladró figurines when she hears someone press the building's doorbell.[26] The bell has been rung by some Haitians, who are fleeing a "quarantine" in Haiti. Activating a security camera—which, with future technology, is connected to her own eyes—Acilde witnesses the following: "Al reconocer el virus en el negro, el dispositivo de seguridad de la torre lanza un chorro de gas letal e informa a su vez al resto de los vecinos, que evitarán la entrada al edificio hasta que los recolectores automáticos, que patrullan calles y avenidas, recojan el cuerpo y lo desintegren" (11) ["Recognizing the virus in the Black man, the security mechanism in the tower releases lethal gas and simultaneously informs the neighbors, who will now avoid the building's entrance until the automatic collectors patrolling the streets and avenues pick up the body and disintegrate it" (9)].[27] Long characterized by a racist line of national discourse as the Dominican Republic's negative other, Haitians in Indiana's 2027 reality are a literal source of contamination. Their expendable bare lives exist alongside—and in fortification of—the tranquil world of armored apartment buildings full of Lladró figurines.

This first scene of Haitian genocide is chilling not for its exceptionalism but rather for its normalcy. Katherine Snyder, in a study of postapocalyptic fiction in English, notes that these fictions achieve their desired effect by crafting a future reality that is at once recognizable and unrecognizable: "Thus, the reader of such fiction must sustain a kind of double consciousness with respect to both the fictionality of the world portrayed and to its potential as to our own world's future" (470). The environmentally devastated world in which Acilde resides is in a number of ways a logical extension of current realities: the ecologically devastated coastline is a more intense, chemically inflected version of recent photographs documenting the plastic trash clogging the country's beaches, and the extermination of infected Haitians might be seen as an extension of the racist and nationalist impulses behind "La Sentencia," the September 2013 ruling (known officially as TC 168-13) by the Constitutional Court of the Dominican Republic that denied Dominican citizenship to anyone born of Haitian parents since 1929 and has served as a rationale for subsequent mass deportations of Haitians.[28] Another element of the novel's opening scene that might be considered an extension of current reality is "Price Spy," an implanted app (applications, like an expanded version of Google Glasses, are occularly implanted) that allows someone to see the monetary value of anything within their view. Price Spy takes away the ability to create the illusion of wealth based on cheap imitations; as Ginsburg notes, it "connects to official or legitimized modes of consumption, not informal economies" (*Cyborg Caribbean* 121). The Lladró figurines in Esther's apartment thus not only communicate a particularly bourgeois sense of taste; thanks to Price Spy, they also convey an immediate measure of social status based purely on how much money she might have paid for them. These futuristic additions do not so much diverge from our present-day reality as carry the exclusionary tendencies of late capitalism to their logical conclusion.

Although these future possible extensions of our current present connect the reader to the novel's dystopian future of 2027, the postapocalyptic time loop that Indiana's novel establishes is more than a "double" consciousness; in fact, *La mucama* moves back and forth between four different points in time and space. These include 2027 (Acilde's present); 1991, when the ocean being that will become Acilde is reborn in the coral reefs of Sosúa, on the northern Dominican coast; Sosúa in 2001, when the ocean being (Acilde), who has now become wealthy Italian émigré Giorgio Menicucci, runs an artists' residency as a fundraising project for his wife's marine-biology laboratory, and the same location in the early seventeenth century, when he is alive as Roque, the leader of a ragtag band of buccaneers who make their living tanning hides and selling them to English pirates. Given that 1991 and 2001 are both pasts with regard to the novel's date of publication (2015), this means that the plot is at no point anchored in an identifiable "present" from the reader's point of view. Rather, it zigzags between what is currently a near future and a series of largely recent pasts. The reader observes these multiple temporalities from a distance, with no way to locate herself in this layering. These distinct temporal scenarios loosen the tension on Berger's "temporal loop," since any causal relationship between postapocalyptic 2027 and another moment in time is spread out over several temporal stages whose connecting points, beyond Acilde's presence in all of them, are not always clear.

Acilde/Giorgio/Roque is not, however, the only character in the novel who has the ability to travel in time. Argenis, one of the artists recruited by Giorgio for his artists' residency, awakens from an allergic reaction to a sea-anemone sting to discover that he is simultaneously living lives in two historical moments: his own life as Giorgio's guest in Sosúa, and another as a member of Roque's band of buccaneers, where he finds himself falling in love with Roque. Although he has failed to produce anything of substance in 2001, in his seventeenth-century lifetime Argenis will go on to complete a series of drawings that have tremendous value not at the time of their creation but rather in the future 2001. The text thus establishes a causal relationship between Argenis's two temporal experiences that is not initially apocalyptic (though it could be argued that what we witness is the collapse of both his present world and his personal worldview).

In addition to Argenis's sudden ability to exist in two temporal moments simultaneously, he could be considered a person "out of time" with his own moment in other ways. Argenis displays an aptitude for draftsmanship from a young age, and eventually earns a scholarship to Altos de Chavón, an exclusive art school on the southern Dominican coast. Once at Altos de Chavón, however, Argenis discovers that his technical skills are not as useful as he had thought, as his peers are primarily concerned with art's conceptual dimension. Argenis has little knowledge of contemporary art theory, and no real desire to "say" anything in his work; but after a helpful professor takes him under her wing, he eventually adapts to his peers' expectations. His most successful painting, a kind of Kehinde Wylie take-off, is a modern *pietá* in which the Jesus figure reads a comic book (Jack Kirby's *New Gods,* a tongue-in-cheek gesture toward what is to come in Indiana's novel), while Mary appears dressed in Nike. Yet the fusion of a pop aesthetic with classical painting carries no real meaning for Argenis himself, and he is unable to build this gesture into a career. When Giorgio, who admired his talent at Chavón, seeks him out to invite him to participate in the artists' residency, Argenis is divorced, living with his mother, and has been recently fired from his job at a call center. He is, in short, trapped in his own kind of personal stasis.

At Giorgio and Linda's house in Playa Bo, however, Argenis finds himself to be as out of sync among his fellow artists as he was in his first months at Chavón. He is too conservative to follow trends, unlike Elizabeth, a video artist who approaches art with dilettantish pleasure, moving from fad to fad (certain that her wealthy family will bankroll her next whim). He is not as knowledgeable—nor as interested in knowledge—as Iván, a Cuban émigré who is viewed as the expert in good taste, his finger on the trends of the moment. Nor is he as fresh and enthusiastic as Malagueta, a former baseball player who fell into performance art without any real preparation or education, and who seems to succeed through pure savant-like grace. Indeed, despite his desire to be an artist, Argenis is not really interested in art or in the creative process, only in the success that a good piece of art might bring him. He spends most of his time fantasizing about sleeping with Linda, Giorgio's Jewish-Dominican wife, and has racist and sexist thoughts about nearly every member of the group, in particular Malagueta, with whom he would seem to have the most in common (164). In comparison to the other members of the residency, both his *machista* mentality and his ambivalent artistic engagement mark him as "out of time" within his moment, albeit in different ways.

Timing, however, is everything. As Guillermina De Ferrari observes, "Time travel relies on the fact that fate has alternatives and therefore is not inevitable" (1). De Ferrari sees Indiana's novel as "an exploration of possible futures" (1); it is also, in the case of Argenis, an exploration of possible pasts. Although Argenis seems unable to produce any artwork of significance in 2001, as a companion to Roque and the other buccaneers, however, he becomes a remarkably productive sketch artist, working in charcoal and blood on velum and paper that Roque trades for the English pirates. In the context of the seventeenth-century Dominican coast, what was talent without a message in the late twentieth and early twenty-first century becomes an extraordinary find—the work of an unusual artist producing technically excellent documentary work in highly unlikely circumstances. For Giorgio, Argenis's time travel is "más que un accidente . . . un golpe de suerte" (174) ["more than an accident . . . a stroke of luck" (127)]. Buried in the seventeenth century and found and dug up in the twenty-first, Giorgio anticipates that the sales of Argenis's artwork to collectors will net him more than what he needs to build Linda's marine laboratory.

In choosing the seventeenth century as the temporal setting for this section of the novel, Indiana connects the late twentieth century with an earlier moment of temporal freedom and flexibility. Roque's buccaneers inhabit the northern Dominican coast after what has come to be known in Dominican history as "The Devastations." In this period, which began around 1605, the Spanish government forced the depopulation of large swaths of the northern part of the country, as an effort to centralize (and, in so doing, control) populations farther south (Moya Pons 45–50). This spatial—and political—opening created the space for French buccaneers to profit from lands that had been previously under Spanish control. The world that Roque and his comrades inhabit is lawless and dangerous, but this very lawlessness allows them the freedom to create a new kind of community, if only temporarily. Although Argenis's mindset is at odds with the more liberatory tendencies of his twentieth-century moment, in the seventeenth century he is able to pursue creative practices that are ahead of their time. In the distance from his own era, he is also able to act on his desire for Roque, somehow liberated from the homophobic construction of masculinity he articulates in 2001.

Spiral Time, Mythic Time

Indiana's narrative seems at first glance to follow Frank Kermode's observation that "apocalyptic thought belongs to rectilinear rather than cyclical views of the world" (4). Despite its expansion of the preapocalyptic past to include various temporal moments, the novel still leads us to see how social conditions visible in 1991 and 2001—the hypocrisies, prejudices, and exclusionary racial and class hierarchies at the heart of a contemporary culture of taste—set up the Dominican Republic for the disaster in 2024. Against this linear historical progression toward disaster, or what Decker and Oloff term "the cyclical periodicity of the 500-year durée of colonialist capitalism" (9), *La mucama* introduces a conceptual counterweight in the form of Regla de Ocha-Ifá, the Afro-Caribbean religious practice popularly known as Santería. As exemplified in Esther Escudero's prophesies regarding Acilde, time in Regla de Ocha-Ifá does not operate in teleological historical terms, but in circular—or, perhaps more accurately, spiral—ones. This spiritual conceptualization of time comes closer to Glissant's view of mythic time, in which linearity is not operative and in which history appears as what he terms "a premonition of the past" (72). As Shane Vogel observes, for Glissant, "myth retemporalizes temporality and time is rendered pliable" (187). Glissant describes myth as a literary form that "*coils* meaning around the image itself" (*Caribbean Discourse* 72), a description that echoes Allison Glassie's observation that *La mucama*'s own curving structure and spiral sense of time both echo the shape of the giant sea anemone who facilitates Acilde's ritual transformation. As Paul Humphrey notes, the pliability of Ocha's spiral time is what makes it possible for Acilde to render temporal boundaries fluid, allowing him not only to exist simultaneously as the reborn ocean being in 1991, Giorgio Menicucci in 2001, and Acilde in 2027 but also to be conscious of the actions of these different selves ("El manto que cubre el mar" 110).

The pliable temporality of spiritual time offers a way out from the "temporal loop" of apocalyptic cause and effect. As Dominican scholar Lorgia García-Peña notes in a review of the novel, the future that Acilde's reincarnation holds open "is also a place where humanity—in all its complexity—can regenerate as past consciousness becomes embodied through the sacred and oft-forgotten spiritual link between the corporal and the disembodied that inhabit Afro-diasporic and Native epistemes" ("Book Review"). Interestingly, Indiana does not draw on practices of Afro-Caribbean religiosity native to Hispaniola—*Gagá* or *Vodou*—to establish an alternative temporal paradigm. Rather, she draws on the highly visible—and thus potentially more legible—Ocha as a system with the strength to counterbalance the weight of history. As the appointed "hijo de Olokun," Acilde will connect back to this oceanic divinity and use the spiritual power of the ocean to, in effect, heal itself.

Yet the promise of a spiritual-material salvation that Indiana's text sets up is a tenuous one almost from the beginning. To begin with, Acilde is a strange protagonist for this mission, as his initial motivation is entirely personal: he joins Esther's household solely on the promise that he will earn enough to be able to purchase the Rainbow Bright pill. Even when the physical gender-confirmation procedure he so desires is finally complete and he is reborn, it is not clear to what extent he is committed to the project of saving the country. As Glassie observes, once Acilde acquires a biologically male body, his new more privileged subject position "distances him from the marginalized forms of maritime knowledge whose transformative potential he is prophesied to seek" (3). It should also be noted that the orisha that Indiana tasks with saving the sea (and the island) is not Yemayá, the maternal orisha connected to the ocean's surface, but Olokun, the orisha of the ocean depths, one of the orishas associated with "great transitions of life and death" (David H. Brown, 370). Olokun, understood to be androgynous (Tsang 119), is a powerful but notoriously ambivalent orisha. One traditional *patakí* describes how Olokun is tied to the sea floor to prevent the orisha from unleashing destruction. Indeed, the one significant deviation that Indiana makes from standard Ocha practice is in having Acilde immediately initiated as an *hijo de Olokun;* many Ocha practitioners insist that an initiate must first receive Yemayá before receiving Olokun, because Yemayá generally serves as an intermediary for the other orisha (Tsang 118). In contrast to Esther Escudero, an *hija de Yemayá*, who takes Acilde in and sets in motion the prophecy she has received, Acilde's connection to Olokun hints at both the powers he possesses and the uncertainty of the outcome for the task he has been assigned.

For indeed, the novel's ending suggests that the rescue project will not succeed as prophesied. Flush with the satisfaction of the discovery of Argenis's art, high on ecstasy, and fresh from a pleasurable session of lovemaking with his wife, Giorgio finds himself a contented spectator at the party-event that represents the culmination of his artists' residency. His eye lights on a young dancer, only to realize that it is Said Bona, future president of the Dominican Republic, and the leader who will be responsible for agreeing to store Venezuela's chemical weapons. Giorgio immediately recognizes the significance of this encounter: "Repentina y aplastante, tenía enfrente la verdadera meta de su misión: darle un mensaje a Said Bona, evitar que, cuando fuese electo presidente, aceptara esas armas biológicas de Venezuela" (177) ["Quickly and overwhelmingly, he had before him the real goal of his mission: to give Said Bona a message—as president, to avoid accepting biological weapons from Venezuela" (129)]. This is clearly the way in which Acilde is being asked to intervene; only someone with knowledge of the future can recognize the significance of this moment, and Giorgio is well placed to use his meeting with Bona to effect positive change. After considering his options, however, Giorgio decides to do nothing: "Tras hablar de rap y política, había despedido a Said sin decirle una palabra sobre su futuro" (180) ["After chatting about rap and politics, he'd said goodbye to Said without a word about his future" (132)]. Although the novel does not confirm that Giorgio/Acilde rejects his sacred charge completely, his refusal to take advantage of this important chance meeting implies it, as does the fact that Giorgio's reflection is accompanied by his witnessing of the deaths of Roque and Acilde, who commits suicide to ensure that Giorgio will survive. To alter the history leading up to the chemical accident would mean altering or even erasing his life as Giorgio, and that, in the end, is a sacrifice he is unprepared to make. Indeed, the presence of Argenis as the protagonist in Indiana's subsequent novel, *Hecho en Saturno* (2018; *Made in Saturn,* 2020)—in which he remembers the experience with Roque as a kind of fever dream—serves to further emphasize that *La mucama*'s ending rejects the temporal opening created by spiritual time and the possibility of salvation that it offers.

Of course, it could be argued that Giorgio can still attempt to avoid disaster in another way. With the money earned from the sale of Argenis's art, Giorgio can fund Linda's marine laboratory, which he calls "el altar que voy a erigirle a Olokun" (176) ["the altar I'm going to build for Olokun" (128)], and help save certain marine species. With the laboratory's prominence and his well-established social capital, he can attempt to influence policy and decisions at other levels as well. Yet these measures can only hope to mitigate the effects of the environmental disaster; they are not oriented toward the prevention of the political conditions that lay the groundwork for the crisis. Fredric Jameson observes that the fundamental anxiety surrounding utopia is "the fear of losing that familiar world in which all our vices and virtues are rooted (very much including the longing for Utopia itself) in exchange for a world in which all these things and experiences—positive as well as negative—will have been obliterated" (*Archaeologies* 97). In the case of Acilde, neither the spiritual contract in which he is a participant nor his own previous experiences as a marginalized subject—and the possibility of sparing others that suffering—are a match for the comfort and pleasure to be had as a wealthy, middle-aged white man living in a world of social and financial privilege, aesthetic pleasures, and physical comfort. Or, as Giorgio/Acilde himself puts it, "Podía sacrificarlo todo menos esta vida, la vida de Giorgio Menicucci, la compañía de su mujer, la galería, su laboratorio" (180–81) ["He could sacrifice everything except this life, Giorgio Menicucci's life, his wife's company, the gallery, the lab" (132).] De Ferrari observes, "While Giorgio does not make the right choice, it is only in choosing that he becomes the man he needed to be to become a man" (5). Giorgio/Acilde's choice to let Giorgio live confirms that he has acquired not only the gender but also the power and position he has so desired. Saving the world is nothing compared with retaining, for however short a time, the well-heeled comforts of home.

Read one way, *La mucama de Omicunlé* presents the reader with an ambivalent, worrisome ending. The addition of multiple temporalities expands and complicates the postapocalyptic time loop, but the connections between the various temporal settings of Indiana's novel make it possible to see how conditions and events from both the 1990s and the early 2000s could lead to an environmental apocalypse in the Dominican Republic. Rather than showing us how this crisis might be averted, however, the novel's ending reaffirms the nearness of catastrophe. Although his ability to save the island by preventing the weapons accident was uncertain in any case, Giorgio/Acilde refuses to accept his appointed role as preordained savior. In *Living in the End Times*, Žižek presents five stages—modeled on the five stages of grief—that allow the world's "social consciousness" to avoid thinking about (and thus facing) impending disaster (xvii). Giorgio/Acilde seems to be stuck between the third stage, "attempts at bargaining," and the last stage, where the apocalypse is perceived as "the chance of a new beginning." The difference here is that Giorgio, as Acilde, is intimately aware of the conditions of the postapocalyptic dystopia that will arise if he fails to act. If the environmental disaster actually occurs "again" as it did in Acilde's lifetime, it will be far from a space of emancipatory possibility. In this sense, we might argue that what is revealed in the lead up to this apocalypse is the way in which the figure of the white European man, initiator of the Caribbean's apocalyptic processes, perpetuates an always already catastrophic status quo. The spiral time of Afro-Caribbean religious experience is left in the realm of still-unrealized possibility.

With Giorgio/Acilde's refusal to assume the role of a savior and forestall a national catastrophe, Indiana removes the possibility of an easy resolution to the coming crisis. And yet, the novel's ending is not entirely devoid of hope. As De Ferrari observes, "Even though it seems practically inevitable, that fatal fate has not happened yet. Reasonable anticipation is not experienced as certainty. The future could still be otherwise" (10). Njelle Hamilton concurs: "The future, fictional disaster of 2024 is still ahead of us as I write in 2020. We readers can change the future—no time machines necessary" (6). Indeed, what the novel shows us is exactly what stands in the way of real change. By removing Acilde as a possible hero, a single savior, Indiana seems to be leaving the possibility of saving the world in the hands of her readers. The Dominican Republic—and, by extension, the planet—will always be at risk, whatever our good intentions, if we cannot let go of our attachments to our current privileges. Will we, like Giorgio, be willing to sacrifice the future for our comfort and privilege in the present?

In fact, the novel's possibility for hope may lie in the narrative's third time traveler: the sea anemone. In postapocalyptic 2027, the anemone is a fixture of Esther Escudero's altar, kept alive—and away from the toxic sludge that is all that remains of its home—by Esther and her assistant Eric's careful attentions. Both in 2027 and in 2001, the anemone facilitates transformation: placed over Acilde's head, it completes his spiritual transformation, allowing him to be incarnated as the *hijo de Olokun* and to be present to his various temporal selves. But the anemone is also present in the waters of Playa Bo in 2001; its sting awakens Argenis to his own past life with Roque. Although it may not be the same anemone in all of these moments, there is clearly a kind of "anemone consciousness" acting to assist Acilde in his mission and in operating outside of linear temporality. Taken together with Giorgio's choices, the anemone's presence and its function as a time-traveling facilitator seems to indicate that the way forward is to "make oddkin" as Donna Haraway urges us, to "require each other in unexpected collaborations and combinations" (4). If neither linear nor spiral time can save us, perhaps it is time to turn to the unexpected tentacularity of cross-species collaboration.

Loop the Postapocalyptic Time Loop: What Is Revealed

For the three narratives this chapter explores, apocalypse is not a break that "wipes the slate clean" (Kaup 52). Indiana's and Mota's novels and Cabral's film reveal not only the historic causes of some catastrophes but also the ways in which the conditions that produced them—illuminated by the apocalypse—continue to follow us into the "post-." In his study of Haiti's histories of catastrophe, Martin Munro identifies what he terms the "four riders of Caribbean apocalypse," conditions that have served as both causes and harbingers of the region's catastrophes: ecological crisis, slavery, the expansion of social divisions, and what he terms the "crisis of criminality" (11). Although in the texts I examine here slavery as a groundwork for current conditions of Caribbean crisis is more implied than explicit, they each in their own way explore how the other three "riders" evolve through an apocalyptic scenario deeply tied to both recent and historic pasts. Mota's and Indiana's novels explore the ways in which ecological disaster is both precipitated by and magnified by human politics. The dystopian futures conjured by *La mucama* and *Arrobá* are easily visible as extensions of the social and racial divisions on display. In *Habana Underguater,* the social divisions are militarily enforced and criminality exists as an acceptable way to circumvent them. In all three texts, money and power continue to be corrupting influences, fragmenting possibilities for broader cooperation and resulting in an environment where present survival trumps thoughts of the future. Time in these texts may be elastic, but place is not.

At the same time, *Habana Underguater, Arrobá,* and *La mucama de Omicunlé* all sidestep or weaken the narrative loop that binds our current present to coming apocalypse, with the result that all three texts share an absence of both pessimism and resolution or salvation. None of these three narratives offers a prescriptive solution for the problems that plague Caribbean cities and islands. The crises in their texts cannot—and will not—be solved by an individual hero or heroes. Autonomous sovereignty (whether personal or national) is not enough. Yet by engaging their readers actively in the construction and development of their scenarios, they create an ethical bond with their audience, leaving open the possibility that we could, together, begin to imagine a different, alternative, better way to move forward.

Epilogue

Future Possibilities

In this study, I argue that contemporary Caribbean writers and artists use science fiction to intervene in constructions and perceptions of Caribbean temporality. I explore the way in which the "future possible" of the science fiction mode, which describes "what has not [yet] happened," inserts itself into recent Hispanic Caribbean cultural production, revealing the constructed nature of what we understand to be both history and present reality, while also offering alternative visions of the future. Until recently science fiction may not have been thought of as a Caribbean genre, but a glance at some of the texts I analyze throughout this study reveals the many ways in which the region's writers, artists, and creatives have taken established elements of the international science fiction "mega-text"—cyberpunk, zombies, and the postapocalyptic, among others—and used them to reveal new aspects of established narratives and views of the region, to show how the past continues to haunt us and to begin to craft alternative stories and glimpse other ways of being.[1] In the texts I have examined in this study, the future possible of science fiction becomes a vantage point from which to expose and explore the effects of colonialism or to reflect critically on the ways in which Cuban revolutionary discourse has stagnated as it has aged. Even in creating literary or cinematic dystopias, the alternate realities offered by these texts open a space for imagining other Caribbean trajectories.

Since I began working on Caribbean science fiction fifteen years ago, both the corpus of cultural artifacts and the communities of cultural creators engaging science fiction have proliferated before my eyes. Texts produced in diverse media and in different national contexts have much to say to one another and are often in direct conversation. Equally impressive has been the way in which the audience for this production has expanded. The circuits of distribution and production that used to limit the circulation of literary production to the writer's national environs—or to the circuits designed by the large publishing houses—have disappeared. Thanks to the development of technologies like Zoom and Facebook Live, performances, conferences, and talks can now bring together interested viewers on several continents simultaneously. Writers and directors can connect with their fans and can read and view one another's work almost as soon as it is produced. A reader in Chicago can connect and listen to a podcast on women writers of science fiction and fantasy produced in Spain by a Cuban writer and her Spanish cocreator.[2] A film director in Miami can tune in to a Zoom conversation sponsored by a Dominican writers' association featuring a speaker from Cuba. A Colombian editor can publish an anthology of Latin American literature featuring writers from around the hemisphere, including two from Cuba.[3]

Of course, neither the creation of these recent Caribbean fictions and communities nor the writing of this study has happened in a vacuum. Much of this book was written during the COVID-19 pandemic, an event that has revealed—as apocalypses do—the great social inequities and the institutional failures present in every nation around the world, and one that has made some of the dystopian imaginings in recent postapocalyptic literature a little too "real" for comfort. As one more crisis to be borne by a region that has a too intimate experience of them, the pandemic exacerbated many of the conditions of crisis in the Caribbean. In a broader sense, it laid bare the ways in which the past is still with us (zombielike), as well as the difficulties that we face moving forward. Any overly optimistic vision of a totally connected world belies the challenges that currently face humanity, not just in the Caribbean but throughout the planet.

I believe that science fiction's rising popularity has to do precisely with the genre's ability to open space for the future possible, what Yomaira Figueroa-Vásquez terms "worlds/otherwise," while still making visible the weight of both past and present. Science fiction texts fall under what Darieck Scott, in his study of superhero comics, terms "fantasy-acts" (35). Asserting that "in fantasy lies, inherently, resistance," Scott sees these works of imagination as meaningful precisely because they constitute "*not* waiting" (36); they are "counterpropositions" to our current reality that urge us to think beyond the limits of the moment. I end this study by examining two such fantasy acts, texts that, though not unconscious of the challenges of Caribbean history and reality, nonetheless engage in acts of imagination as resistance: Rita Indiana's song "Como un dragon" (from *Mandinga Times*, 2020) with its accompanying video, directed by Noelia Quintero Herencia, and Yolanda Arroyo Pizarro's short story "Mûlatresse," from the collection *Prietopunk: antología de afrofuturismo caribeño* (2022). In different ways, these texts urge us to expand our frameworks of imagination and possibility. They also highlight the increasing role female creators are playing in the production of such fantasy acts.

La Montra Returns

"Como un dragón," the first song on Indiana's album *Mandinga Times* and a fusion of dembow and doom metal, opens boldly.[4] The first thing we hear is the beat—"Bum cha, bum cha / Bum-bum cha bum cha"—heavy and electronic. On the video screen, a small round projectile comes flying toward the viewer, moving to dodge a strange shape as it does so. As the camera moves backward, creating distance between the viewer and the object, we see that the shape is a small rocky island set in the middle of a lake. It is nighttime, and a light shines out from a window at the center of the island's rocky promontory. The light comes from a chamber deep within the island, "La Montra's" lair. The camera cuts to the chamber itself, a dimly lit room lined with machines with strange tubes coming out of them and giant beakers containing colored liquids and round shapes. The space functions both as a stage on which La Montra—Indiana herself, in ice-blue hair and sharp blue triangles of makeup that shape the rest of her face into a kind of skeletal mask—sings and dances, and as a laboratory where she engineers surreal creations. In one scene we see La Montra working on one of her projects, a purple ball with dozens of red openings like mouths, out of which pop small eyes. It was one of these eyes that zoomed toward the viewer in the first shot, and they zoom around through other scenes in the video as if they were small, living drones.

On one level, "Como un dragón" is a kind of rap-battle challenge. Moving forcefully around the stage, La Montra touts her skills as a musician and a writer in both the verses and the chorus:

> ¡Suena la sirena!
> Regresó la Montra pa' comérselos de cena
> Como un dragón
> De *Game of Thrones*
> Después que abra a boca vamo' a ver qué queda.
>
> [Sound the siren!
> La Montra's back to eat you all for dinner
> Like a dragon

Figure 6. Rita Indiana as "La Montra" in the video for "Como un dragón" (2020).

From *Game of Thrones*
Once she opens her mouth, we'll see what's left.]

As Paul Humphrey notes, "La Montra" (the Dominican pronunciation of "la monstrua") is slang for "someone particularly skillful at something" (342). A "monster" of music-making and verse, La Montra promises to eat her competitors alive. She also slings put-downs at would-be challengers: "Pi pi, llegaron los camiones / a recoger la mierda que tú crees que son canciones" [Beep, beep, the trucks have arrived / to pick up the shit you think are songs]. Underneath the swagger, however, the listener can also feel the pulse of sheer creative energy. If La Montra is a "monster," she is also the mad scientist, a fusion of Dr. Frankenstein and his monster, controlling everything from her island vantage point. In the video, we see her in the laboratory, pouring a strange blue liquid onto the ball with eyes. As they emerge from the ball, the eyes operate like drone cameras, zooming off to other spaces, allowing the viewer to witness a series of other scenes.

As if echoing La Montra's reference to *Game of Thrones*, the hugely popular TV show based on the book series by George R. R. Martin, in the song's chorus, the scenes that the eyes move through suggest the settings of Westeros, the land where *Game of Thrones* is set. Produced with stop-motion animation, the eyes create a parallel narrative centering on two featureless figures, one dressed in a spiky black dress and carrying a huge javelin, the other with a strangely shaped head and wearing a bright orange-red jacket. Followed by the eyes, these figures travel through a series of interiors and then landscapes, first separately, then together. In a wood of trees dressed in autumnal foliage, they come upon a monitor on which they glimpse La Montra in her lab. The two narratives suddenly come together. We see a brief shot of the two figures on board a small boat—named Desamparo (abandonment)—crossing the waters of the lake, headed, it becomes clear, for La Montra's island. They head into the island, moving closer and closer to La Montra's room. Suddenly, boom! They fall into a pit, where a fierce green dragon (made of papier maché and in stop animation) eats them up in one bite. The paper dragon makes literal the chorus's simile; it devours the competition.

The presence of *Game of Thrones* introduces cross-genre hybridity and intertextuality into both the song itself and the video. The TV series, set in a fictional land whose culture is largely patriarchal and medieval, is clearly a work of fantasy. As seen in the video, La Montra's island could be described as a similarly fantastic setting. Yet amid this fantastic setting, the laboratory setup, the creation of the eye drones, speaks more to a kind of science. As Noelia Quintero Herencia, the video's director, describes it, "In this universe, living beings coexist with lethal technology which La Montra develops in her musical lab" (quoted in Exposito). In this sense, the video is emblematic of the ways in which Caribbean texts commingle science fiction with other genres. The science fiction elements of the video put scientific technology in the lands of La Montra, whose creations emerge from her autochthonous-island setting ready to take on the world. But the island also echoes Caribbean geography, and the intertextual references connect this scene of creation to other circulating imaginaries; this act of creation is not taking place in isolation.

Although "La Montra" is Indiana's popular nickname, she explains in an interview that the character she embodies in the video and for the album is named Mandinga and they are "a queer-gendered creature" ("Rita Indiana, La Monstra, Returns"). The Spanish name for an African ethnic group, *Mandinga* thus connects back to the slave trade and the Dominican population's African origins. But Indiana also provides another meaning: "[W]hen they beat you up, a bunch of people beat you up, it's called, you know, te dieron Mandinga" (ibid). Indiana's appearance in the video plays with the multiple meanings of Mandinga's name. The song's rap posturing suggests that Mandinga is willing to fight someone. If we are living in "Mandinga Times," a moment ready to beat us down, Mandinga, like the dragon, is ready to take on whatever comes.

The song's last verse reinforces the parallels between La Montra's imagined space and other, real islands:

De nube negra 'ta lleno el horizonte
La tormenta se acerca la llamaste por su nombre
Y no te asombre cuando salga de la cueva
Con todo lo podere' y par de vaina' nueva'

[The horizon is full of black clouds
The storm is coming, you called it by name
So don't be surprised when I emerge from the cave
With all my powers and a couple of new tricks]

Indiana has described *Mandinga Times,* her second album, as a kind of "songbook for the apocalypse" (quoted in Herrera). The final verse of "Como un dragón" reminds the listener of the terrible and very real storms—María, Irma—that have battered the Caribbean in recent years, as well as the ongoing crises produced by climate change, a "storm" that will surely only grow stronger. Although "Como un dragón" does not directly address either climate change or other kinds of Caribbean crisis, as Humphrey, Ginsburg, Maillo-Pozo, and others have observed, Indiana's music is connected to and in productive resonance with her literary production.[5] The image of the angry waters in the video resonates with readers of Indiana's novel *La mucama de Omucunlé,* analyzed in the previous chapter, who will be reminded of the importance of the sea in her novel as well as the environmental apocalypse that provides the backdrop for the novel's future setting. La Montra's (and the viewer's) ability to see into other spaces through the flying eyes finds a parallel in Acilde, the novel's protagonist, who is tasked with helping prevent environmental destruction precisely through their ability to see into multiple times at once. Both the novel and the video include creatures—the dragon in the video, the anemone in *La mucama*—who assist the protagonists, thus suggesting the importance of cross-species, post-human relations in these moments of crisis.

Yet "Como un dragón" removes us from the novel's very real Santo Domingo setting, providing the viewer with a parallel space. In a deliberate fantasy act, it presents a space where Mandinga/La Montra is in control, not only of the space itself but also of the scientific technology. A big storm is coming, but La Montra is ready, stronger than ever and with new allies and tricks up her sleeve. The song thus becomes both the declaration of an artist at the top of her game and an affirmation of the power of the imagination as the first step to effect change.

Caribbean Afrofuturism

Published in *Prietopunk: antología de afrofuturismo caribeño* (2022) Yolanda Arroyo Pizarro's story "Mûlatresse" is a narrative clearly engaged with Figueroa-Vásquez's idea of "worlds/otherwise" as "fashion[ing] new possibilities for Black life and ways of being in the world for both the present moment and the future" (148). "Mûlatresse" is set in what appears to be a peaceful future society, even if not all social problems have been resolved. Indeed, the text's narrator-protagonist, a robot who has worked as an official in the "Gobierno Continental" [Continental Government] for the last 150 years, remarks on having witnessed humanity's cyclical advances and setbacks over the decades. Yet humanity continues to fascinate it (them): "Porque al final siempre descubro algo interesante que me mantiene queriendo regresar a la nostalgia, deseando investigar más sobre la existencia de este plano" (28) [Because in the end I always discover something interesting that keeps me wanting to return to nostalgia, wanting to investigate more about existence on this plane]. This fascination—and, it becomes clear, sympathy—with human beings leads the robot narrator to commit small acts of what we might call resistance: giving a human visitor information about how to obtain an illegal baptism, for example.

The crucial connection between the robot government official and a particular human being occurs at the end of a workday one Tuesday. A woman appears at the official's window to request "a termination." The robot takes in the woman's appearance: "La piel era oscura y brillosa. El pelo era un afro corto. Su masa corporal había sido bien cuidada. No poseía arrugas visibles, ni cicatrices quirúgicas, ni golpes o extremidades mecánicas de mala calidad" (30) [Her skin was dark and shiny. Her hair was a short afro. Her body mass had been well cared for. She had no visible wrinkles, no surgical scars, no bumps, or poor-quality mechanical extremities]. Despite the woman's "optimal" physical condition, the tattoo on her arm tells the official that she is well over two hundred years old. Although we might not ascribe feelings to an AI, the robot "feels" some kind of connection to this woman, a connection experienced as a "glitch" in their functioning; they twice repeat the sentence, "Hace años que no tramito una solicitud de terminación eutanacista" (31) [It has been years since I processed a termination through euthanasia]. The connection is reciprocated; the woman, Amora, invites the robot official to "dinner," an encounter that serves as the beginning of a kind of human-robot love affair that takes place over the course of the three days before the woman is scheduled to end her life.

Although both the human woman and her robot lover appear to experience some form of attraction to the other, Amora also enters into this intimate relationship because she needs something from her companion. As part of the "termination" process, she has created a "virtual blueprint," a digital recording that she will view as her life is ending. She asks her robot lover to undress her, to place her on the funeral dais, and to help her watch a "preview" of the virtual blueprint—in short, to help her stage a kind of rehearsal of the death itself. But "Mûlatress" (*sic*), the blueprint she has prepared, is not an overview of her own life but rather the life of one of her ancestors, an African woman who experienced the Middle Passage: "En la pantalla mi humana se convertía en Atawa, luego en Rosalie. Su Nacimiento sucede en 1772. Corría a través de la selva Africana intentando no ser secuestrada. Asesinó a tres de sus captores, pero otros siete sobrevivieron y la encadenaban" (34) [On the screen my human became Atawa, then Rosalie. She was born in 1772. She ran across the African jungle, trying not to be kidnapped. She killed three of her captors, but another seven survived and put her in chains]. For Amora, Atawa/Rosalie's descendant, the virtual blueprint seems to serve less as a memorial than as a kind of ritual enactment, almost like a video game, where the outcome changes and evolves: "Con cada nueva corrida Atawa se hacía más fuerte, más astuta, dirigía cada vez más revueltas y sediciones" (34) [With each new race, Atawa became stronger, smarter; each time she led more revolts and uprisings]. With each replaying of the blueprint, the woman's ancestor evolves, becoming a kind of enslaved superhero capable of nearly impossible feats. Yet her death is always the same.

The woman's inability to resolve her ancestor's death leads her to make a request of her robot lover that goes against the laws of robot-human relations. She wants the robot official to end her life *before* the blueprint portrays Atawa/Rosalie's death, so that her ancestor lives on, even if her descendant dies. This leaves the robot official in a quandary. As they observe in the story's last lines, "No se permite a los no humanos, causar la muerte a humana alguna. Tampoco se nos permite enamorarnos de ellas y heme aquí, en este dilema" (36) [Nonhumans are not allowed to cause death to any human being. Nor are we allowed to fall in love with them, and so here I find myself, in this dilemma]. The narrative ends here on the threshold of the robot functionary's decision. The reader doesn't know whether the narrator will decide to honor their feelings for the woman and end her life as she wishes. But it becomes clear that the three days the robot has spent with the woman—and the repeated views of Atawa/Rosalie's journey—have altered what was previously a distanced view of human relations.

Arroyo Pizarro shows us a future world in which Caribbean colonial history is still casting a long shadow. Although she is living hundreds of years in the future, Atawa/Rosalie's descendant is still living "in the wake," as Christina Sharpe puts it; her view of herself and her family history has been indelibly marked by her ancestor's experience of enslavement. The blueprint functions as what Angela Naimou terms "salvage work"; in creating a personal archive of one Atlantic history (her ancestor's) and exploring the full dimensions of the personhood of the protagonist at the heart of this history, Amora "refashions the objects and subjects of history, creating literary and visual assemblages of historical fragments figuratively pulled from the wreck of the present" (Naimou 9). In this future reality, the blueprint's ability to alter details of this life gives this salvage work an even more active quality. At the same time, Amora's inability to fundamentally alter the blueprint to ensure her ancestor's survival recognizes the nature of salvage as "neither a full nor a failed recuperation" (8). Amora is able to reconstruct Atawa/Rosalie's life as a person with agency, but she cannot completely undo her enslavement nor the other violent events that lead to her death by hanging, just after having given birth to her only child.

Arroyo Pizarro's text also can be seen as "salvage work" in that it reveals the ways in which "the category of the legal slave" continues to "participate in shaping the conditions of contemporary life" (Naimou 7), in this case a contemporary life in the future. Although the little we are shown of this future Caribbean society leads the reader to assume that this is a peaceful, better reality, the robot functionary is proof of the rigidity of the law. Despite the affective relationship she has formed with the robot narrator, Amora's life and death is still subject to the law; she must apply for permission to end her life, and to end her life as she would like to (i.e., before the end of the blueprint), she must make an illegal request of her robot lover. She has lived a long, healthy life, but her fate is still not entirely her own.

The centrality of the past in Arroyo Pizarro's story is in line with what Sofia Samatar has observed about Afrofuturism in Africa. She states, "[Afrofuturism] is always about all times: past, present, and future. The excavation of the past is essential, for it is from those historical fragments that the data thief or bricoleur constructs visions of what is to come" (178). In gathering these pieces of the present to imagine the worlds/otherwise that might take its place, Arroyo Pizarro, like other Caribbean creators whose fictions I explore in this study, reminds us how where we have been and what we know shapes what we can imagine. At the same time, she leaves us on the threshold of a world in which new and compelling post-human relationships may be just beginning to take hold, in which the actions of both a human protagonist and her robot companion might just open space for something new and previously unimagined.

NOTES

Introduction

1 All translations are mine unless otherwise identified.
2 Jamaica Kincaid writes clearly of the uncomfortable distinction between tourist and native: "That the native does not like the tourist is not hard to explain. For every native of every place is a potential tourist, and every tourist is a native of somewhere. Every native everywhere lives a life of overwhelming and crushing banality and boredom and desperation and depression, and every deed, good and bad, is an attempt to forget this. Every native would like to find a way out, every native would like a rest, every native would like a tour" (18).
3 Of particular note are the five conferences organized by Rafael Acevedo and Melanie Pérez Ortiz in San Juan (in 2014, 2015, 2016, 2017, and 2019); "Caribe Extremófilo," the first Dominican conference on science fiction and fantasy, organized by the group Mentes Extremófilas in Santo Domingo in 2016; and the joint Conferencia Caribeña de Ciencia Ficción in 2023, which featured activities taking place over two weekends in both San Juan and Santo Domingo and was sponsored by the previously mentioned groups, in addition to the Asociación Dominicana de Ficción Especulativa. These encounters were notable for bringing together writers and artists from various parts of the Caribbean and the diaspora.
4 I draw here on anthropologist Arjun Appadurai's definition of a *mediascape* as both "the distribution of the electronic capabilities to produce and disseminate information (newspapers, magazines, television stations, and film-production studios)" and as "the images of the world created by these media" (35). The increased circulation of electronic media has allowed both narratives and visual images of science fiction to proliferate and circulate widely, reaching beyond national or regional borders. In *Caribes 2.0,* Jossianna Arroyo explores the particular dimensions of the Caribbean mediascape, specifically the ways in which viral content creators "negotiate their bodies, subjectivities and agencies in Caribbean landscapes" (7).
5 According to Australian critic Damien Broderick, these are elements of what he terms science fiction's "mega-text" (48), not technically a genre at all but rather an "interlocking web of fictive worlds . . . constructed in rhetorical space" (ibid.).
6 In *Metamorphoses of Science Fiction,* the book-length expansion of his initial, groundbreaking essay, Suvin expands this definition slightly: "*SF is, then, a literary genre whose necessary and sufficient conditions are the presence and interaction of*

estrangement and cognition, and whose main formal device is an imaginative framework alternative to the author's environment" (7–8, italics in the original).

7 In "The Carrier Bag Theory of Fiction," Le Guin argues, "If science fiction is the mythology of modern technology, then its myth is tragic. . . . If, however, one avoids the linear, progressive, Time's-(killing)-arrow mode of the Techno-Heroic and redefines technology and science as primarily cultural carrier bag rather than weapon of domination, one pleasant side effect is that science fiction can be seen as a far less rigid, narrow field, . . . and in fact less a mythological genre than a realistic one. It is a strange realism, but it is a strange reality" (*Dancing at the Edge of the World* 169–70).

8 As Wendy Faris and Lois Parkinson Zamora note, "[M]agical realism is not a Latin American monopoly" ("Introduction" 2); in fact, the term first surfaced in German writing during the Weimar era. Nevertheless, it may be most strongly associated with the writers who defined the Latin American Boom generation, especially Carlos Fuentes, Gabriel García Márquez, and José Donoso.

9 Lim's concept draws heavily on the work of anthropologist Johannes Fabian, who argues that the labeling of conquered peoples as "primitive" was a strategy of conquest and subjugation: "When in the course of colonial expansion a Western body politic came to occupy, literally, the space of an autochthonous body, several alternatives were conceived to deal with that violation of the rule. The simplest one, if we think of North America and Australia, was of course to move or remove the other body. . . . Most often the preferred strategy has been simply to manipulate the other variable—Time. With the help of various devices of sequencing and distancing one assigns to the conquered populations a different time" (29–30).

10 In *Archaeologies of the Future: The Desire Called Utopia and Other Science Fictions*, Fredric Jameson engages in a thorough tracing of the genre's literal engagement with utopia and what he terms the "Utopian form" in a semantic sense. I am less concerned here with recognizing this subgenre—indeed, Caribbean science fiction may fall outside the criteria (temporal and narrative) that Jameson establishes—than I am in recognizing a kind of utopian potential in a Blochian sense inherent in the genre's temporal aspects.

11 Bloch distinguishes between unproductive or static "daydreams" and what he calls "forward dreaming," based in hope and actively oriented toward the future: "The imagination and the thoughts of future intention described in this way are utopian, this again not in a narrow sense of the word which only defines what is bad (emotively reckless picturing, playful form of an abstract kind), but rather in fact in the newly tenable sense of the forward dream, of anticipation in general" (*Principle of Hope* 12).

12 A desire to highlight the development of these communities of Spanish-language producers and consumers of science fiction is also the reason why this study is limited to work from the Hispanophone Caribbean. Although there has also been significant recent production from Anglophone and Francophone Caribbean communities—work consumed by the Hispanophone Caribbean—I do not see these creators as participating in Hispanophone science fiction networks in the same way. Furthermore, in the case of Anglophone Caribbean writers like Nalo

Hopkinson, Travis Buckle, and Karen Lord, their location in the diaspora means that they are often read more within the broader Anglo-American corpus of science fiction and speculative literature. For more on Anglophone and Francophone science fiction, see Shaw Nevins.

Chapter 1. Shades of *Destiempo*

1 Carpentier's essay is, at least in part, a critique of what he perceives as the artificiality of European avant-garde art. For him, the marvelous real and the "naturalness" of the Caribbean's excess stand in contradistinction to the forced and inauthentic excess of European surrealism.
2 See the introduction for a deeper discussion of the difference between science fiction and magical realism.
3 For more on this transition, especially in Cuban filmmaking, see Stock, *On Location in Cuba*; and Álvarez Pitaluga, "Brief Notes."
4 For more on the long tradition of science fiction in Argentina and Brazil, see Page, *Science Fiction in Argentina*; and Ginway, *Brazilian Science Fiction*. Teresa López-Pellisa and Silvia G. Kurlat Ares's *Historia de la ciencia ficción en la literatura latinoamericana I: desde los orígenes hasta la modernidad*, which dedicates a chapter to each Latin American country, demonstrates the depth of the science fiction tradition in some countries as well as its paucity in others.
5 After declaring independence from Spain in 1821, Dominican leaders aligned themselves with Haiti a year later. However, Dominican resistance to what was perceived as a mismanagement of the country, particularly by Haitian president Jean-Pierre Boyer, led the Dominicans to declare independence from Haiti in 1844. Between 1844 and 1865, Haiti sought to regain control over the other half of the island through a series of military incursions. Although the Dominicans were eventually successful in repelling the Haitian advances, the toll that this defense effort took on the economy forced Dominican leadership to seek assistance from Spain, leading to the country's reannexation by Spain in 1861. Clashes between Dominican nationalists and Spanish troops finally forced the Spanish to relinquish control of the Dominican Republic in 1865.
6 Until 2015, the most notable of these challenges was Cubans' restricted access to the internet due to a combination of government restrictions as well as the slow connection to the internet through an aging cable connection to the United States. Although that began to change in 2013 with the opening of the ALBA-1 fiber optic cable connection provided by Venezuela, it was not until the establishment of public Wi-Fi hot spots in 2015 that more users began to have sustained access to the technology.
7 See Lauren Derby for a careful analysis of the ways in which Trujillo maintained control through systems of both patronage and fear. Derby observes: "The very invasiveness of the state and its multiple roles endowed it with many meanings that transcended Trujillo himself, even if he became the master trope for a new regime of state penetration" (7).

8   By referring to Puerto Rico as "islands," rather than "island," I follow recent scholarship that recognizes Puerto Rico's identity as an archipelago that includes Vieques and Culebra, in addition to other smaller islands.
9   As Hilda Lloréns and Maritza Stanchich argue, these practices set the islands up for an escalating series of crises: "As a US territory, Puerto Rico's municipal bonds were touted as triple tax exempt from federal, state and local taxes since 1917. . . . When the debt far outsized the country's gross national product (GNP), ratings agencies in 2014 downgraded Puerto Rico's bonds to junk status. Vulture hedge funds that were also players in Greece, Argentina, and Detroit debt crises preyed upon the broken system, with bonds purchased pennies to the dollar and loans made to the tune of 746% interest rates" (86).
10 For more information on the history of science fiction writing in Cuba, see Maguire, "Ficciones científicas"; Soltero Sánchez, "La ciencia ficción cubana"; Yoss, "Marcianos"; and Román, *Universo*.
11 The "Quinquenio Gris" is normally understood to be the period from 1971 through 1975. However, in a 2003 reflection on the period—known popularly as "la guerrita de los emails" (the little email war), critic Ambrosio Fornet acknowledged that one could also speak of "la década negra" (the black decade), as the climate of censorship had, in fact, lasted far longer than a lustrum.
12 Between 1979 and 1989, the Premio David, the Premio Luis Rogelio Nogueras, and the Premio Juventud Técnica facilitated the publication of a number of science fiction novels and short story collections. The first of these was the 1979 awarding of the Premio David, a prize given for an author's first book, to Bruno Henríquez's *Aventura en el laboratorio: cuentos de ciencia ficción* (Adventure in the lab: science fiction stories, 1987).
13 Among the members of the Oscar Hurtado workshop, Yoss lists Féliz Lizárraga, Arnoldo Águila, Roberto Estrada, Julián Pérez, Eduardo Frank, Ileana Vicente, Raúl Aguiar, Ricardo Fumero, and Georgina (Gina) Picart (Yoss, "Marcianos" 71). However, Soltero Sánchez notes that sources disagree on the full membership of this workshop.
14 Personal communications with Raúl Aguiar and Yoss, 2008, 2014.
15 Before the installation of the fiber-optic cable connection to Venezuela, the island had the lowest rate of internet access of anywhere in the hemisphere, and internet connection speeds averaged a mere 329 Mbps. See Maguire, "Islands in the Slipstream"; Henken, "Introduction."
16 Ahmel Echevarría Peré, in an interview with Laura V. Sández, distinguishes between "Generación Año Cero" as a group and "Generación Cero" as a generation: "De ahí la idea de Generación Cero, que además trae como consecuencia cierta confusión porque Generación Cero o Generación Año Cero, no era el nombre de una generación sino de un grupo. Mucho tiempo después algunos críticos cubanos utilizaron esa idea de Orlando, o ese nombre, para nombrar a un grupo más amplio de escritores cubanos, ya no concebido como grupo sino como generación, pero del nombre eliminaron año y se quedó como generación. Inicialmente era Generación

Año Cero, que era para nombrar a un grupo de escritores, no a una generación" ("En cada libro cambio de rostro").
17 For a deeper discussion of Palacios Ramé's work, see Ginsburg, "La adaptación afrofuturista."
18 For more on the process that brought about this transition in filmmaking, see Stock, *On Location in Cuba*.
19 Produced over a ten-year period of what Coyula calls "guerrilla filmmaking," *Corazón azul* has been censured in Cuba but well received on the international film festival circuit; see Rialta Staff, "Mención para 'Corazón azul.'"
20 "Mundos Alternos: Art and Science Fiction in the Americas" opened at the UCR ARTSblock in Riverside, California, as part of the Getty Foundation's "Pacific Standard Time: LA/LA" initiative. It later traveled to the Queens Museum (see Durón).
21 In his entry on Dominican science fiction for the science fiction encyclopedia, Juan Carlos Toledano Redondo notes that the characterization of De la Cruz's novel as science fiction "cannot be accepted without controversy owing to its generic ambivalence," adding that its originality is "based on its focus on the akashic records" ("Dominican Republic"). This "generic ambivalence" could be seen as a prefiguration of the more recent hybrid texts that I examine in this study.
22 Some criticism on Afrofuturism includes writing by Anglophone Caribbean writers in the corpus of Anglo-American Afrofuturism, without distinguishing their Caribbeanness. For more on Caribbean Afrofuturism, see Hunte and Shaw Nevins.
23 See Maguire, "Caribbean Afrofuturism."

Chapter 2. The View from the Future Possible

1 See López-Nussa, "El buey cansao."
2 "El baile del buey cansao" makes oblique reference to the 10 Million Ton Harvest, an effort by Cuba's revolutionary government to prop up the economy by harvesting a record 10 million tons of sugar in 1971, a project that required the participation of nearly every able-bodied Cuban.
3 Given that Vint describes ab-realism as revealing "the absurdities of 'real' life under capitalism," some readers may question my application of the term to Cuban fictions, produced under what is ostensibly a socialist system. I believe that Vint's emphasis on capitalism comes in part from her coinage of the term in relation to the work of Miéville, an explicitly Marxist writer. In a purely economic sense, however, Cuba is no longer exclusively socialist (if it ever was); rather, its economy incorporates a combination of socialist and capitalist practices. I would also argue that in a broader sense we are all living in a postsocialist world dominated by late capitalism. I believe that Cuban fictions are as engaged as capitalist fictions in exposing the cracks in this postsocialist reality.
4 See chapter 1 for a more extensive explanation of Carpentier's term.
5 Rather than separating science fiction from realist narrative, Chu identifies science fiction as what she terms "high-intensity realism," a realism that requires more "energy" to describe the world because so many elements "defy straightforward representation" (7). For Chu, science fiction does not argue necessarily for the existence

of things beyond our worldview; rather, its "intensity" (to use Chu's description) is a function of needing to explain things within our worldview that *do not yet* exist.

6   For more on Papá Liborio and the subsequent "Palma Sola" movement, see Lauren Derby's chapter "Papá Liborio and the Morality of Rule" in her *Dictator's Seduction* (227–56).

7   By *criollo* here, I am referring to descendants of Spanish settlers in the Americas.

8   Vlak himself articulates something of this anxiety in an interview with Cuban writer Elaine Vilar Madruga when he states, "El ciclo de *Crónicas historiológicas* es el primer fruto de ese reconocimiento de que un future proyectado desde el Caribe es tan válido como el *yanqui*—aunque no hayamos desarrollado el Proyecto Manhattan—, y que los mitos taínos y los importados de África son tan fantásticos como los que inspiraron a Tolkein"; see Vilar Madruga, "Odilius Vlak."

9   See Bobes et al., *Los nuevos caníbales*; Rosado, *El rostro y la máscara*; Santos Febres, *Ma(h)ab(l)ar*. Liboy has also published stories and poems in the literary journals *Filo de juego, Tríptico,* and *La Habana Elegante*.

10   For a summary of Puerto Rico's socioeconomic and environmental problems, see Lloréns and Stanchich; and Bonilla.

11   This mixture of the real and the fictional begins with the book's cover, in which the title appears slapped broadly across the front in a font reminiscent of those used for B horror films. In the background, there is an aerial view of what could be a plantation. A photographic image of Liboy's own face appears in the foreground, surrounded by an areola of light, so that Liboy appears almost as if he were a god observing the scene from the heavens. The juxtaposition suggests a pulp magazine, but Liboy's image adds a realist touch.

12   As Freedman observes, "The future is crucial to science fiction not as a specific chronological register, but as a locus of radical *alterity* to the mundane status quo, which is thus estranged and historicized as the concrete past of potential future" (54).

13   Here I am thinking of both Deleuze and Guattari's discussion of the rhizome and Édouard Glissant's take on this figure in his elaboration of a "poetics of Relation."

14   For more about this history—and its environmental effects—see Dietrich.

15   The writer Pedro Cabiya (1971), whose work is explored elsewhere in this study, published his first book *Historias tremendas* (1999) under the nom de plume Diego Deni, the name that is referenced in *El Informe Cabrera*.

16   A Cuban-German coproduction, *El viaje* was produced by the same Cuban production company, Producciones de la 5ta Avenida, that produced *Juan de los muertos*.

17   For more on the history of Cuban immigration, see Lamrani, "Cuban emigration"; and Masud-Piloto, *From Welcomed Exiles to Illegal Immigrants*.

18   See Rodríguez, "El viaje extraordinario."

19   The inside joke is that actor Jorge Molina, who also played Lázaro in *Juan de los muertos*, is himself a director who is well known for making films that limn the borders of horror and erotica.

Chapter 3. The Countertimes of Caribbean Cyberpunk

1 Born in Guines, a small town south of Havana, Achon emigrated to the United States at age fifteen and settled in Miami, where he currently resides. In a personal communication with the artist in May 2023, he stated, "I currently work in retail as a salesperson while I do art in my free time. In the last few years, I found out [about] web3 and the benefits it offers for artists. I have artworks listed on Foundation, Makersplace, Knownorigin, NiftyGateway, and OBKJKT."

2 An NFT (an acronym for nonfungible token) is a piece of digital artwork that is produced as a one-of-a-kind, single edition. NFTs were originally introduced as part of the blockchain of the Etherium cryptocurrency, but similar kinds of digital art are now sold on the blockchains of other cryptocurrencies. For more on NFTs, see Clark, "NFTs Explained."

3 Released in February of 2021, the song and the accompanying video by Asiel Babstro are explicitly critical of the Cuban government, in particular the government response to the Movimiento San Isidro (the San Isidro Movement), a group of writers and artists pushing for greater artistic freedom. At the time of the song's release, several of the group's members were under house arrest and one, Luis Manuel Otero Alcántara, was on hunger strike. Otero Alcántara was later sentenced to five years in prison and is still incarcerated as of the time of this writing (Dafoe). https://www.youtube.com/watch?v=a1C25ReHHKQ.

4 See the auction record at the Foundation website: https://foundation.app/@undefined/foundation/112503. Accessed 2 February 2022.

5 Mota has since expanded his "Cyberpunk" series to include photos of Santiago de Cuba and Bogotá, Colombia, as well as additional images of Havana.

6 The genre drew its name from the eponymous story by British writer Bruce Bethke. For more on the genesis of the movement, see Latham, "Literary Precursors"; and Murphy, "Mirrorshades Collective."

7 Although the internet as most people recognize it did not emerge until the 1990s, internet or internet-like systems were in existence as early as the 1960s. In the United States, the Defense Department's Advanced Research Projects Agency created the ARPANET. And Chile under Salvador Allende experimented with another early form of internet connection with Project Cybersyn. See Hafner and Lyon, *Where Wizards Stay Up Late*; and Medina, *Cybernetic Revolutionaries*.

8 See Maguire, "El hombre lobo en el espacio."

9 Benjamin West notes that Gibson's descriptions in *Neuromancer* were in fact influenced by the illustrations in the French graphic novel *Métal Hurlant* (198). For more on cyberpunk and visual culture, see Murphy and Schmeink, *Cyberpunk and Visual Culture*.

10 As Cadoga notes, a second wave of Anglo-American cyberpunk, of which Pat Cadigan was very much the forerunner, provided a response to the "boys club" of early cyberpunk. Cadoga observes, "Feminist cyberpunk envisions something that femi-

nist theory badly needs: fragmented subjects who can, despite their multiple positionings, negotiate and succeed in a high-tech world" (357).

11 As Steven Levy observes, the stereotype of the hacker as "an antisocial geek whose identifying attribute is the ability to sit in front of a keyboard and conjure up a criminal kind of magic" (432) emerged largely from the ways in which hackers were portrayed on television and in film. According to Levy, the emergence of the cyberpunk genre marked the moment when "[f]inally, true hackers became cool" (433). In contrast to illegal hacking, many groups of hackers have created their own codes of conduct. For one such example, see MIT's "Hacker Ethic," http://hacks.mit.edu/Hacks/misc/ethics.html.

12 As M. Elizabeth Ginway observes, the appearance of cyberpunk in Latin America varies by country. The earliest text that might be identified as cyberpunk is Brazilian author Alfredo Sirkis's novel *Silicone XXI* (1985), published only a year after Gibson's *Neuromancer*. However, cyberpunk truly gained popularity in Latin America in the 1990s. See Ginway, "Latin America."

13 Cyberpunk, and science fiction in general, took longer to be taken up by writers in the Dominican Republic, something I discuss in greater detail in chapter 1. For more on cyberpunk in Cuba, see Aguiar, "Ciberpunk Cubano."

14 Although Aguiar's *La estrella bocarriba* (2001) departs significantly from the classic cyberpunk style in terms of its relationship to technology, it fully embraces the genre's "punk" aspect. A crucial member of El Establo, Aguiar has also served as a shepherd of the genre in Cuba and Latin America from his position as a staff member at the Centro Onelio Jorge Cardoso de Escritura Jóven. From personal interviews with Raúl Aguiar and Yoss, June 2008. For more on the history of Cuban science fiction in the 1980s and '90s, see Yoss, "Marcianos en el platanar de Bartolo"; and Rinaldo Acosta.

15 Espacio Abierto has turned out to be one of the longest-lasting workshops. Housed in the Centro Onelio Jorge Cardoso, a cultural institution focused on supporting young and emergent writers, the workshop is still operating as of the time of this writing.

16 "El Periodo Especial en Tiempos de Paz" (The Special Period in Peacetime) was the name Fidel Castro gave to the economic austerity measures the Cuban government imposed in 1990 following the economic crisis brought on by the Soviet Union's collapse. The Cuban government has never declared an official end to the Special Period. Scholars of Cuba have taken to calling the years since 2000 the post-Soviet era.

17 For more on the ambivalent nature of the hacker in Encinosa Fu's fiction and its use of noir elements, see Maguire "El hombre lobo."

18 The economic scarcity of the Special Period caused a decline in the material conditions of life on the island, as was reflected in a deterioration of many buildings, particularly those in historic neighborhoods in Havana. The "ruins" of Havana—and the idea of Havana as a ruin—was a prevalent topic of both critical discourse and fiction, in such texts as Antonio José Ponte's *La fiesta vigilada* and "Un arte de hacer

ruinas." See also *Havana Beyond the Ruins: Cultural Mappings After 1989*, edited by Anke Birkenmaier and Esther Whitfield.

19 Before *Exquisito cadáver,* Acevedo had published *Contracanto de los superdecidores* (1982), *El retorno del ojo pródigo* (1986), *Libro de islas* (1989), and *Instrumentario* (1996). However, the publication of *Exquisito cadáver* initiated a period of experimentation with the novel form; his subsequent novels, *Sexo y cura/Carnada de cangrejo en Manhattan* (2008), *Flor de ciruelo y el viento* (2011), *Al otro lado del muro hay carne fresca* (2014), and *Guaya guaya* (2016) play with other styles and subgenres such as the zombie novel, gang fiction, and Orientalist fantasy.

20 Together with Melanie Pérez Ortiz, Acevedo also went on to found and serve as one of the primary organizers for the Congreso de ciencia ficción y literatura fantástica del Caribe, which ran annually from 2014 to 2019, bringing together writers and scholars of Caribbean science fiction in San Juan. For examples of Puerto Rican writing with speculative elements contemporaneous to *Exquisito cadáver,* see José Liboy Erba's *Cada vez te despides mejor* (2003); and Pedro Cabiya's *Historias tremendas* (1999) and *Historias atroces* (2003).

21 For more on Section 936 and the beginning of Puerto Rico's long financial crisis, see Greenberg and Ekins, "Tax Policy Helped Create"; and Morales, "Puerto Rico's Unjust Debt."

22 For more on the history of Sánchez's "La guagua aérea," see Mitchell, "Carving Place."

23 Slipstream, according to Seo-Young Chu, is "a type of science-fictional mimesis whose cognitively estranging referent is the partially virtual reality of living in a mainstream hypermediated and rendered half-surreal by technology" (9).

24 Levinas says elsewhere that the ethical response that this connection calls forth is specifically *not to kill* (*Ethics and Infinity*, 86).

25 In thinking about how taste and smell structure the heterotopias in Acevedo's text, I am drawing on Dvinge's study of Candace Allen's novel *Valaida* (2004), in which she shows how Allen uses tempo, both textual and musical, to structure the novel's heterotopias. In both cases, the texts play with reading as synesthetic experience.

26 One might say that this begins with the title of Acevedo's novel itself; the name *Exquisite Corpse* apparently comes from one of the first collage poems produced from the game: "Le cadavre / exquis / boira / le vin / nouveau."

27 Acevedo's text is not without its moments of humor. What follows the discovery of the System Administrator's body, in the next chapter, is the recipe for *spaghetti ai frutti di mare,* in the original Italian.

28 The original Orion Project, run by the US Defense Department in the 1950s and '60s, was a project to design a spacecraft powered by nuclear propulsion. See Dyson, *Project Orion*.

Chapter 4. In the Time of the Zombie

1 In her study, Lauro also deals with another, more specific form of zombie remake: "reanimated texts that are pressed into service by a different author to express the concerns of a new generation, or even another culture" (148). In this category, Lauro

includes both metaphorical zombie remakings, such as Jean Rhys's *Wide Sargasso Sea* (1966), the retelling of the *Jane Eyre* story from the perspective of Rochester's Caribbean-born wife, as well as the more literal zombification of canonical works, such as *Pride and Prejudice and Zombies* (2009).

2   The Italian zombie film tradition, most active during the 1980s, is anchored by the multiple zombie films of Lucio Fulci, beginning with *Zombi 2* (Zombie 2, 1979), but includes work from directors such as Umberto Lenzi and Dario Argento. Like early American zombie films, Fulci's films also drew on the Haitian zombie paradigm. For recent foreign zombie films, see Wilson Yip's *Bio Zombie* (Hong Kong, 1998); Omar Khan's *Zibahkhana* (Hell's ground, Pakistan, 2007); Tommy Wirkola's *Dead Snow* (Norway, 2009); Krishna D. K. and Raj Nidimoru's *Go Goa Gone* (India, 2013); Ming Jin Woo's *KL Zombi* (Indonesia, 2013), and *Zombitopia* (2021); and Yeon Sang-ho's *Train to Busan* (Korea, 2016). Interestingly, *Dead Snow, Bio Zombie, KL Zombie,* and *Go Goa Gone,* like *Juan de los muertos,* are parodies of the genre. When one of the characters in *Go Goa Gone* asks why there should be zombies in India, his friend responds, "It's globalization!"

3   I am referring here to the concept of "bare life" that Giorgio Agamben develops in *Homo Sacer: Sovereign Power and Bare Life* (1998), which explores the biopolitical borders of citizenship. In his study, Agamben uses two ancient Greek terms to distinguish between two different ideas of "life": *zoe*, or mere biological existence, and *bios,* "a qualified form of life" (1), or political life. For Agamben, sovereign power is defined through the border between those who have bios, a political life, an existence as citizens, and those for whom access to political existence is denied. Those who exist for the state solely as zoe, as biological life, are reduced to "bare life," in which they are denied political existence and are vulnerable to being sacrificed at any time.

4   Critics have frequently read zombies in US narratives as metaphors of mindless conformity, as an allegory for contemporary citizens "enslaved" to capitalism. However, because of the zombie's particular connection to Caribbean history, this is not a critique that I see in the narratives I analyze here. For more on zombies and consumerism, see Bishop.

5   Mota published this story in an earlier version in Spanish, "Memorias de un país zombi." However, for the English version published in the anthology *Cuba in Splinters* in 2014, he significantly revised and expanded the narrative. I have chosen to analyze this more recent version.

6   Lauro argues that the Haitian zombie, in its potential to represent both slavery and rebellion from it, "is itself a representation of the people's history" (9).

7   See Renda, *Taking Haiti,* for an exploration of how these narratives were stimulated by and in turn fortified discourses of US imperialism.

8   For examples of these pulp fictions, see Roscoe, "Grave Must Be Deep!"; and Goddard, *Whistling Ancestors.*

9   An exception to this kind of zombie occurs in the string of movies and TV shows, including *Zombieland* (2009), *Warm Bodies* (2013), *iZombie* (2014–19), and *Santa Clarita Diet* (2017–19), that feature zombie protagonists who can think and feel.

Some of these screen zombie narratives, *Warm Bodies* and *iZombie* in particular, distinguish between less-zombified zombies (the protagonists, who are capable of thinking and feeling) and more-zombified zombies, who adhere more closely to the unconscious, hungry Romero type.

10 Scholars such as John Rieder and Istvan Csicsery-Ronay Jr. have remarked on the connections between imperial narratives and the development of science fiction literature. It is interesting to note that despite their differences from Haitian zombies, in their cannibal aspect, Romero's zombies are still closely tied to colonial images of the primitive savage.

11 Although, as Ann Marie Stock notes, Juan Padrón's animated vampire comedies, *¡Vampiros en la Habana!* (1985) and *Más vampiros en la Habana* (2003), might be considered precursors to Brugués's *Juan de los muertos* is the first live action Cuban film of its kind (61).

12 As Bianka Ballina puts it, Brugués "deploy[s] transnational resources to produce a critical mediation of the current Cuban reality" (198).

13 The term "zom-com" appears in the promotional materials of the Bollywood film *Go Goa Gone* (D. K. and Nidimoru, 2013), another film that provides a nationally specific riff on Edgar Wright's *Shaun of the Dead*.

14 Sara Potter notes, "While it is never confirmed that the United States is responsible for the zombie [outbreak] in Brugués's Cuba . . . , the country is never declared entirely innocent" (12). Indeed, that the first zombie that Juan and Lázaro encounter in their fishing expedition is wearing an orange jumpsuit typical of US prisoners—and Guantanamo detainees—suggests that the outbreak may have arrived via Cuba's neighbor to the north.

15 I deal more fully with the question of revolutionary "destiempo" in chapters 1 and 2.

16 For a text that lays out Guevara's ideals of the socialist New Man, see his seminal essay "Socialismo y el hombre en Cuba."

17 For more on the repression and "reeducation" of those deemed "dissident" or "antirevolutionary," see Sierra Madero, *El cuerpo nunca olvida*.

18 Gutiérrez Alea's film was itself based on the novel *Memorias del subdesarrollo* (1965; *Inconsolable Memories*, 1965; later, *Memories of Underdevelopment*) by Edmundo Desnoes.

19 Gutiérrez Alea outlines his goals for producing a cinematic "coming to consciousness" in his essay "Appendix: Memories of *Memories*."

20 Like *Memorias del subdesarrollo*, *Fresa y chocolate* is the cinematic adaptation of a contemporary literary text, in this case Senel Paz's short story "El lobo, el bosque, y el hombre nuevo."

21 See *Nada +*, (*Nothing More*, 2001), directed by Juan Carlos Cremata Malberti; *Viva Cuba* (2005), also directed by Cremata Malberti; *Habana Blues* (2005), directed by Benito Zembrano, and *Personal Belongings* (2008), directed by Alejandro Brugués.

22 Ann Marie Stock interprets this as an optimistic ending that shows Juan as "self-reliant and determined" (63). Despite Juan's determination, however, his solitude, and the fact that he is vastly outnumbered by the zombies, seems to set a more ambivalent tone.

23 See, e.g., the "Advertencias preliminares" with which Cuban intellectual Fernando Ortiz begins his study *Hampa afrocubana* (1906).

24 This is a term first coined by Fernando Ortiz in his *Contrapunteo cubano del tabaco y el azúcar* (1940), to refer to the processes of cultural exchange, adaptation, and synthesis that happen in an encounter between two cultures. Ortiz argues that even when one culture occupies a "dominant" position with respect to another, the encounter between them involves not only the loss of culture (deculturation) and the taking up of aspects of another (acculturation) but also "la consiguiente creación de nuevos fenómenos culturales que pudieran denominarse de neoculturación" (260) ["the consequent creation of new cultural phenomena, which could be called neoculturation" (103, in the 1995 edition from Duke UP)]. The coming together of all these processes across the power differential is understood to be transculturation.

25 Calle G (G Street), also known as Avenida de los Presidentes (Avenue of the Presidents) is one of the main boulevards in the Vedado neighborhood. The area where G Street and 23rd Street meet has long been a place where young people from various social groups congregate during the evening.

26 Significant events in the history of US interventions include the attempted annexation of then–Santo Domingo by Ulysses S. Grant in 1869, the US occupation of the country between 1916 and 1924, and the invasion of the country in 1965.

27 Candelario sees this triangulation as visible in Dominican constructions of race as well: "[D]espite the country's African heritage, Dominican identity formations negotiated the fraught space between U.S.-dominant notions of white supremacy that defined mixture as degeneration and the geopolitical positioning of Dominicans as '*los blancos de la tierra* [the whites of the land]' relative to Haitians" (38).

28 In an interview with Néstor E. Rodríguez, Cabiya notes how his time in the Dominican Republic has expanded his perspective in relation to the Caribbean: "Vivir en la República Dominicana me puso en contacto con otras fuentes, muy ricas, que tuvieron un efecto sensibilizador y enriquecedor; la religiosidad popular, el panteón caribeño, la farmacopea de las islas . . . el contraband y la piratería, la astucia del hambre, las complejidades de la identidad racial, el dinamismo de los creoles, la potencia indiscutible de la brujería, la pobreza extrema y, lo más importante de todo, la inquebrantable alegría" (Rodríguez, "Impredicible oficio" 4).

29 Readers of Julio Cortázar's novel *Rayuela* (1963; *Hopscotch*, 1966) are informed in the text's first pages that they can read it in two ways: moving sequentially from the first chapter to the last, or in a "snapshot" fashion according to an order determined by the author.

30 Belisle observes that the upper-class Haitian exiles are former officials in the regime of Jean-Claude "Baby Doc" Duvalier, who governed Haiti between 1971 and 1986, continuing many of the repressive techniques established by his father, François "Papa Doc" Duvalier (37–38).

31 As Belisle notes, Isadore's scientific studies are an extension of the work by ethnobotanist Wade Davis, first published in *The Serpent and the Rainbow* (1985) and then in *The Passage of Darkness* (1988). Although Davis began his investigations into the plants and chemical compounds that might produce an effect of "zombification," his

work also reveals the extent to which zombiism was a socially produced phenomenon, as well as the ways in which it was utilized as a mechanism of social control by both François and Jean-Claude Duvalier.

Chapter 5. After World's End

1 "Broadly speaking, apocalyptic thought belongs to rectilinear rather than cyclical views of the world" (Kermode 4). Kermode goes on to add, "The Bible is a familiar model of history. It begins at the beginning ('In the beginning . . .') and ends with a vision of the end ('Even so, come, Lord Jesus'); the first book in Genesis, the last Apocalypse. Ideally, it is a wholly concordant structure, the end is in harmony with the beginning, the middle with beginning and end" (5–6).

2 Martin Munro observes, "The fact they are identified as black women suggests too that there is some kind of internal exoticism at play, that Benítez Rojo is projecting onto them qualities and ways of thinking that he believes he sees, but which must to some extent be the product of his own imagination and the social and cultural distance that exists between the women and him" (17).

3 Radical "world endings" are a feature of dystopian allegories like Cuban writer Yoss's novelized short story collection *Se alquila un planeta* (2001), which imagines Earth as colonized by a federation of more powerful planets, or Cuban director Miguel Coyula's film *Corazón azul* (2021), in which genetically bred "New Men" rebel against their makers; of parables set in the wake of environmental disasters, such as Eduardo del Llano's film *Omega 3* (2015), Anabel Enríquez Piñeiro's "Nada que declarar" (in *Nada que declarar*, 2008), Nuria Ordas's *Entremundos* (2010), Rita Indiana's *La mucama de Omicunlé* (2015), and José Acosta's *La multitud* (2011); of apocalyptic extensions of current political and economic crises, such as Luis Othoniel Rosa's *Caja de fractales* (2017; *Down with Gargamel,* 2020); and, of course, of texts dealing with zombie invasions, such as Puerto Rican writer Rafael Acevedo's *Al otro lado del muro hay carne fresca* (2014), Dominican American writer Junot Díaz's short story "Monstro," Cuban director Alejandro Brugués's *Juan de los muertos* (2011), and Puerto Rican writer Pabsi Livmar's "Golpe de agua" (in *Teoremas turbios,* 2018), the last two of which I examine in another part of this study. Radical world endings also appear, notably, in texts that posit new futures by exploring different pasts, such as Erick Mota's *Habana Underguater* (2011), analyzed here, and his second novel, *El colapso de las Habanas infinitas* (2017), which takes us through various alternate histories for Cuba.

4 While there are too many works to list here, a very brief survey of recent fiction would include Margaret Atwood's *MaddAdam* trilogy (*Oryx and Crake,* 2003; *The Year of the Flood,* 2009; and *MaddAdam,* 2013), David Mitchell's *Cloud Atlas* (2004), Cormac McCarthy's *The Road* (2006), Edan Lepucki's *California* (2014), Colson Whitehead's *Zone One* (2011), and Emily St. John Mandel's *Station Eleven* (2014). TV series include the television version of Mandel's *Station Eleven* as well as *The 100, The Leftovers, The Rain, The Last Man on Earth,* and *The Last of Us.*

5 See García Canclini, *Culturas híbridas,* and Quijano, "Coloniality of Power."

6 This marking by the abyss is what African American cultural critic Christina Sharpe

has termed being or living "in the wake," though Sharpe traces the "wake" specifically to African American experience: "Transatlantic slavery was and is the disaster. The disaster of Black subjection was and is planned: terror is disaster . . . and it is deeply atemporal. The history of capital is inextricable from the history of Atlantic chattel slavery. The disaster and the writing of disaster are never present, are always present" (5).

7 Posmentier notes that Berlant's and Nixon's ideas "run parallel to and are interconnected with scientific attempts to account for an environmental change" (16).

8 In his examination of the concept of apocalypse in his essay "Of an Apocalyptic Tone," Derrida emphasizes apocalypse's connection not only to revelation in a biblical or epiphanic sense but also to a revealing of the physical, particularly that which is habitually hidden: "I disclose, I uncover, I unveil, I reveal the thing that can be a part of the body, the head or the eyes, a secret part of the sex or whatever might be hidden, a secret thing, the thing to be dissimulated, a thing that is neither shown nor said, signified perhaps but that cannot or *must* not first be delivered up to self-evidence" (4, italics in the original).

9 "[Science fiction's] primary orientation . . . is towards the future; it is thus capable of engaging the matter of historicity without the same kind of post-1848 ideological baggage that the historical novelist carries" (57).

10 As de Cristofaro explains, the critical temporality that contemporary postapocalyptic narratives introduce both "deconstruct[s] the apocalyptic model of narrative" (which emphasizes closure) and "expose[s] the hegemonic apocalyptic temporality at the core of Western modernity as a narrative enmeshed with power structures" (10).

11 Examples of these ambivalent—if not outright dystopian—uchronia include Philip K. Dick's *The Man in the High Castle* (1962), which imagines a World War II in which Japan successfully invades the United States; Michael Chabon's *The Yiddish Policeman's Union* (2007), set in a world in which a postwar Jewish free state was established in Alaska rather than Palestine; Roberto de Sousa Causo's *Selva Brasil* (2010), which explores what might have happened if Jânio Quadros, president of Brazil for six months in 1961, had ordered the invasion of Guyana; and Jorge Baradit's novel *Synco* (2008), which posits what would have happened if General Augusto Pinochet had not been successful in his a coup d'état against then-President Salvador Allende in 1973.

12 Mota capitalizes "Orishas" in *Habana Underguater*, perhaps to allude to the specific role they play in Underguater society as both religious and civic figures. I have maintained this capitalization in my discussion of his novel, but use the lowercase "orisha" elsewhere in the chapter when referring exclusively to the Afro-Cuban deities, as is the general practice.

13 In "Walking in the City," De Certeau compares the path of a pedestrian moving through a city to a "speech act": "Walking affirms, suspects, tries out, transgresses, respects, etc., the trajectories it 'speaks'" (99). This "enunciation" then affects what

the pedestrian engages: "The long poem of walking manipulates spatial organizations. . . . It creates shadows and ambiguity within them" (101).

14 Perhaps the most famous of the Soviet-style housing projects, Alamar was conceived of as a model urban development east of Havana, and was constructed largely with the help of volunteer builders (including the Venceremos brigades). Transportation problems between the community and Havana proper resulted in a kind of ghettoization. In recent years, however, the community has become a center of Havana's hip-hop music scene and home to a vibrant arts community.

15 See, e.g., Wim Wenders's documentary *The Buena Vista Social Club* or Florian Borchmeyer's *Habana—Arte nuevo de hacer ruinas* (Havana: The art of making ruins, 2007), which draws at least in part from the work of writer Antonio José Ponte, in particular his short story "Un arte de hacer ruinas" and his novel *La fiesta vigilada*. In her 2002 article "Picturing Havana," Ana María Dopico argues that Havana has become synonymous with the photograph: "This visual scrutiny, selective and seductive, has a banal and ominous significance for a city that lives in multiple temporalities, a capital that is negotiating survival and ideology, improvising its daily life amid the shifting and mixed economies of third-world tourism and Cold War symbolism" (451).

16 The Callejón de Hamel, a small street in the historically Afro-Cuban Central Havana neighborhood of Cayo Hueso, has become the location of weekly rumba sessions that have come to be marketed to tourists. As Price notes (85), in Mota's novel a digital version of the Callejón de Hamel is also coded as a setting for the Orishas (34).

17 Given its poor reception, the film may also be Cabral's least known. His subsequent films *Carpinteros* (2017) and *El proyeccionista* (2019), both of which were features of the international festival circuit, have garnered more attention and critical praise (De Pablos).

18 Rivera uses the term "*rasquache* aesthetic" to refer to his cinematic technique, "which repurposes animation, archival, and interview footage in a collage form" (Decena and Gray, 131). But as Rivera explains, his term references the practice (which he identifies as Latinx) of creative recycling and repurposing of materials. For more on Rivera's own *rasquachismo*, see also Castillo.

19 In the words of historian Lauren Derby, "Trujillo established one of the longest and most repressive authoritarian regimes in Latin America, characterized by bouts of extreme carnage interspersed with everyday forms of terror such as random abductions, pervasive surveillance, and institutionalized forms of ridicule" (108).

20 Trujillo was not entirely wrong to be paranoid; the previous year (1959), Dominican exiles in Cuba had attempted to overthrow him. Although the attempt was not successful, dissent against Trujillo was growing. In November 1960, Trujillo had the Mirabal sisters, anti-Trujillo revolutionaries, killed in cold blood. And on 30 May 1961, Trujillo himself was assassinated.

21 Derby notes that Trujillo's maternal grandmother "was an *hija de la calle* (illegitimate child) of a Haitian couple who migrated westward during the Haitian occupation in the 1840s" (369). Both Rodríguez and García-Peña see Trujillo's racist ideas

as amplifying a kind of latent racism present in national discourse since the country's founding. Rodríguez refers to this as a kind of "colonización interna" (*Escrituras* 12) [internal colonization]; García-Peña argues that this amplified racism is in part due to the fact both the country and *Dominicanidad* exist "in a geographic and symbolic border between the United States and Haiti" (*Borders* 3).

22 For more on the 1937 Haitian massacre and its function in state building, see Turits, "World Destroyed."

23 "Dios y Trujillo" was also the title of a 1954 essay written by Joaquín Balaguer, who was not only Trujillo's successor but also the regime's intellectual architect. Balaguer begins his essay chronicling the fortuitous arrival of Columbus to Hispaniola, highlighting the admiral's strong connections to the island. He ends by asserting that it is only after 1930, with the beginning of the *Trujillato*, "cuando el pueblo dominicano deja de ser asistido exclusivamente por Dios para serlo igualmente por una mano que parece tocada desde el principio de una especie de predestinación divina: la mano providencial de Trujillo" (170).

24 Frank Kermode observes that "a majority of interpretations of Apocalypse assume the End is pretty near" (8).

25 See Cuban writer Roberto Fernández Retamar's *Calibán* takes the figure of Calibán as a symbol of the colonized subject (with Prospero as the colonizer). Martinican intellectual Aimé Césaire also locates a pointed critique of colonialism in his own reworking of Shakespeare's drama, *Une Tempéte*.

26 Although Acilde identifies as male, Indiana uses feminine pronouns to refer to her character before the scene of gender confirmation. I have followed suit.

27 All translations of *La mucama* are taken from the English translation, *Tentacle*, translated by Achy Obejas (2018).

28 In an interesting intersection, *Arrobá*'s director José María Cabral went on to direct *Isla de plástico* (2019), a documentary about the Dominican Republic's waste management problem and the pollution of its beaches.

Epilogue

1 For more on Damien Broderick's concept of the mega-text, see my explanation in the introduction; or Broderick 48.

2 This is an oblique reference to the podcast *Las escritoras de Urras*, directed by Maielis González Fernández and Sofía Barker.

3 See *El tercer mundo después del sol* (2021), edited by Rodrigo Bastidas Pérez.

4 For Indiana's own description of the song, see Villegas.

5 See Humphrey, "Rita Indiana's Fluid Temporalities" (325); Maillo-Pozo (49–51); Ginsburg, *Cyborg Caribbean* (118).

BIBLIOGRAPHY

2001: A Space Odyssey. Directed by Stanley Kubrick, Metro-Goldwyn Mayer, 1968.
Acevedo, Rafael. *Al otro lado del muro hay carne fresca.* La secta de los perros, 2014.
———. *Contracanto de los superdecidores.* Plus Ultra, 1982.
———. *Exquisito cadáver.* Ediciones Callejón, 2001.
———. *Flor de ciruelo y el viento: novela china tropical.* Folium, 2011.
———. *Guaya guaya.* La secta de los perros, 2012.
———. *Instrumentario.* Isla Negra, 1996.
———. *Libro de islas.* 1989.
———. *El retorno del ojo pródigo.* 1986.
———. *Sexo y cura/Carnada de cangrejo en Manhattan.* Isla Negra, 2008.
Ackermann, Hans W., and Jeanine Gauthier. "The Ways and Nature of the Zombie." *Journal of American Folklore,* vol. 104, no. 414, 1991, pp. 466–94.
Acosta, José. *La multitud.* 2011. Techo de Papel Editores, 2015.
Acosta, Rinaldo. "La ciencia ficción cubana de los noventa: entre la provocación y el cambio." *Rialta Magazine,* 8 July 2020, https://rialta.org/la-ciencia-ficcion-cubana-de-los-noventa-entre-la-provocacion-y-el-cambio/.
Adrover Lausell, Miguel. *Quantum Weaver Yocahú.* Disonante, 2015.
Agamben, Giorgio. *Homo Sacer: Sovereign Power and Bare Life.* Translated by Daniel Heller-Roazen, Stanford UP, 1998.
Aguiar, Raúl. "Ciberpunk cubano en cuarto creciente. Variantes y herederos ¿Lo que vendrá?" *Qubit,* vol. 35, June 2008, pp. 25–29.
———. "Ciberpunk cubano en cuarto creciente: variantes y herederos." *Latin American Literature Today,* February 2018, https://latinamericanliteraturetoday.org/es/2018/02/cuban-cyberpunk-rise-variations-and-successors-raul-aguiar/.
———. *La estrella bocarriba.* Letras Cubanas, 2001.
Ahmad, Aalya. "Gray Is the New Black: Race, Class, and Zombies." *Generation Zombie: Essays on the Living Dead in Modern Culture,* edited by Stephanie Boluk and Wylie Lenz, MacFarland, 2014, pp. 130–46.
Alcocer, Rudyard. *Narrative Mutations: Discourses of Heredity and Caribbean Literature.* Routledge, 2005.
———. *Time Travel in the Latin American and Caribbean Imagination: Re-reading History.* Palgrave Macmillan, 2011.
Allred, Michael, and Chris Roberson. *iZombie.* Vertigo Comics, 2010–12.

Altman, Rick. "A Semantic/Syntactic Approach to Film Genre." *Cinema Journal,* vol. 23, no. 3, Spring 1984, pp. 6–18.
Álvarez Pitaluga, Antonio. "Brief Notes on the History of Cuban Cinema." *The Cinema of Cuba: Contemporary Film and the Legacy of Revolution,* edited by Guy Baron and Ann Marie Stock, with Antonio Álvarez Pitaluga, I.B. Tauris, 2017, pp. 9–29.
Amphibian Man. Directed by Vladimir Chebotaryov and Gennadi Kazansky, Lenfilm, 1962.
Angulo Guridi, Francisco Javier. *La ciguapa.* 1866. Colección Obras Clásicas Dominicanas, Mann Ediciones Digitales, 2017.
———. *La fantasma de Higüey.* 1857. Libros Caribe, 2009.
Appadurai, Arjun. *Modernity at Large: Cultural Dimensions of Globalization.* U of Minnesota P, 1996.
Arango, Ángel. *¿Adónde van los cefalomos?* Ediciones R, 1964.
Armengot, Sara. "Creatures of Habit: Emergency Thinking in Alejandro Brugués' *Juan de los muertos* and Junot Díaz's 'Monstro.'" *Trans,* vol. 14, no. 4, 2012, http://trans.revues.org/566.
Arrobá. Directed by José María Cabral, Bronter Media, 2013.
Arroyo, Jossianna. *Caribes 2.0: New Media, Globalization, and the Afterlives of Disaster.* Rutgers UP, 2023.
———. "Cities of the Dead: Performing Life in the Caribbean." *Journal of Latin American Cultural Studies,* vol. 27, no. 3, 2018, pp. 331–56.
Atwood, Margaret. *MaddAddam.* Doubleday, 2013.
———. *Oryx and Crake.* 2003. Anchor Books, 2004.
———. *The Year of the Flood.* 2009. Anchor Books, 2010.
Bakhtin, M. M. "Forms of Time and Chronotope in the Novel." *The Dialogic Imagination: Four Essays,* edited by Michael Holquist, translated by Caryl Emerson and Michael Holquist, U of Texas P, 1981, pp. 84–258.
Balaguer, Joaquín. "Dios y Trujillo. Una interpretación realista de la historia dominicana." *CLIO: Órgano de la Academía Dominicana de la Historia,* year 22, no. 101, October–December 1954, pp. 165–70.
Ballina, Bianka. "*Juan of the Dead*: Anxious Consumption and Zombie Cinema in Cuba." *Studies in Spanish and Latin American Cinemas,* vol. 14, no. 2, 2017, pp. 193–213.
Balseros. Directed by Carles Bosch and Josep Maria Domènech, Bausan Films and TVC, 2002.
Baradit, Jorge. *Synco.* 2008. Plaza & Janes, 2018.
Barlow, John Perry. "Declaration of the Independence of Cyberspace." *Humanist,* May–June 1996, pp. 18–19.
Bastidas Pérez, Rodrigo, editor. *El tercer mundo después del sol: antología de ciencia ficción latinoamericana.* Bogotá: Minotauro, 2022.
Belisle, Natalie. "Passing Life, Playing Dead: Zombification as Juridical Shapeshifting in Pedro Cabiya's *Malas hierbas.*" *Journal of Latin American Cultural Studies,* vol. 30, no. 1, May 2021, pp. 25–45.
Benítez Rojo, Antonio. *La isla que se repite: El Caribe y la perspectiva posmoderna.* 1989. 2nd ed., Ediciones del Norte, 1996.

———. *The Repeating Island: The Caribbean and the Post-Modern Perspective.* Translated by James Maraniss, Duke UP, 1996.
Berger, James. *After the End: Representations of Post-Apocalypse.* U of Minnesota P, 1999.
Berlant, Lauren. *Cruel Optimism.* Duke UP, 2011.
Bethke, Bruce. "Cyberpunk." *Amazing Stories,* November 1983.
Bill and Ted's Excellent Adventure. Directed by Stephen Herek, starring Keanu Reeves and Alex Winter, Orion Pictures, 1989.
Bio Zombie. Directed by Wilson Yip, Media Blasters, 1998.
Blade Runner. Directed by Ridley Scott, starring Harrison Ford, Rutger Hauer, Sean Young, and Edward James Olmos, The Ladd Company, Shaw Brothers, and Warner Brothers, 1982.
Birkenmaier, Anke, and Esther Whitfield, "Introduction: Beyond the Ruins." *Havana Beyond the Ruins: Cultural Mappings After 1989,* edited by Anke Birkenmaier and Esther Whitfield, e-book ed., Duke UP, 2011, pp. 1–10.
Bishop, Kyle William. "The Idle Proletariat: *Dawn of the Dead,* Consumer Ideology, and the Loss of Productive Labor." *Journal of Popular Culture,* vol. 43, no. 2, 2010, pp. 234–49.
Blanco, María del Pilar. "Reading the Novum World: The Literary Geography of Science Fiction in Juno Díaz's *The Brief Wondrous Life of Oscar Wao.*" *Surveying the American Tropics: A Literary Geography from New York to Rio,* edited by María Cristina Fumagalli, Peter Hulme, Owen Robinson, and Leslie Wylie, Liverpool UP, 2013, pp. 49–74.
Blaustein, Eduardo. *Cruz diablo.* Editorial Emecé, 1997.
Bloch, Ernst. *The Principle of Hope.* Translated by Neville Plaice, Stephen Plaice, and Paul Knight, vol. 1, MIT P, 1986.
———. "Something's Missing: A Conversation between Ernst Bloch and Theodor Adorno on the Contradictions of Utopian Longing." 1964. *The Utopian Function of Art and Literature,* MIT P, 1987, pp. 1–17.
Bobes, Marilyn, Pedro Antonio Valdés, and Carlos R. Gómez Beras, editors. *Los nuevos caníbales: antología de la más reciente cuentística del Caribe hispano.* Isla Negra, 2003.
Bonilla, Yarimar. "The Coloniality of Disaster: Race, Empire, and the Temporal Logics of Emergency in Puerto Rico, USA." *Political Geography,* vol. 78, 2020, https://doi.org/10.1016/j.polgeo.2020.102181.
Boon, Kevin Alexander. "Ontological Anxiety Made Flesh: The Zombie in Literature, Film, and Culture." *Monsters and the Monstrous: Myths and Metaphors of Enduring Evil,* edited by Niall Scott, Rodopi, 2007, pp. 32–43.
Boym, Svetlana. *The Future of Nostalgia.* Basic Books, 2001.
Briggs, Laura. *Reproducing Empire: Race, Sex, Science and U.S. Imperialism in Puerto Rico.* U of California P, 2002.
Broderick, Damien. *Reading by Starlight: Postmodern Science Fiction.* Routledge, 1994.
Brown, David H. *Santería Enthroned: Art, Ritual and Innovation in an Afro-Cuban Religion.* U of Chicago P, 2003.
Brown, J. Andrew. "Sampling and Remixing in Recent Latin American Narrative." *Revista Hispánica Moderna,* vol. 71, no. 1, June 2018, pp. 7–22.

Buena Vista Social Club. Directed by Wim Wenders, Road Movies/Kintop Pictures/ICAIC, 1999.

Bukatman, Scott. *Blade Runner.* BFI Film Classics Series. British Film Institute, 2012.

———. *Terminal Identity: The Virtual Subject in Postmodern Science Fiction.* Duke UP, 1993.

Burges, Joel, and Amy J. Elias, editors. "Introduction: Time Studies Today." *Time: A Vocabulary of the Present,* New York UP, 2016, pp. 1–34.

Cabiya, Pedro. *Ánima sola.* Zemí Comics, 2013.

———. *La cabeza.* Editorial Isla Negra, 2005.

———. *The Head.* Translated by Daniela Paiwonsky, Zemí Book, 2014.

———. *Historias atroces.* 2002. Zemí Book, 2011.

———. *Historias tremendas.* 1999. Zemí Book, 2011.

———. *Malas hierbas.* 2010. Zemí Book, 2011.

———. *María V.* Zemí Book, 2013.

———. *Phantograms.* Evil Ministries, 2013.

———. *Tercer Mundo.* Zemí Book, 2019.

———. *Trance.* Editorial Norma, 2007.

———. *Wicked Weeds.* Translated by Jessica Ernst Powell, Mandel Vilar Press, 2016.

Cadoga, Karen. "Feminist Cyberpunk." *Science Fiction Studies,* vol. 22, no. 3, November 1995, pp. 357–72.

Canavan, Gerry. "We *Are* the Walking Dead: Race, Time, and Survival in Zombie Narrative." *Extrapolation,* vol. 51, no. 3, 2010, pp. 431–53.

Candelario, Ginetta. *Black behind the Ears: Dominican Racial Identity from Museums to Beauty Shops.* Duke UP, 2007.

Carpentier, Alejo. *De lo real maravilloso americano.* Colección Pequeños Grandes Ensayos. Universidad Autónoma de México, 2003.

Carpinteros. Directed by José María Cabral, Tabula Rasa, 2017.

Casamayor-Cisneros, Odette. *Utopía, dystopia e ingravidez: Reconfiguraciones cosmológicas en la narrativa postsoviética cubana.* Iberoamericana/Vervuert, 2013.

Castillo, Debra A. "Rasquache Aesthetics in Alex Rivera's 'Why Cybraceros?'" *Nordlit,* no. 31, 2014, pp. 1–23.

Castillo, Efraim. *Inti Huamán, o Eva Again.* 1968. Últimos Monstruos, 2019.

Castro Ruz, Fidel. *Palabras a los intelectuales.* 1961. Departamento de Ediciones de la Biblioteca Nacional José Martí, 1991.

Cedeño Rojas, Maribel. "Apocalipsis revolucionario en *Juan de los muertos* de Alejandro Brugués." *Terra zombi: el fenómeno transnacional de los muerto vivientes,* edited by Rosana Díaz-Zambrana, Isla Negra, 2016, pp. 276–95.

La central azucarera en Puerto Rico, 1898–1952. Vol. 1, Oficina Estatal de Preservación Histórica de Puerto Rico, 1991.

Chabon, Michael. *The Yiddish Policeman's Union: A Novel.* Harper, 2007.

Chaviano, Daína. *Fábulas de una abuela extraterrestre.* 1987. Ediciones Huso, 2018.

———. *Los mundos que amo.* 1980. Gente Nueva, 1982.

Chu, Seo-Young. *Do Metaphors Dream of Literal Sleep? A Science Fictional Theory of Representation.* Harvard UP, 2010.

Clark, Mitchell. "NFTs Explained." *Verge*, 18 August 2021, https://www.theverge.com/22310188/nft-explainer-what-is-blockchain-crypto-art-faq.
Cohen, Jeffrey Jerome. "Monster Culture (Seven Theses)." *Monster Theory: Reading Culture*, edited by Jeffrey Jerome Cohen, e-book ed., U of Minnesota P, 1996, pp. 3–25.
Collazo, Miguel. *El libro fantástico de Oaj*. Ediciones Unión, 1966.
———. *The Journey*. Translated by David Frye. Introduction by Yoss, Restless Books, 2020.
———. *El viaje*. 1968. Colección Radar Letras Cubanas, 1981.
Cooper, Brenda. *Magical Realism in West African Fiction*. Routledge, 1998.
Corazón azul. Directed by Miguel Coyula, with Lynn Cruz and Carlos Gronlier, Producciones Pirámide, 2021.
Córdoba Conejo, Antonio. *¿Extranjero en tierra extraña? El género de la ciencia ficción en América Latina*. Universidad de Sevilla Secretariado de Publicaciones, 2011.
Cortázar, Julio. *Hopscotch*. Translated by Gregory Rabassa, Pantheon, 1966.
———. *Rayuela*. 1963. Alfaguara, 2013.
Cortés-Rocca, Paola. "Etnología ficcional. Brujos, zombis, y otros cuentos caribeños." *Revista Iberoamericana*, vol. 75, no. 227, April–June 2009, pp. 333–47.
Csicsery-Ronay, Jr., Istvan. "Science Fiction and Empire." *Science Fiction Studies*, vol. 30, no. 2, 2003, pp. 231–45.
———. *The Seven Beauties of Science Fiction*. Wesleyan UP, 2012.
Cua Lim, Bliss. *Translating Time: Cinema, the Fantastic, and Temporal Critique*. Duke UP, 2009.
Dafoe, Taylor. "Jailed Artist Luis Manuel Otero Alcántara Has Penned an Op-Ed Calling for Support in the 'Just' Fight against the Cuban Government." *Artnet News*, 12 July 2023, https://news.artnet.com/news/luis-manuel-otero-alcantara-op-ed-2335950. Accessed 8 December 2023.
Dalton, David. "*Antropofagia*, Calibanism, and the Post-Romero Zombie: Cannibal Resistance in Latin America and the Caribbean." *Alambique: Revista Académica de Ciencia Ficción y Fantasía*. vol. 6, issue 1, no. 6, 2018, https://scholarcommons.usf.edu/alambique/vol6/iss1/6.
Danowski, Déborah, and Eduardo Viveiros de Castro. *Há um mundo por vivir? Ensaio sobre os Medos e os Fins*. Desterro, Cultura e Barbárie e Instituto Socioambiental, 2014.
Davis, Wade. *Passage of Darkness: The Ethnobiology of the Haitian Zombie*. U of North Carolina P, 1988.
———. *The Serpent and the Rainbow*. Warner Books, 1985.
Dead Snow. Directed by Tommy Wirkola, Euforia Film, 2009.
De Andrade, Oswald. "Manifesto Antropófago." *Vanguarda européia e modernismo brasileiro: apresentação e crítica dos principais manifestos vanguardistas*, edited by Gilberto Mendonça Tele, 3rd ed., Vozes, INL, 1976.
Decena, Carlos Ulises, and Margaret Gray. "Putting Transnationalism to Work: An Interview with Alex Rivera." *Social Text*, vol. 24, no. 3, 2006, pp. 131–38.
De Certeau, Michel. "Walking in the City." *The Practice of Everyday Life*, translated by Steven Rendell, U of California P, 1980, pp. 91–110.

Decker, Sharae, and Kerstin Oloff. "'The One Who Comes from the Sea': Marine Crisis and the New Oceanic Weird in Rita Indiana's *La mucama de Omicunlé.*" *Humanities*, vol. 9, no. 3, pp. 1–14.

De Cristofaro, Diletta. *The Contemporary Post-Apocalyptic Novel: Critical Temporalities and the End Times*. Bloomsbury, 2019.

De Ferrari, Guillermina. "Science Fiction and the Rules of Uncertainty." *Small Axe* 61, March 2020, pp. 1–10.

De galipotes y robots: Primera selección de la Asociación Dominicana de Ficción Especulativa. Edited by Rodolfo Báez. Últimos Monstruos, 2019.

De la Cruz, Josefina. *Una casa en el espacio*. 1986.

Delany, Samuel L. "About 5,760 Words." *The Jewel-Hinged Jaw: Notes on the Language of Science Fiction*. 1978. Introduction by Michael Cheney, Wesleyan UP, 2009, pp. 1–15.

———. "Science Fiction and 'Literature'—or, The Conscience of the King." *Starboard Wine: More Notes on the Language of Science Fiction*. 1984. Introduction by Michael Cheney, e-book ed., Wesleyan UP, 2012, pp. 61–80.

De la Torre Rodríguez, Javier. "En busca de la ucronía perdida." *La isla y las estrellas: El ensayo y la crítica de la ciencia ficción en Cuba*. Edited by, Rinaldo Acosta, e-book ed., Editorial Cubaliteraria, 2015, pp. 338–52.

Deleuze, Gilles, and Félix Guattari. "Introduction: Rhizome." *A Thousand Plateaus: Capitalism and Schizophrenia*. Translation and foreword by Brian Massumi, U of Minnesota P, 1987, pp. 3–25.

De Maessener, Rita. "New Approaches to the Puerto Rican Short Story in the Nineties." *Journal of West Indian Literature*, vol. 12, nos. 1–2, November 2004, pp. 135–48.

Dendle, Peter. "The Zombie as Barometer of Cultural Anxiety." *Monsters and the Monstrous: Myths and Metaphors of Enduring Evil*, edited by Niall Scott, Rodopi, 2007, pp. 45–57.

De Pablos, Emilio. "Sony Pictures Nabs Latin American Rights to Cabral's 'Hotel Coppelia' from Latido." *Variety*, 18 February 2022, https://variety.com/2022/film/global/sony-pictures-hotel-coppelia-latido-films-1235185751/.

Derby, Lauren Hutchinson. *The Dictator's Seduction: Politics and the Popular Imagination in the Era of Trujillo*. Duke UP, 2009.

De Rojas, Agustín. *El año 200*. Letras Cubanas, 1990.

———. *Espiral*. 1982. Letras Cubanas, 2014.

———. *Una leyenda del futuro*. 1985. Restless Books, 2015.

———. *Spiral*. Translated by Nick Caistor and Hebe Powell, Restless Books, 2020.

Derrida, Jacques. "Of an Apocalyptic Tone Recently Adopted in Philosophy." *Oxford Literary Review*, vol. 6, no. 2, 1984, pp. 3–37.

Dery, Mark. "Black to the Future: Interviews with Samuel R. Delany, Greg Tate, and Tricia Rose." *South Atlantic Quarterly*, vol. 92, 1993, pp. 735–78.

Desnoes, Edmundo. *Inconsolable Memories*. Translated by the author, foreword by Jack Gelber, The New American Library, 1967.

———. *Memorias del subdesarrollo*. 1965. Ediciones Mono Azul, 2013.

———. *Memories of Underdevelopment*. Translated by Al Schaller, Latin American Literary Review Press, 2004.

De Sousa Causo, Roberto. *Selva Brasil*. E-book ed., Editora Drago, 2010.
Díaz, Junot. "Apocalypse." *Boston Review*, 1 May 2011, http://bostonreview.net/junot-diaz-apocalypse-haiti-earthquake.
———. *The Brief Wondrous Life of Oscar Wao*. Riverhead Books, 2007.
———. "Monstro." *New Yorker*, 4 and 11 June 2012, https://www.newyorker.com/magazine/2012/06/04/monstro.
Díaz Grullón, Virgilio. *Más allá del espejo*. Universidad Autónoma de Santo Domingo, 1975.
Dick, Philip K. *The Man in the High Castle*. 1962. Harper Voyager, 2017.
Dietrich, Alexa S. *The Drug Company Next Door: Pollution, Jobs, and Community Health in Puerto Rico*. New York UP, 2013.
Doctor Who. Created by Newman, Sydney, C. E. Webber, and Donald Wilson, BBC Studios and Bad Wolf, 1963–89; 2005–present.
Dopico, Ana. "Picturing Havana: History, Vision, and the Scramble for Cuba." *Nepantla: Views from the South*, vol. 3, no. 3, 2002, pp. 451–93.
Dorta, Walfrido. "Conversa en Benefit Street (sobre literatura cubana reciente)." *Diario de Cuba*, 14 March 2015, https://diariodecuba.com/cultura/1426285786_13395.html.
———. "Políticas de la distancia y del agrupamiento: Narrativa cubana de las últimas dos décadas." *Istor. Revista de Historia Internacional*, vol. 63, 2015, pp. 115–35.
Duany, Jorge. *Puerto Rican Nation on the Move: Identities on the Island and in the United States*. U of North Carolina P, 2002.
Duchesne-Sotomayor, Dafne. *¿Qué ocurre cuando el zombie habla? Lo posthumano en* Malas hierbas *de Pedro Cabiya*. Editora Educación Emergente, 2020.
Duchesne Winter, Juan. "Noticias de un país que desaparece, 'raros' puertorriqueños de hoy." *América Latina Hoy*, vol. 58, 2011, pp. 31–50.
Duong, Paloma. *Portable Postsocialisms: Cuban Mediascapes After the End of History*. U of Texas P, 2023.
Durón, Maximiliano. "ADÁL, Key Photographer Whose Work Imagined New Futures for Puerto Rico, Has Died at 72." *ArtNews*, 11 December 2020, https://www.artnews.com/art-news/news/adal-maldonado-dead-1234579063/. Accessed 8 December 2023.
Dvinge, Anne. "Keeping Time, Performing Place: Jazz Heterotopia in Candace Allen's *Valaida*." *Journal of Transnational American Studies*, vol. 4., no. 2, 2012, https://escholarship.org/uc/item/79w3r5ck.
Dyson, George. *Project Orion: The Atomic Spaceship, 1957–1965*. Gardners Books, 2004.
Echevarría Peré, Ahmel. "En cada libro cambio de rostro. Entrevista con Laura V. Sández." *Diario de Cuba*, 1 February 2015, https://diariodecuba.com/cultura/1422655847_12625.html. Accessed, 8 December 2023.
Echevarría Peré, Ahmel, and Jorge Enrique Lage. "(De)Generación. Un mapa de la narrativa cubana más reciente." *Diario de Cuba*, 15 December 2013, https://diariodecuba.com/de-leer/1386613604_6269.html. Accessed 7 December 2023.
Eckstein, Susan Eva. *Back From the Future: Cuba Under Castro*. 2nd ed., Routledge, 2003.
El proyeccionista. Directed by José María Cabral, Tabula Rasa, 2019.

El viaje extraordinario de Celeste García. Directed by Arturo Infante, Producciones de la 5ta Avenida-/FassB Filmproduktion, 2018.
Encinosa Fu, Michel. *Dioses de neón.* Letras Cubanas, 2006.
———. *Niños de neón.* Letras Cubanas, 2001.
Enríquez Piñeiro, Anabel. *Nada que declarar.* Editorial Abril, 2007.
Escape from New York. Directed by John Carpenter, starring Kurt Russell, Lee Van Cleef, and Ernest Borgnine, AVCO Embassy Pictures, 1981.
Espírito Santo, Diana. "Liquid Sight, Thing-like Words, and the Precipitation of Knowledge Substances in Cuban Espiritismo." *Journal of the Royal Anthropological Institute,* vol. 21, no. 3, September 2015, pp. 579–96.
———. "Turning Outside In: Infolded Selves in Cuban Creole *Espiritismo*." *Ethos,* vol. 43, no. 3, pp. 267–85.
Exposito, Suzy. "Rita Indiana Gets Back in the Game with New Single, 'Como un dragón.'" *Rolling Stone,* 24 April 2020, https://www.rollingstone.com/music/music-latin/rita-indiana-como-un-dragon-mandinga-times-988874/.
Extraterrestres. Directed by Carla Cavina, Pulsar Productions, 2016.
Fabian, Johannes. *Time and the Other: How Anthropology Makes Its Object.* 1983. Columbia UP, 2002.
Faris, Wendy. *Ordinary Enchantments: Magical Realism and the Re-Mystification of Narrative.* Vanderbilt UP, 2004.
Faris, Wendy, and Lois Parkinson Zamora. "Introduction: Daiquiri Birds and Flaubertian Parrot(ies)." *Magical Realism: Theory, History, Community,* edited by Wendy Faris and Lois Parkinson-Zamora, Duke UP, 1995, pp. 1–11.
Fawcett, Fausto. *Santa Clara Poltergeist.* 1990. Editora Encrenca, 2014.
Fehimović, Dunja. *National Identity in 21st Century Cuban Cinema: Screening the Repeating Island.* Palgrave Macmillan, 2018.
———. "Zombie Nation: Monstrous Identities in Three Cuban Films." *The Cinema of Cuba: Contemporary Film and the Legacy of Revolution,* edited by Guy Baron, Ann Marie Stock, and Antonio Álvarez Pitaluga, Tauris, 2017, pp. 147–70.
Fernández Retamar, Roberto. *Calibán; apuntes sobre la cultura en nuestra América.* Editorial Diógenes, 1971.
Figueroa-Vásquez, Yomaira C. *Decolonizing Diasporas: Radical Mappings of Afro-Atlantic Literature.* Northwestern UP, 2020.
Fornet, Ambrosio. "El quinquenio gris: revisitando el término." *Revista Criterios,* 2 February 2007, https://rebelion.org/el-quinquenio-gris-revisitando-el-termino/.
Forte, Will, creator. *The Last Man on Earth.* The Si Fi Company, Lord Miller Productions, and 20th Century Fox Television, 2015–2018.
Foucault, Michel. "Of Other Spaces." Translated by Jay Miscowiec, *Diacritics,* vol. 16, no. 1, Spring 1986, pp. 22–27.
Freedman, Carl. *Critical Theory and Science Fiction.* Wesleyan UP, 2000.
Frelik, Pawel. "'Silhouettes of Strange Illuminated Mannequins': Cyberpunk's Incarnations of Light." *Cyberpunk and Visual Culture,* edited by Graham J. Murphy and Lars Schmeink, Routledge, 2017, pp. 80–99.

Fresa y chocolate. Directed by Tomás Gutiérrez Alea and Juan Carlos Tabío, starring Jorge Perugorría, Vladimir Cruz, and Mirta Ibarra, ICAIC, 1993.
Game of Thrones. Created by David Benioff and D. B. Weiss, HBO Entertainment, 2011–19.
Gamerro, Carlos. *Las islas*. 1998. EDHASA, 2012.
García, Hernán. "Tecnociencia y cibercultura en México: *Hackers* en el cuento *cyberpunk* mexicano." *Revista Iberoamericana*, vol. 78, nos. 238–39, January–June 2012, pp. 329–48.
———. "Texto y contexto del ciberpunk mexicano en la década de los noventa." *Alambique: Revista Académica de Ciencia Ficción y Fantasía*, vol. 5, no. 2, 2018, http://dx.doi.org/10.5038/2167-6577.5.2.5.
García Canclini, Néstor. *Culturas híbridas. Estrategias para salir y entrar de la modernidad*. Grijalbo, 1989.
García-Peña, Lorgia. "Book Review: Rita Indiana's *La mucama de Omicunlé*." *Aster(ix) Journal*, 26 July 2016, https://asterixjournal.com/book-review-rita-indiana/.
———. *The Borders of Dominicanidad: Race, Nation, and Archives of Contradiction*. Duke UP, 2016.
Gikandi, Simon. *Slavery and the Culture of Taste*. Princeton UP, 2011.
Ginsburg, Samuel. "La adaptación afro-futurista y el placer como supervivencia en 'Los pueblos silenciosos de Elena Palacios Ramé." *Alambique: Revista Académica de Ciencia Ficción y Fantasía*, vol. 5, no. 2, 2018, http://dx.doi.org/10.5038/2167-6577.5.2.3.
———. *The Cyborg Caribbean: Techno-Dominance in 21st Century Cuban, Dominican, and Puerto Rican Science Fiction*. Rutgers UP, 2023.
———. "Future Visions of Dominican History in Odilius Vlak's *Crónicas historiológicas*." *Latin American Literary Review*, vol. 46, no. 91, 2019, pp. 12–21.
Ginway, M. Elizabeth. *Brazilian Science Fiction: Cultural Myths and Nationhood in the Land of the Future*. Bucknell UP, 2004.
———. *Cyborgs, Sexuality, and the Undead: The Body in Mexican and Brazilian Speculative Fiction*. Vanderbilt UP, 2020.
———. "Latin America." *The Routledge Companion to Cyberpunk Culture*, edited by Anna McFarlane, Lars Schmeink, and Graham Murphy, Routledge, 2020, pp. 385–94.
Glassie, Allison. "Into the Anemone: Ocean, Form, and the Anthropocene in *Tentacle*." *SX Salon*, vol. 34, June 2020, http://smallaxe.net/sxsalon/discussions/anemone.
Gledhill, Christine. "Re-thinking Genre." *Reinventing Film Studies*, edited by Christine Gledhill and Linda Williams, Bloomsbury, 2000, pp. 221–43.
Glissant, Édouard. *Caribbean Discourse: Selected Essays*. 1981. Translated by J. Michael Dash, U of Virginia P, 1989.
———. *Poetics of Relation*. Translated by Betsy Wing, U of Michigan P, 1997.
Goddard, Richard E. *The Whistling Ancestors*. 1936. Dancing Tuatara Press, 2009.
Go Goa Gone. Directed by Krishna D. K. and Raj Nidimoru, Eros International, 2013.
Goldman, Dara. "Trans-Formation: The Remaking of the 'New Man' in Queer Representations." Unpublished book chapter. Shared with the author in 2017.

Gomel, Elana. "Recycled Dystopias: Cyberpunk and the End of History." *Arts*, vol. 7, no. 3, 2018, pp. 1–8, https://www.mdpi.com/2076-0752/7/3/31. Accessed 5 August 2021.

González Fernández, Maielis. "Distopías en el cyberpunk cubano: 'CH,' 'Ofidia,' y 'Habana Underguater.'" *La isla y las estrellas: El ensayo y la crítica de la ciencia ficción en Cuba*, edited by Rinaldo Acosta, Letras Cubanas, 2015, pp. 238–58.

——. *Sobre los nerds y otras criaturas mitológicas*. Guantanamera, 2016.

Grahame-Smith, Seth, and Jane Austen. *Pride and Prejudice and Zombies*. Quirk Books, 2009.

Greenberg, Scott, and Gavin Ekins. "Tax Policy Helped Create Puerto Rico's Fiscal Crisis," The Tax Foundation, 30 June 2015, https://taxfoundation.org/tax-policy-helped-create-puerto-rico-fiscal-crisis/.

Guevara, Ernesto "Che." "Socialismo y el hombre en Cuba." 1965. Ocean Sur/Ocean Press, 2011.

Gutiérrez Alea, Tomás. "Appendix: Memories of *Memories*." *The Viewer's Dialectic*. José Martí, 1988, pp. 69–85.

Hafner, Katie, and Matthew Lyon. *Where Wizards Stay Up Late: The Origins of the Internet*. Simon and Schuster, 1998.

Habana—Arte nuevo de hacer ruinas. Directed by Florian Borchmayer, Glueck Auf Film/Koppfilm/Raros Media, 2006.

Habana Blues. Directed by Benito Zembrano, 2005. Polychrome Pictures, 2007.

Hamilton, Njelle W. "'Another Shape to Time': *Tentacle's* Spiral Now." *SX Salon*, vol. 34, June 2020, pp. 1–9.

Haraway, Donna. *Staying with the Trouble: Making Kin in the Chthulucene*. Duke UP, 2016.

Hartman, Saidiya. "The Time of Slavery." *South Atlantic Quarterly*, vol. 101, no. 4, Fall 2002, pp. 757–77.

Haywood Ferreira, Rachel. *The Emergence of Latin American Science Fiction*. Wesleyan UP, 2011.

Heise, Ursula. *Sense of Place and Sense of Planet: Environmental Imagination of the Global*. Oxford UP, 2008.

Hellekson, Karen. *The Alternate History: Reconfiguring Historical Time*. Kent State UP, 2001.

Henken, Ted A. "Introduction: *In Medias Res*: Who Will Control Cuba's Digital Revolution?" *Cuba's Digital Revolution*, edited by Ted A. Henken and Sara Garcia Santamaria, UP of Florida, 2021, pp. 1–25.

Henríquez, Bruno. *Aventura en el laboratorio: cuentos de ciencia ficción*. Editorial Oriente, 1987.

Hernández Medina, Aníbal, editor. *Prietopunk: antología de afrofuturismo caribeño*. Aníbal Hernández Medina, 2022.

Hernández Pacín, Vladimir. *Nova de cuarzo*. Extramuros, 1999.

——, editor. *Onda de choque*. Extramuros, 2005.

Herrera, Isabelia. "The Return of Rita Indiana: A Singular Icon of Dominican Music." *Pitchfork*, 11 September 2020, https://pitchfork.com/thepitch/the-return-of-rita-indiana-a-singular-icon-of-dominican-music/.

Heuser, Sabine. *Virtual Geographies: Cyberpunk at the Intersection of the Postmodern and Science Fiction.* Brill, 2003.
Hicks, Heather J. *The Post-Apocalyptic Novel in the Twenty-first Century: Modernity beyond Salvage.* Palgrave Macmillan, 2016.
Horn, Maja. *Masculinity after Trujillo: The Politics of Gender in Dominican Literature.* UP of Florida, 2017.
Humphrey, Paul. "'El manto que cubre el mar': Religion, Identity, and the Sea in Rita Indiana's *La mucama de Omicunlé.*" *Sargasso.* nos. 1–2, 2016-17, pp. 109–25.
———. "Rita Indiana's Fluid Temporalities and the Queering of Bodies, Time, and Place." *Caribbean Quarterly,* vol. 68, no. 3, 2022, pp. 325–47.
Hunte, Nicola. "Encountering Others across Science Fiction, Afrofuturism and Anglophone Caribbean Speculative Fiction." *Journal of West Indian Literature,* vol. 27, no. 2, November 2019, pp. 15–28.
Hurston, Zora Neale. *Tell My Horse: Voodoo and Life in Haiti and Jamaica.* 1938. Harper Perennial, 2008.
Hurtado, Oscar. *La ciudad muerta de Korad.* Ediciones R, 1964.
———, editor. *Cuentos de ciencia ficción.* Instituto del Libro, 1969.
———, editor. *Introducción a la ciencia ficción.* Julián Benita, 1971.
Indiana, Rita. *Ciencia succión.* Amigo del Hogar, 2001.
———. "Como un dragón." Directed by Noelia Quintero Herencia, HQ Storytelling and Diptongo, 2020.
———. *Hecho en Saturno.* Periférica, 2018.
———. *Made in Saturn.* Translated by Sydney Hutchinson, And Other Stories, 2020.
———. *Mandinga Times.* Eduardo Cabra (Visitante), 2020.
———. *La mucama de Omicunlé.* Periférica, 2015.
———. "Rita Indiana, La Monstra, Returns with 'Black Sabbath Dembow.'" Interview by Jasmine Garsd, Alt.Latino, NPR, 17 June 2020, https://www.npr.org/transcripts/879316231. Accessed 7 December 2023.
———. *Tentacle.* Translated by Achy Obejas, And Other Stories, 2018.
Indiana, Rita y Los Misterios. *El juidero.* Premium Latin Music, 2010.
Irizarry, Guillermo. "Tecnologías discursivas del pensamiento posnacional en *Exquisito cadáver,* de Rafael Acevedo." *CENTRO Journal,* vol. 21, no. 1, Spring 2009, pp. 201–17.
Isla de plástico. Directed by José María Cabral, Cacique Films, 2019.
I Walked with a Zombie. Directed by Jacques Tourneur, RKO Radio Pictures, 1943.
iZombie. Created by Ruggiero-Wright, Diane, and Rob Thomas, The CW, 2015–present.
Jameson, Fredric. *Archaeologies of the Future: The Desire Called Utopia and Other Science Fictions.* Verso, 2005.
———. *Postmodernism, or, the Cultural Logic of Late Capitalism.* Duke UP, 1991.
Jáuregui, Carlos. *Canibalia. Canibalismo, calibanismo, antropofagia cultural y consumo en América Latina.* Fondo Editorial Casa de las Américas, 2005.
Juan de los muertos. Directed by Alejandro Brugués, Producciones de la 5ta Avenida, 2011.
Kalogridis, Laeta, creator. *Altered Carbon.* 2018–2020. Netflix, www.netflix.com.
Kaup, Monika. *New Ecological Realisms.* Edinburgh UP, 2021.

Kawin, Bruce. *Horror and the Horror Film*. Anthem, 2012.

———. "The Mummy's Pool." *Dreamworks*, vol. 1, no. 4, Summer 1981, pp. 291–301.

Kermode, Frank. *The Sense of an Ending: Studies in the Theory of Fiction*. 1966. Oxford UP, 2000.

Ketterer, David. *Canadian Science Fiction and Fantasy*. Indiana UP, 1992.

Kincaid, Jamaica. *A Small Place*. Farrar, Straus and Giroux, 1988.

Kincaid, Paul. *What It Is We Do When We Read Science Fiction*. Beccon, 2008.

King, Edward. *Science Fiction and Digital Technologies in Argentine and Brazilian Culture*. Palgrave Macmillan, 2013.

KL Zombi. Directed by Woo Ming Jin, Grand Brilliance, 2013.

Koselleck, Reinhart. *Futures Past: On the Semantics of Historical Time*. 1979. Translated and with an introduction by Keith Tribe, Columbia UP, 2004.

Kuhn, Annette. "Introduction." *Alien Zone: Cultural Theory and Contemporary Science Fiction Cinema*, Verso, 1990, pp. 1–12.

Lage, Jorge Enrique. *Archivo*. Hypermedia, 2015.

———. *Carbono 14. Una novela de culto*. 2010. Letras Cubanas, 2012.

———. *Everglades*. Hypermedia, 2020.

———. *Vultureffect*. Ediciones Union, 2011.

Lamrani, Salim. "Cuban Emigration to the United States from 1860 to 2019: A Statistical and Comparative Analysis." *Études caribéennes*, 7 July 2021, https://doi.org/10.4000/etudescaribeennes.23031.

Las escritoras de Urras. Directed by Maielis González Fernández and Sofía Barker. See https://escritorasdeurras.blogspot.com/.

The Last of Us. Created by Mazin, Craig, and Neil Druckman, Playstation Productions and Sony Pictures Television, 2023.

Latham, Rob. "Literary Precursors." *The Routledge Companion to Cyberpunk Culture*, edited by Anna McFarlane, Lars Schmeink, and Graham Murphy, Routledge, 2020, pp. 7–14.

Lauro, Sara Juliet. *The Transatlantic Zombie: Slavery, Rebellion, and Living Death*. Rutgers UP, 2015.

Lauro, Sara Juliet, and Karen Embry. "A Zombie Manifesto: The Nonhuman Condition in the Era of Advanced Capitalism." *Boundary 2*, vol. 35, no. 1, 2008, pp. 85–108.

Leandro Hernández, Lucía. "La ciencia ficción en Puerto Rico (1872–1960) y República Dominicana (1967–1984)." *Historia de la ciencia ficción latinoamericana I: Desde los orígenes hasta la modernidad*, edited by Teresa López-Pellisa and Silvia Kurlat Ares, Iberoamericana/Vervuert, 2021, pp. 343–69.

Lechuga, Carlos. "Con los sentimientos bajo cero," *El estornudo*, 28 March 2022, https://revistaelestornudo.com/emocion-sentimiemntos-bajo-cero-emigrar-cuba/. Accessed 28 March 2022.

The Leftovers. Created by Lindelof, Damon, and Tom Perrota, White Rabbit Productions and HBO Entertainment, 2014–17.

Le Guin, Ursula. *Dancing at the Edge of the World: Thoughts on Words, Women, Places*. Grove Press, 1989.

Lepucki, Edan. *California*. 2014. Back Bay Books, 2015.

Levinas, Emmanuel. *Ethics and Infinity: Conversations with Philippe Nemo.* 1982. Translated by Richard A. Cohen, Duquesne UP, 1985.

———. *Totality and Infinity.* An Essay on Exteriority. 1961. Translated by Alfonso Lingis, Duquesne UP, 1969.

Levy, Steven. *Hackers: Heroes of the Computer Revolution.* 1984. Penguin Books, 2001.

Lezama Lima, José. "Muerte del tiempo." *La fijeza,* edited by Rado Molina, Lingkua Ediciones, 2024, p. 87.

Liboy Erba, José. *Cada vez te despides mejor.* Isla Negra, 2004.

———. *El informe Cabrera.* Concepción 8, 2009.

Lim, Bliss Cua. *Translating Time: Cinema, the Fantastic, and Temporal Critique.* Duke UP, 2009.

Lima, Chely, and Alberto Serret. *Espacio abierto.* Colección Radar, Letras Cubanas, 1983.

Livmar, Pabsi. "Golpe de agua." *Teoremas turbios,* Editorial EDP University, 2018, pp. 7–42.

Lloréns, Hilda, and Maritza Stanchich. "Water Is Life, but the Colony Is a Necropolis: Environmental Terrains of Struggle in Puerto Rico." *Cultural Dynamics,* vol. 31, nos. 1–2, 2019, pp. 81–101.

López-Nussa, Harold. "El buey cansao." Directed by Raupa, Mala, and Nelson Ponce, Mack Avenue Records, 2020, https://www.youtube.com/watch?v=-fcgrG2sSu4.

López-Pellisa, Teresa, and Silvia Kurlat Ares. *Historia de la ciencia ficción latinoamericana I: Desde los orígenes hasta la modernidad.* Iberoamericana/Vervuert, 2021.

Lovecraft, H. P. "The Colour Out of Space," *Amazing Stories,* vol. 2, no. 6, September 1927, pp. 556–67.

Löwy, Michael. "The Current of Critical Irrealism: 'A Moonlight Enchanted Night.'" *A Concise Companion to Realism,* edited by Matthew Beaumont, Wiley-Blackwell, 2010, pp. 211–24.

Maguire, Emily A. "A Caribbean Afrofuturism." Under review at *Revista de Estudios Hispánicos.*

———. "Ficciones científicas para un país emergente: los 'eslabones perdidos' de la ciencia ficción cubana." *Historia de la ciencia ficción en la literatura latinoamericana I: desde los orígenes hasta la modernidad,* edited by Teresa López-Pellisa and Silvia G. Kurlat Ares, Iberoamericana/Vervuert, 2020, pp. 211–32.

———. "El hombre lobo en el espacio: el *hacker* como monstruo en el *cyberpunk* cubano." *Revista Iberoamericana,* April–June 2009, pp. 501–17.

———. "Islands in the Slipstream: Diasporic Allegories in Cuban Science Fiction Since the Special Period." *Latin American Science Fiction: Theory and Practice,* edited by M. Elizabeth Ginway and J. Andrew Brown, Palgrave Macmillan, 2012, pp. 19–34.

———. "Walking Dead in Havana: *Juan de los muertos* and the Zombie Film Genre." *Simultaneous Worlds: Global Science Fiction Cinema,* edited by Jennifer Feeley and Sarah Ann Wells, U of Minnesota P, 2015, pp. 171–88.

Maillo-Pozo, Sharina. "Diálogos músico-literarios y discursos contrahegemónicos en dos novelas de Rita Indiana Hernández." *Cuadernos de Literatura,* vol. 23, no. 45, January–June 2019, pp. 47–72.

Mallarmé, Stéphane. "Hérodiade." *Oeuvres Completes,* Gallimard, 1945, pp. 41–49.

Mandel, Emily St. John. *Station Eleven.* 2014. Vintage Books, 2015.
Martí, José. "El padre suizo." *Obras completas,* edición crítica, vol. 14, Centro de Estudios Martianos, pp. 126–27.
Massumi, Brian. "The Autonomy of Affect." *Cultural Critique* 31, Autumn 1995, pp. 83–109.
Masud-Piloto, Félix. *From Welcomed Exiles to Illegal Immigrants: Cuban Emigration to the U.S., 1959–1995.* Rowman and Littlefield, 1996.
Más Vampiros en la Habana. Directed by Juan Padrón, ICAIC, 2003.
The Matrix. Directed by the Wachowskis, starring Keanu Reeves, Laurence Fishburne, Carrie-Anne Moss, and Hugo Weaving, Warner Brothers and Vintage Roadshow Pictures, 1999.
The Matrix Reloaded. Directed by the Wachowskis, starring Keanu Reeves, Laurence Fishburne, Carrie-Anne Moss, and Hugo Weaving, Warner Brothers and Vintage Roadshow Pictures, 2003.
The Matrix Revolutions. Directed by the Wachowskis, starring Keanu Reeves, Laurence Fishburne, Carrie-Anne Moss, and Hugo Weaving, Warner Brothers and Vintage Roadshow Pictures, 2003.
McAlister, Elizabeth. "Slaves, Cannibals, and Infected Hyper-Whites: The Race and Religion of Zombies." *Zombie Theory: A Reader,* edited by Sarah Juliet Lauro, U of Minnesota P, 2014, pp. 63–84.
McCarthy, Cormac. *The Road.* Knopf Doubleday, 2006.
McHale, Brian. "Towards a Poetics of Cyberpunk." *Beyond Cyberpunk: New Critical Perspectives,* edited by Graham J. Murphy and Sherryl Vint, Routledge, 2010, pp. 3–28.
Medina, Eden. *Cybernetic Revolutionaries: Technology and Politics in Allende's Chile.* MIT P, 2014.
Melocotones. Directed by Héctor Valdez, Emmett Industries, 2017.
Memorias del subdesarrollo [Memories of Underdevelopment]. Directed by Tomás Gutiérrez Alea, ICAIC, 1968.
Métraux, Alfred. *Voodoo in Haiti.* Translated by Hugo Charteris. 1959. Schocken Books, 1972.
Miéville, China. "Afterward/Cognition as Ideology: A Dialectic of SF Theory." *Red Planets: Marxism and Science Fiction,* edited by Mark Bould and China Miéville, Wesleyan UP, 2009, pp. 231–48.
Mitchell, David. *Cloud Atlas.* Random House, 2004.
Mitchell, Tamara. "Carving Place Out of Non-place: Luis Rafael Sánchez's 'La Guagua aérea' and Postnational Space." *Chasqui,* vol. 47, no. 1, 2018, pp. 275–92.
Mond, F. *Cecilia después, o ¿por qué la Tierra?* Gente Nueva, 1987.
———. *Con el perdón de las terrícolas.* Letras Cubanas, 1983.
———. *¿Dónde está mi Habana?* Letras Cubanas, 1985.
Moore, Robin. *Music and Revolution: Cultural Change in Socialist Cuba.* U of California P, 2006.
Mora, Marie T., Alberto Dávila, and Havidán Rodríguez. "Migration, Geographic Destinations, and Socioeconomic Outcomes of Puerto Ricans during *La Crisis Boricua:*

Implications for Island and Stateside Communities Post-María." *Centro Journal*, vol. 30, no. 3, 2018, pp. 208–29.

Morales, Ed. *Fantasy Island: Colonialism, Exploitation, and the Betrayal of Puerto Rico.* Bold Type Books, 2019.

———. "Puerto Rico's Unjust Debt." *Aftershocks of Disaster: Puerto Rico Before and After the Storm,* edited by Yarimar Bonilla and Marisol LeBrón, Haymarket Books, 2019, 246–58.

Morales Cabrera, Pablo. *Cuentos populares.* 2nd ed., Prologue by Emilio S. Belaval, Baldrich, 1939.

Moraña, Mabel. *El monstruo como máquina de guerra.* Iberoamercana/Vervuert, 2017.

Morgan, Richard K. *Altered Carbon.* Victor Gollancz, 2002.

Morton, Timothy. *Dark Ecology: For a Logic of Future Coexistence.* Columbia UP, 2018.

Mota, Erick J. "Afrofuturismo del Caribe: diferencias con el *afrofuturism* y el futurismo africano." Asociación Dominicana de Ficción Especulativa, 16 December 2021, Zoom presentation.

———. *El colapso de las Habanas infinitas.* Editorial Hypermedia, 2017.

———. "El cyberpunk, una deconstrucción de la realidad: Apuntes sobre un possible 'neo-cyberpunk cubano.'" *Istmo: Revista Virtual de Estudios Literarios y Culturales Centroamericanos,* num. 23, July–December 2011, pp. 1–15.

———. *Habana Underguater. Novela y cuentos.* Atom Press, 2010.

———. "Memorias de un país zombi." *Terranova: antología de ciencia ficción contemporánea,* Sportula, 2012.

———. "That Zombie Belongs to Fidel!" *Cuba in Splinters: Eleven Stories from the New Cuba.* OR Books, 2014, pp. 133–50.

Moya Pons, Frank. *The Dominican Republic: A National History.* Markus Wiener, 2010.

Munro, Martin. *Tropical Apocalypse: Haiti and the Caribbean End Times.* U of Virginia P, 2015.

Muñoz, José Esteban. *Cruising Utopia: The Then and There of Queer Futurity.* New York UP, 2009.

Murphy, Graham J. "The Mirrorshades Collective." *The Routledge Companion to Cyberpunk Culture,* edited by Anna McFarlane, Lars Schmeink, and Graham Murphy, Routledge, 2020, pp. 15–23.

Murphy, Graham J., and Lars Schmeink, editors. *Cyberpunk and Visual Culture.* Routledge, 2017.

Nada +. Directed by Juan Carlos Cremata Malberti, ICAIC, 2001.

Naimou, Angela. *Salvage Work: U.S. and Caribbean Literatures amid the Debris of Legal Personhood.* Fordham UP, 2015.

Nazare, Joe. "Marlowe in Mirrorshades: The Cyberpunk (Re-)Vision of Chandler." *Studies in the Novel,* vol. 35, no. 3, Fall 2003, pp. 383–404.

Nixon, Rob. *Slow Violence and the Environmentalism of the Poor.* Harvard UP, 2011.

Noya, Elsa. "El palpitar de la cultura. Los años noventa del campo cultural puertorriqueño." *Escrituras en contrapunto: Estudios y debates para una historia crítica de la literatura puertorriqueña,* edited by Marta Aponte Alsina, Juan Gelip, and Malena Rodríguez Castro, Editorial de la Universidad de Puerto Rico, 2015, pp. 765–99.

Oloff, Kerstin. "'Greening' the Zombie: Caribbean Gothic, World Ecology, and Socio-Ecological Degradation." *Green Letters: Studies in Ecocriticism,* vol. 16, no. 1, 2012, pp. 31–45.

———. "Lo humano es una historia, un cuento de hadas: Entrevista a Pedro Cabiya." *La Habana Elegante* 51, Spring–Summer 2012, http://www.habanaelegante.com/Spring_Summer_2012/Entrevista_Oloff.html.

———. "Towards the World-Zombie: The Monstrous, the 'Human' and the Dominican-Haitian Frontier in Pedro Cabiya's *Malas hierbas* (2010) and Junot Díaz's 'Monstro' (2012)." *Rethinking 'Identities': Cultural Articulations of Alterity and Resistance in the New Millennium,* edited by Lucille Cairns and Santiago Fouz-Hernández, Peter Lang, 2014, pp. 189–211.

Omega 3. Directed by Eduardo del Llano, ICAIC, 2014.

Ordas Matos, Nuria Dolores. *Entremundos.* Editorial Gente Nueva, 2010.

Ortega, Gregorio. *Kappa15.* Colección Radar, Letras Cubanas, 1982.

Ortiz, Fernando. *Contrapunteo cubano del tabaco y el azúcar.* 1940. Consejo Nacional de Cultura, 1973.

———. *Cuban Counterpoint: Tobacco and Sugar.* Translated by Harriet de Onís, introduction by Fernando Coronil. 1947. Duke UP, 1995.

———. *Hampa afrocubana. Los negros brujos.* 1906. Ediciones Universal, 1973.

Othoniel Rosa, Luis. *Caja de fractales.* Entropía, 2017.

———. *Down with Gargamel.* Translated by Noel Black, Argos Books, 2020.

OVNI. Directed by Raúl Marchand Sánchez, Bonter Media Group, 2016.

Padilla Cárdenas, Gilberto. "El factor Cuba. Apuntes para una semiología clínica." *Temas* 80, October–December 2014, pp. 114–20.

Page, Joanna. *Science Fiction in Argentina: Technologies of the Text in a Material Multiverse.* U of Michigan P, 2016.

Pardo Lazo, Orlando Luis, editor. "Generación Cero: *nuevarrrativa* en la literatura cubana e-mergente," *Sampsonia Way,* 29 July 2013, http://www.sampsoniaway.org/features/2013/08/06/antologia-nuevarrativa-cubana.

———, editor. *Generation Zero: An Anthology of New Cuban Fiction.* Sampsonia Way, 2014.

———. "Preface." *Cuba in Splinters: Eleven Stories from the New Cuba.* OR Books, 2014.

Patterson, Orlando. *Slavery and Social Death: A Comparative Study, with a New Preface.* 2nd ed., Harvard UP, 2018.

Paz, Senel. "El lobo, el bosque, y el hombre nuevo." Ediciones Era, 1991.

Pérez Ortiz, Melanie. *La revolución de las apetencias: El tráfico de muertos en la literatura puertorriqueña contemporánea.* Ediciones Callejón, 2021.

Personal Belongings. Directed by Alejandro Brugués, 2008, Maya Entertainment, 2009.

Ponte, Antonio José. *La fiesta vigilada.* Anagrama, 2007.

———. "Un arte de hacer ruinas." *Un arte de hacer ruinas y otros cuentos,* Fondo de Cultura Económica, 2005, pp. 56–73.

Porcayo, Gerardo Horacio. *La primera calle de la soledad.* 1993. Editorial Planeta Mexicana, 2020.

Posmentier, Sonya. *Cultivation and Catastrophe: The Lyric Ecology of Modern Black Literature.* Johns Hopkins UP, 2017.

Potter, Sara. "Postcolonial Pandemics and Undead Revolutions: Contagion as Resistance in *Con z de zombie* and *Juan de los muertos.*" *Alambique: Revista Académica de Ciencia Ficción y Fantasía,* vol. 6, no. 1, https://digitalcommons.usf.edu/alambique/vol6/iss1/5/.

Press, Larry. "The Past, Present, and Future of the Cuban Internet." *Cuba's Digital Revolution,* edited by Ted A. Henken and Sara Garcia Santamaria, UP of Florida, 2021, pp. 29–49.

Price, Rachel. *Planet/Cuba: Art, Culture, and the Future of the Island.* Verso, 2015.

———. "Planet/Cuba. On Jorge Enrique Lage's *Carbono 14: una novela de culto* and Vultureffect." *La Habana Elegante,* Fall–Winter 2012, http://www.habanaelegante.com/Fall_Winter_2012/Invitation_Price.html#nota1

Prietopunk. Edited by Luis Reynaldo Pérez, Asociación Dominicana de Ficción Especulativa, 2021.

Pulgar, E. R. "Rita Indiana Foretells the End on 'Mandinga Times.'" *Ladygunn.com,* 25 September 2020, https://www.ladygunn.com/music/interviews-music/rita-indiana-interview/.

Quesada, Sarah. "A Planetary Warning? The Multilayered Caribbean Zombie in 'Monstro.'" *Junot Díaz and the Decolonial Imagination,* edited by Monica Hanna, Jennifer Harford Vargas, and José David Saldívar, Duke UP, 2016, pp. 291–318.

Quijano, Aníbal. "Coloniality of Power, Eurocentrism, and Latin America," *Nepantla: Views from the South,* vol. 1, no. 3, 2000, pp. 533–80.

Quintero Herencia, Juan Carlos. *De la queda(era). Imagen, tiempo y detención en Puerto Rico.* El Cangrejo, 2021.

———. "Extranjería, comunidad y escucha: escenas contemporáneas de autoridad literaria puertorriqueña." *Centro Journal,* vol. 22, no. 2, 2010, 151–71.

Quiroga, José. *Cuban Palimpsests.* U of Minnesota P, 2005.

The Rain. Created by Tai Mosholt, Jannick, Esben Toft Jacobsen, and Christian Potalivo, Miso Film, 2018–20.

Ramírez, Dixa. *Colonial Phantoms: Belonging and Refusal in the Dominican Americas, from the 19th Century to the Present.* New York UP, 2018.

Renda, Mary. *Taking Haiti: Military Occupation and the Culture of U.S. Imperialism (1915–1940).* U of North Carolina P, 2001.

Rhys, Jean. *Wide Sargasso Sea.* Norton, 1966.

Rialta staff. "Mención para 'Corazón azul', de Miguel Coyula, en el Festival de Cine Latino de la Universidad de Yale." *Rialta,* 16 November 2022, https://rialta.org/mencion-para-corazon-azul-de-miguel-coyula-en-el-festival-de-cine-latino-de-la-universidad-de-yale/. Accessed 8 December 2023.

Ricoeur, Paul. *Time and Narrative.* Translated by Kathleen McLaughlin and David Pellauer, vol. 1, U of Chicago P, 1984.

Rieder, John. *Colonialism and the Emergence of Science Fiction.* Wesleyan UP, 2012.

———. *Science Fiction and the Mass Cultural Genre System.* Wesleyan UP, 2017.

Rivera, Ángel. *Ciencia ficción en Puerto Rico: Heraldos de la catástrofe, el apocalipsis y el cambio.* La secta de los perros, 2019.

Rivera, Ángel, and María Teresa Vera-Rojas. "Ciencia ficción en Puerto Rico (1960–2019) y República Dominicana (1986–2020)." *Historia de la ciencia ficción latinoamericana II,* edited by Teresa López-Pellisa and Silvia G. Kurlat Ares, Iberoamericana/Vervuert, 2021, pp. 592–637.

Rivera Montes, Zorimar. *¿Quién le debe a quién? Debt and Coloniality in Contemporary Puerto Rican Culture.* 2022. Northwestern U, PhD dissertation.

Rodríguez, Ileana Margarita. "El viaje extraordinario de Arturo Infante," *ADN Cuba,* 6 July 2019, https://adncuba.com/noticias-de-cuba-cultura/cine-y-audiovisual/el-viaje-extraordinario-de-arturo-infante. Accessed 20 December 2021.

Rodríguez, Néstor E. *Escrituras de desencuentro en la República Dominicana.* Siglo XXI Editores, 2005.

———. "Impredicible oficio el de la maravilla: entrevista al escritor puertorriqueño Pedro Cabiya." *Revista Iberoamericana,* vol. 74, no. 222, January–March 2008, pp. 1–8.

Rogers, Charlotte, "Rita Indiana's Queer Interspecies Caribbean and the Hispanic Literary Tradition." *SX Salon,* vol. 34, June 2020, http://smallaxe.net/sxsalon/discussions/rita-indianas-queer-interspecies-caribbean-and-hispanic-literary-tradition.

Rojo, Pepe. *Ruido gris.* 1996. Fondo de Cultura Económica, 2020.

Román, N. V. *Universo de la ciencia ficción cubana.* Ediciones Extramuros, 2005.

Rosado, José Ángel, editor. *El rostro y la máscara: Antología alterna de cuentistas puertorriqueños contemporáneos.* Editorial de la Universidad de Puerto Rico, 1995.

Roscoe, Theodore. "A Grave Must Be Deep!" *Argosy Weekly,* December 1934–January 1935.

Rothenberg, Jason, creator. *The 100.* Alloy Entertainment, CBS Television Studios, and Warner Bros. Television, 2014–20.

Ruggiero-Wright, Diane, and Rob Thomas, creators. *iZombie.* The CW. 2015–present.

Samatar, Sofia. "Toward a Planetary History of Afrofuturism." *Research in African Literatures,* vol. 48, no. 4, Winter 2017, pp. 175–91.

Santiago-Valles, Kelvin A. *"Subject People" and Colonial Discourses: Economic Transformation and Social Disorder in Puerto Rico, 1898–1947.* State U of New York P, 1994.

Sánchez, Luis Rafael. "The Flying Bus." *Herencia,* edited by Nicolás Kanellos, translated by Elpidio Laguna Díaz, Oxford UP, 2003, pp. 631–38.

———. *La guagua aérea.* San Juan: Editorial Cultural, 2000.

Santa Clarita Diet. Created by Victor Fresco, *Netflix,* www.netflix.com, 2017–19.

Santos Febres, Maya, editor. *Ma(h)ab(l)ar.* Fundación Puertorriqueña de las Humanidades, 1997.

Scott, Darieck. *Keeping It Unreal: Black Queer Fantasy and Superhero Comics.* New York UP, 2022.

Scott, David. *Omens of Adversity: Tragedy, Time, Memory, Justice.* Duke UP, 2014.

Seabrook, William. *The Magic Island.* 1929. Kessinger Publishing, 2003.

Sharpe, Christina. *In the Wake: On Blackness and Being.* Duke UP, 2016.

Shaun of the Dead. Directed by Edgar Wright, Universal Studios, 2004.

Shaw Nevins, Andrea. *Working Juju: Representations of the Caribbean Fantastic.* U of Georgia P, 2019.

Sierra Madero, Abel. *El cuerpo nunca olvida: Trabajo forzado, hombre nuevo y memoria en Cuba (1959–1980).* Rialta, 2022.

Sirkis, Alfredo. *Silicone XXI.* Editora Record, 1985.

Siskind, Mariano. "Towards a Cosmopolitanism of Loss: An Essay About the End of the World." *World Literature, Cosmopolitanism, Globality,* edited by Gesine Müller and Mariano Siskind, DeGruyter, 2019, pp. 205–36.

Sklodowska, Elzbieta. *Invento, luego resisto: El Período Especial en Cuba como experiencia y metáfora.* Cuarto Propio, 2016.

Soares, Kristie. "Dominican Futurism: The Speculative Use of Negative Aesthetics in the Work of Rita Indiana." *Meridians: Feminism, Race, Transnationalism,* vol. 19, no. 2, October 2020, pp. 401–26.

Soltero Sánchez, Evangelina. "La ciencia ficción cubana desde la Revolución a nuestros días (1957–2019)." *Historia de la ciencia ficción latinoamericana II,* edited by Silvia Kurlat Ares and Teresa López-Pellisa, Iberoamericana/Vervuert, 2021, pp. 287–338.

Sommer, Doris. *Foundational Fictions: The National Romances of Latin America.* U of California P, 1993.

Sommerville, Patrick, creator. *Station Eleven.* Paramount Television Studios, 2021–22.

Sterling, Bruce. Preface. *Mirrorshades: The Cyberpunk Anthology.* Ace Books, 1986, pp. ix–xvi.

Stock, Ann Marie. *On Location in Cuba: Street Filmmaking During Times of Transition.* U of North Carolina P, 2009.

———. "Resisting Disconnectedness in *Larga distancia* and *Juan de los muertos*: Cuban Filmmakers Create and Compete in a Globalized World," *Revista Canadiense de Estudios Hispánicos,* vol. 37, no. 1, Autumn 2012, pp. 49–66.

Suite Habana. Directed by Fernando Pérez, ICAIC and Cinema Tropical, 2003.

Suvin, Darko. "On the Poetics of the Science Fiction Genre." *College English,* vol. 34, no. 3, December 1972, pp. 372–82.

Toledano Redondo, Juan Carlos. "Cuba's Cyberpunk Histories." *The Routledge Companion to Cyberpunk Culture,* edited by Anna McFarlane, Graham J. Murphy, and Lars Schmeink, Routledge, 2020, pp. 395–400.

———. "Dominican Republic." *SF Encyclopedia: The Encyclopedia of Science Fiction,* 4th ed., https://sf-encyclopedia.com/entry/dominican_republic. Accessed 8 December 2023.

———. "From Socialist Realism to Anarchist Capitalism: Cuban Cyberpunk." *Science Fiction Studies,* vol. 32, 2005, pp. 442–66.

———. "Lo que se llevó el Ciclón del 16 en la Cuba cyberpunk *Underguater* de Erick Mota." *Co-Herencia: Revista de Humanidades,* vol. 16, no. 30, January–June 2019, pp. 79–104.

Tolentino, Adriana, and Patricia Tomé. "En busca de una identidad fílmica: El proceso evolutivo del emergente cine dominicano." *La gran pantalla dominicana: Miradas críticas al cine actual,* edited by Adriana Tolentino and Patricia Tomé, Almenara, 2017, pp. 9–28.

Torres, John. *Undead.* 2013. 2nd ed., Disonante, 2017.
Train to Busan. Directed by Yeon Sang-ho, Next Entertainment World and Red Peter Film, 2016.
Tsang, Martin. "A Different Kind of Sweetness: Yemayá in Afro-Cuban Religion." *Yemoja: Gender, Sexuality, and Creativity in the Latina/o and Afro-Atlantic Diasporas,* edited by Solimar Otero and Toyin Falola, SUNY Press, 2013, pp. 113–29.
Tundra. Directed by José Luis Aparicio, Esen Studios, 2021.
Turits, Richard Lee. "A World Destroyed, a Nation Imposed: The 1937 Haitian Massacre in the Dominican Republic," *Hispanic American Historical Review,* vol. 82, no. 3, August 2002, pp. 589–635.
Últimos días en la Habana. Directed by Fernando Pérez, with Jorge Martínez, Gabriela Ramos and Patricio Wood, ICAIC, Besa Films, and Wanda Vision, 2016.
Valdéz, Diógenes. *Todo puede suceder en un día.* Taller, 1984.
¡Vampiros en la Habana! Directed by Juan Padrón, ICAIC, 1985.
Vázquez, Alexandra T. *Listening in Detail: Performances of Cuban Music.* Duke UP, 2013.
Vázquez, Karina. "Brazilian Cyberpunk and Latin American Neobarroque: Political Critique in a Globalized World." *Luso-Brazilian Review,* vol. 49, no. 1, pp. 208–24.
Vilar Madruga, Elain. "Odilius Vlak: La escritura no es para lobos solitarios." Website of the Asociación Hermanos Sainz, 1 March 2021, http://www.ahs.cu/?p=32265.
Villegas, Richard. "Rita Indiana Breaks Down Every Track on Her Apocalyptic New Album, 'Mandinga Times,'" *Remezcla,* 8 September 2020, https://remezcla.com/lists/music/rita-indiana-track-by-track-review-mandinga-times-album-interview/.
Vint, Sherryl. "Ab-realism: Fractal Language and Social Change." *China Miéville: Critical Essays,* edited by Caroline Edwards and Tony Venezia, Glyphi, 2016, pp. 39–60.
———. *Bodies of Tomorrow: Technology, Subjectivity, Science Fiction.* U of Toronto P, 2007.
Viva Cuba. Directed by Juan Carlos Cremata Malberti, Film Movement 2005.
Vlak, Odilius. "Ciencia ficción y fantasía dominicana: más ficción y fantasía que realidad." *Tiempos Oscuros,* no. 4, January–June 2015, pp. 389–99.
———. *Crónicas historiológicas.* Disonante, 2017.
———. *Exoplanetarium.* Disonante, 2015.
Vogel, Shane. *Stolen Time: Black Fad Performance and the Calypso Craze.* U of Chicago P, 2018.
Warm Bodies. Directed by Jonathan Levine, starring Nicholas Hoult and Teresa Palmer, Lionsgate Films, 2013.
Warren, Charles W., Charles F. Westoff, Joan M. Herold, Roger W. Rochat, and Jack C. Smith. "Contraceptive Sterilization in Puerto Rico." *Demography,* vol. 23, no. 3, August 1986, pp. 351–65.
Wells, H. G. *The Time Machine.* 1895. Bantam Classics, 1984.
West, Benjamin. "*Bladerunner* and *Altered Carbon*: Aesthetic and Setting in Cyberpunk." *Film Matters,* vol. 10, no. 3, 2019, pp. 198–205.
Whitehead, Colson. *Zone One.* 2011. Anchor Books, 2012.
White Zombie. Directed by Victor Halperin, United Artists, 1932.

Williams, Rosalind. "Crisis: The Emergence of Another Hazardous Concept." *Technology and Culture,* vol. 62, no. 2, April 2021, pp. 521–46.
Wittenberg, David. *Time Travel: The Popular Philosophy of Narrative.* Fordham UP, 2013.
Wolfe, Gary K. *The Known and the Unknown.* Kent State UP, 1979.
Womak, Ytasha L. *Afrofuturism: The World of Black Sci-Fi and Fantasy Culture.* Lawrence Hill Books, 2013.
Yoss. "La épica farsa de los sobrevivientes: O varias consideraciones casi sociológicas sobre la actualidad y el más reciente cine cubano, disfrazadas de ¿simple? reseña del filme *Juan de los muertos.*" *Korad* 7, October–December 2011, pp. 48–55.
———. "Marcianos en el platanar de Bartolo: un análisis de la historia y perspectivas de la ciencia ficción en Cuba al final del segundo milenio." *La quinta dimensión de la literatura: Reflexiones sobre la ciencia ficción en Cuba y el mundo,* Letras Cubanas, 2012, pp. 62–81.
———, editor. *Reino eterno.* Letras Cubanas, 1999.
———. *Planet for Rent.* Translated by David Frye, Restless Books, 2015.
———. *Se alquila un planeta.* 2001. Restless Books, 2015.
———. *Timshel.* Letras Cubanas, 1989.
Zambrana, Rocío. *Colonial Debts: The Case of Puerto Rico.* Duke UP, 2021.
Zibahkhana. Directed by Omar Khan, Mondo Macabro, 2007.
Žižek, Slavoj. *Living in the End Times.* 2nd ed., Verso, 2011.
Zombi 2. Directed by Lucio Fulci, Variety Distribution, 1979.
Zombieland. Directed by Ruben Fleischer, featuring Woody Harrelson, Jessie Eisenberg, Emma Stone, and Abigail Breslin, Columbia Pictures, 2009.
Zombitopia. Directed by Woo Ming Jin, Greenlight Pictures, Sunstar Entertainment, and Lobo Pictures, 2021.

INDEX

Page numbers in *italics* refer to illustrations.

Ab-realism: definition of, 12–13, 41–42; in Caribbean literature, 42, 43–69, 70, 197n3
Acevedo, Rafael, 31, 50, 95–96, 193n3, 201n19, 205n3; *Al otro lado del mundo hay carne fresca*, 205n3; *Exquisito cadáver*, 13, 31, 82, 95–107, 201n26, 201n27
Acevedo, Ricardo, 27
Acevedo, David Caleb, 32
Achon, Frank, 72–74, 107, 199n1; "Havana Cyberpunk 2059" (NFT image), 72, *73*
Ackerman, Hans, 108
Acosta, José, 205n3
Acosta, Rinaldo, 11, 27, 200n14
ADÁL (Adál Maldonado), 30, 31; "Coconauts in Space" (photographic series), 30; "Coconauta Interrogation/ Intelligence Center" (video), 30, *31*
Adrover Lausell, Miguel, 32
Adyanthaya, Aravind, 50
Afrofuturism. *See under* Science fiction (genre); Science fiction in the Hispanic Caribbean
Agamben, Giorgio, 202n3
Aguiar, Raúl, 26, 27, 28, 83, 196n13, 200n13, 200n14
Águila, Arnaldo, 196n13
Alamar (Havana housing project), 207n14
Alcocer, Rudyard, 18, 54, 164
Allen, Candace, 201n25
Allende, Salvador, 206n11
Alonso, Alicia, 26
Al otro lado del mundo hay carne fresca (Acevedo). *See under* Acevedo, Rafael

Altered Carbon (novel by Richard Morgan), 77
Altered Carbon (TV series), 77
Amazing Stories (magazine), 74
Aparicio, José Luis, 29
Apocalypse and apocalyptic thought, 151, 152, 205n1, 206n8; in the Caribbean region, 147–52. *See also* Apocalyptic and postapocalyptic narrative in literature and film
Apocalyptic and postapocalyptic narrative in literature and film, 35, 114, 141, 148–49, 152–53, 206n10; in the Caribbean region, 14–15, 148–51, 153–55, 205n3. *See also* Apocalypse and apocalyptic thought; Cabral, José María: *Arrobá*; Indiana, Rita: *La mucama de Omincunlé*; Mota, Erick: *Habana Underguater*
Aponte Alsina, Marta, 95
Appadurai, Arjun, 35, 193n4
Arango, Arturo, 25
Argento, Dario, 202n2
Aristotle, 40
Armengot, Sara, 122
Arrobá (Cabral). *See under* Cabral, José María
Arroyo, Jossianna, 3, 22, 24, 111, 193n4
Arroyo Pizarro, Yolanda, 15; "Mulâtresse" (short story), 183, 188–91
Asociación Dominicana de Ficción Especulativa (ADFE), 33, 34, 193n3

Babstro, Asiel 199
Báez, Rodolfo 33
Bakhtin, Mikhail, 40
Balaguer, Joaquín, 21, 165, 167, 208n23
Ballina, Bianka, 203n12

Balseros (documentary film), 63
Bardit, Jorge, 206n11
Barker, Sofía, 208n2
Barlow, Peter Paul, 76
Bastidas Pérez, Rodrigo, 208n3
Batalla de Mal Tiempo (Cuba), 67
Batista, Fulgencio, 19
Battle of March 19th (Dominican Republic), 44, 47
Bef (Bernardo Fernández), 79
Belisle, Natalie, 110, 131, 139, 204n30, 204n31
Benítez Rojo, Antonio, 18–19, 147, 152, 155, 205n2
Berger, James, 14, 149, 152–53, 154, 155, 169, 173
Berlant, Laura, 151, 206n7
Bestia (Vilar Madruga), 107
Bethke, Bruce, 199
Bill and Ted's Excellent Adventure (film), 9
Birkenmaier, Anka, 160, 200n18
Bishop, Kyle William, 202n4
Blade Runner (film), 77, 85, 97
Blanco, María del Pilar, 17
Blaustein, Eduardo, 80
Bloch, Ernst, 9, 153, 194n11
Bobes, Marilyn, 198n9
Bonilla, Yarimar, 150, 151, 152, 198n10
Borchmeyer, Florian, 207n15
Bosch, Juan, 32
Boyer, Jean-Pierre, 195n5
Boym, Svtlana, 38–39, 40
Brief Wondrous Life of Oscar Wao, The (Díaz). See under Díaz, Junot
Briggs, Laura, 55
Broderick, Damien, 193n5
Brown, Andrew J., 116
Brown, David, 162, 176
Brugués, Alejandro, 29, 111, 115, 117, 203n21. See also *Juan de los muertos*
Buckell, Tobias, 35
Buckle, Travis, 195n12
Buena Vista Social Club, The (film), 207n15
Bueno, Descemer, 72
Bukatman, Scott, 76, 77, 78, 85
Burges, Joel, 24
Burguet, Daniel, 28

Cabiya, Pedro, 30–31, 60, 95, 96, 129, 139, 204n28; *Malas hierbas*, 31, 111, 128–40; *Historias tremendas* (published under pseud. "Diego Deni"), 30, 198n15, 201n20
Cabral, José María, 34, 207n17; *Arrobá* (film), 154–55, 207n17
Cadigan, Pat 74, 199n10
Cadoga, Karen, 199n10
Caja de fractales (Rosa), 205n3
Calibán (Fernández Retamar), 208n25
Canavan, Gerry, 130
Candelario, Ginetta, 204n27
Capek, Karel, 26
Caribbean region: history of, 18–24; literature and film of, 17–18, 148–51; and modernity, 149; temporality and, 2, 16–17, 18, 148. See also Ab-realism; Apocalypse and apocalyptic thought; Apocalyptic and postapocalyptic narrative in literature and film; Cuba; Dominican Republic; Environmental disaster; Magical realism and fantastic literaure; Puerto Rico; Science fiction in the Hispanic Caribbean; Zombie
Caribe Extremófilo (conference), 193n3
Carpentier, Alejo. See "De lo real maravilloso americano" (Carpentier)
Carroll, Lewis, 98
Casamayor-Cisneros, Odette, 84, 116
Castillo, Debra, 207n18
Castillo, Efraim, 32
Castro, Fidel, 19, 20, 119, 128
Castro, Raúl, 20
Castro, Eduardo Viveiros de, 149
Catastrophe. See Apocalypse and apocalyptic thought; Apocalyptic and postapocalyptic narrative in literature and film
Causo, Roberto de Sousa, 206n11
Cavina, Carla, 32
Cedeño Rojas, Maribel, 120
Central Soller (Cuban sugar plantation), 56
Centro Onelio Jorge Cardoso, 28, 200n14, 200n15
Certeau, Michel de, 158, 206n13
Césaire, Aimé, 208n25
Chabon, Michael, 206n11

Chandler, Raymond, 78
Chaviano, Daína, 25, 26
Chebotaryov, Vladimir, 26
Checo Estévez, Yubany Alberto, 33
Chico, Kattia, 60
Chu, Seo-Young, 45, 59–60, 197n5, 201n23
Cimafunk (musician), 37, 38, 39
Cineteca Nacional (Puerto Rico), 34
Clark, Mitchell, 199n2
"Coconauta Interrogation/ Intelligence Center" (video by ADÁL). *See under* ADÁL
"Coconauts in Space" (photographic series by ADÁL). *See under* ADÁL
Collazo, Miguel, 25
Colonialism and postcolonialism, and science fiction, 56
Columbus, Christopher, 48, 166
"Como un dragón" (song and video by Rita Indiana). *See under* Indiana, Rita
Conferencia Caribeña de Ciencia Ficción (2023 conference), 193n3
Congreso de Ciencia Ficción Caribeña, 31, 201n20
Contrapunteo cubano del tabaco y el azúcar (Ortiz), 204n24
Corazón azul (film), 197n19, 205n3
Córdoba Cornejo, Antonio, 11, 52
Cortázar, Julio 130
Cosmos Burlesco (Pruné), 107
COVID-19 pandemic, 183
Coyula, Miguel, 29, 30
Cremata Malberti, Juan Carlos, 123
Cristofaro, Diletta de, 149, 153, 206n10
Crónicas historiológicas (Vlak), 42, 43–50
Cruz, Ariel, 83
Cruz, Josefina de la, 32, 197n21
Cruz diablo (Blaustein), 80
Csicsery-Ronay Jr., Istvan, 203n10
Cuando despierte (Burguet), 107
Cuba: Cuban cinema, 29–30; Cuban music, 20; Cuban Revolution, 19, 84; economic crisis (*see* Special Period *below*); emigration, 62–63; Foreign Investment Law of 1995 (Ley de Inversión Extranjera), 28; foreign tourism in, 20, 28, 63, 84; history of, 19–21, 147–48; internet connectivity in, 195n6, 196n15; Cuban Missile Crisis, 147–48; Quinquenio Gris (Gray Period, 1971–975), 25, 83, 196n11; Special Period (Periodo Especial en Tiempos de Paz), 19–10, 27, 28, 38, 62–63, 83–84, 151, 200n16. *See also* Caribbean region
Cuba in Splinters: Eleven Stories from the New Cuba (anthology), 13, 20, 29, 84, 111, 202n5
Culebra (island in Puerto Rico), 196n8
Cyberpunk: as a literary genre, 74–83; hackers and hacking (cybernetic) in, 78, 200n11; in the Caribbean region, 27, 80–82, 106–7; in Cuba, 27, 80–82, 83, 84–85, 200n13; in the Dominican Republic, 200n13; in film, 77–83; in Latin American literature, 78–80, 200n12; in Puerto Rico, 80–82, 96–96; "Tupinipunk" (Brazilian cyberpunk movement), 79, 200n12. *See also* Heterotopia

Dafoe, Taylor, 199
Dalton, David, 112, 143
Danowski, Déborah, 149
Davis, Wade, 204n41
Decena, Carlos Ulises, 207n18
Decker, Sharae, 171, 175
De Ferrari, Guillermina, 174, 178, 179
Delaney, Samuel, 40, 41
Deleuze, Gilles, 198n13
"De lo real maravilloso americano" (Carpentier), 16–17, 18–19, 43 195n1
Dendle, Peter, 112
Deni, Diego. *See* Cabiya, Pedro
Derby, Lauren, 166, 195n7, 198n6, 207n19, 207n21
Derrida, Jacques, 206n8
Dery, Mark, 35
Desnoes, Edmundo, 203n18
Díaz, Junot: on apocalypse, 152; *The Brief Wondrous Life of Oscar Wao*, 16–17; "Monstro" (short story), 35, 205n3
Díaz, María Isabel, 62
Díaz-Canel, Miguel, 20
Díaz Grullón, Virgilio, 32
Dick, Phillip K., 206n11
Dietrich, Alexa S., 198n14

Dioses de neón (film). *See under* Encinosa Fu, Michel
Disparo en red (magazine), 28
Doctor Who (TV series), 9
Domínguez, Peter, 33
Dominican Republic: economic crisis, 165; history of, 21, 47, 165, 175; independence struggle, 19, 44, 195n5; nationalism in, 48–49, 129; racial positioning of, 129, 204n27; relations with Haiti, 129, 172 (*see also* Cabiya, Pedro: *Malas hierbas*); relations with the U.S., 21, 129; U.S. military invasions of, 204n26. *See also* Caribbean region; Balaguer, Joaquín; Guzmán, Antonio; Trujillo, Rafael Leónidas
Donoso, José, 194n8
Dopico, Ana Maria, 73, 207n15
Duaney, Jorge, 97
Duarte Cano, Carlos, 28
Duchesne Winter, Juan, 51
Duong, Paloma, 20, 24, 151
Durón, Maximiliano, 197n20
Duvalier, François, "Papa Doc," 136, 138, 204n30, 205n31
Duvalier, Jean-Claude "Baby Doc," 204n30, 205n31
Dvinge, Anne, 82, 201n25
Dyson, George, 201n28

Echevarría Peré, Ahmel, 28, 196n16
Eckstein, Susan, Eva 84
"El baile del buey cansao" (song and album by Los Van Van), 37, 38, 39, 197n2
"El buey cansao" (song and video by López-Nussa), 37–40, 39, 42, 70
El Establo (Cuban writing group), 83
El Funky (musician), 72
El hueco negro (Cuban writers' workshop), 27
Elias, Amy J., 24
El Informe Cabrera (Liboy Erba), 42, 50–61; contamination in, 56–57; cover image 198n11; embryology in, 54–61; environmental pollution in, 57–58; geneology in, 53; science fictional aspects of, 52; spiritism (espiritismo) in, 54
Elkins, Gavin, 201n21
"El padre suizo" (poem by Martí), 59–60

El viaje extraordinario de Celeste García (film). *See under* Infante, Arturo
Embry, Karen, 109
Encinosa Fu, Michel, 27, 28, 29, 82–95, 200n17; *Niños de neón*, 82–95, 98, 106; *Dioses de neón*, 28, 86
Enríquez Piñeiro, Anabel, 28, 205n3
Entremundos (Ordas), 205n3
Environmental disaster, 151–52. *See also* Hurricane Irma; Hurricane María
Escape from New York (film), 77
Escuelas al campo (Cuba), 65
Espiral (Cuban writers' workshop), 28
Espíritu Santo, Diana, 55
Estrada, Roberto, 196n13
Estrella bocarriba (Aguiar), 200n14
Exquisito cadáver (Acevedo). *See under* Acevedo, Rafael

Fabian, Johannes, 194n9
Faris, Wendy, 194n8
Fawcett, Fausto, 79
Fehimović, Dunja, 115, 117, 120
Feria del Libro de Santo Domingo, 34
Fernández de Oviedo, Gonzalo, 102
Fernández Retamar, Roberto, 208n25
Figueroa-Vásquez, Yomaira, 35, 183, 188
Flores Iriarte, Raúl, 28, 29
Flores Taylor, Erick, 28
Formell, Juan, 38
Fornet, Ambrosio, 196n11
Foucault, Michel, 81–82, 99, 104
Franco, Omar, 66
Frank, Eduardo, 196n13
Freedman, Carl, 7, 49, 109, 153, 198n12
Frelik, Pawel, 74, 77
Fresa y chocolate (film), 123, 203n20
Fuentes, Carlos, 194n8
Fulci, Lucio, 202n2
Fumero, Ricardo, 196n13

Gagá. *See* Vodou
Gala, Leonardo, 28
Game of Thrones (TV series), 185–86
Gamerro, Carlos, 80
García, Hernán, 79
García Canclini, Néstor, 205n6

Index · 235

García Márquez, Gabriel, 194n8
García Padilla, Alejandro, 22, 141
García-Peña, Lorgia, 21, 129, 176, 207n21
Gauthier, Jeanine, 108
Generación Año Cero, 28–29, 196n16
Generation Zero: An Anthology of New Cuban Fiction, 29
Gente de Zona (Cuban music group), 72
Gibson, William, 74–75, 76, 77
Gikandi, Simon, 129
Ginsburg, Samuel, 3, 11, 44–45, 164, 167–68, 172, 197n17, 208n5
Ginway, M. Elizabeth, 79, 109, 195n4, 200n12
Glassie, Allison, 175, 176
Gledhill, Christine, 52
Glissant, Édouard: on history: 43; on myth: 137–38, 175–76; on the significance of the Middle Passage (in *Poetics of Relation*), 150–51, 171, 198n13
Goddard, Richard E., 202n8
Go Goa Gone (film) 202n2, 203n13
Goldman, Dara, 123
"Golpe de agua" (short story by Livmar). *See under* Livmar, Pabsi
Gomel, Elana, 85
González Fernández, Maielis, 1–2, 28, 81, 84–85, 107, 208n2
González Neira, Fabricio, 27, 83
Goth, Marcus E., 33
Grant, Ulysses S., 204n26
Gray, Margaret, 207n18
Greenberg, Scott, 201n21
Guatari, Félix, 198n13
Guevara, Ernesto "Che," 120, 203n16
Guridi, Francisco Javier, 32
Gutiérrez Alea, Tomás, 122, 123, 203n19
Guzmán, Antonio, 165

Habana—Arte nuevo de hacer ruinas (documentary film), 207n15
Habana Blues (film), 63, 123, 203n21
"Habana Cyberpunk" (photographic series). *See under* Mota, Erick
Habana Underguater (Mota). *See under* Mota, Erick
Hackers and hacking (cybernetic). *See under* Cyberpunk

Haiti. *See* Caribbean region; Dominican Republic; Vodou; Zombie: in Haitian folklore
Hale, Brian, 76
Halperin, Victor, 112
Haraway, Donna, 180
Hartman, Saidiya, 110
"Havana Cyberpunk 2059" (NFT image by Achon). *See under* Achon, Frank
Heise, Ursula, 41, 149
Hellekson, Karen, 164
Henríquez, Bruno 27, 196n12
Heras León, Eduardo, 33
Herbert, Frank, 46
Hernández Pacín, 27, 28, 83
"Hérodiade" (poem by Mallarmé), 99
heterotopia, 81–82, 87, 99, 104
Heuser, Sabine 76, 77–78
Hicks, Heather, 149
Historia general de las Indias (Fernández de Oviedo), 102
Historias tremendas. *See under* Cabiya, Pedro
Hopkinson, Nalo, 35, 194n12
Horn, Maja, 169
Humphrey, Paul, 176, 185, 208n5
Hurricane Irma, 151, 187
Hurricane Maria, 141, 142, 151, 152, 187
Hurston, Zora Neale, 112
Hurtado, Oscar, 25, 26

Indiana, Rita 33; *La mucama de Omincunlé,* 155, 170–81, 187; "Como un dragón" (song and music video), 183–87, 185
Infante, Arturo, 12, 29, 70; *El viaje extraordinario de Celeste García,* 42, 62–70, 198n16
Instituto Cubano de Arte e Industria Cinematográfica (ICAIC), 29, 30
Internet 199n7. *See also* Cuba: internet connectivity in
Irizarry, Guillermo, 98
I Walked with a Zombie (film), 112
iZombie (film), 202n9

Jameson, Fredric, 75, 85, 178, 194n10
Jaque Mate (film), 163
Jáuregui, Carlos, 143
Juan de los muertos (film by Brugués), 13, *121,* 114–28, 146, 203n12, 203n22; contagion

Juan de los muertos—continued
in, 203n14; relation to earlier Cuban cinema, 114–15, 122–24, 203n11; relation to international zombie films, 114–16, 117; representation of Cuban society and governance, 63, 111, 117–22, 124
Juan of the dead (film by Brugués). See *Juan de los muertos*
Juventud Técnica (magazine), 26

Kalogridis, Laeta, 77
Kardec, Allan, 55
Kaup, Monica, 149, 152, 155, 180
Kawin, Bruce, 114
Kazansky, Gennadi, 26
Kermode, Frank, 148, 175, 205n1, 208n24
Ketterer, David, 77
Kincaid, Jamaica, 193n1
King, Edward, 79, 80
Korad (magazine), 28
Kubrick, Stanley, 38
Kurlat-Ares, Silvia, 11, 195n4

La fiesta vigilada (Ponte), 207n15
Lage, Jorge Enrique, 28, 29
La isla que se repite (Benítez Rojo). See Benítez Rojo, Antonio
Lala, Eduardo, 51
Lamrani, Salim, 63, 198n17
La mucama de Omincunlé. See under Indiana, Rita
La multitud (José Acosta), 205n3
La primera calle de la soledad (Porcayo), 79–80
Las escritoras (podcast), 208n2
Las islas (Gamerro), 80
Latham, Rob, 199n6
Lauro, Sara Juliet, 108, 109, 112, 138, 139, 201n1, 202n6
Lechuga, Carlos, 69
Le Guin, Ursula, 194n7
Lem, Stanislaw, 26
Lenzi, Umberto, 202n2
Levinas, Emmanuel, 101, 201n24
Levy, Steven, 200n11
Ley de Cine (Puerto Rican law, 2010), 34

Lezama Lima, José, 99
Liboy Erba, José ("Pepe"), 31, 95, 198n9, 201n20. See also *El Informe Cabrera*
Liceaga, Yara, 50, 60–61
Lim, Bliss Cua, 7, 109
Lima, Chely, 25, 27
literary genre, 4–6, 49, 52, 78
Livmar, Pabsi, 111; "Golpe de agua" (short story), 111, 140–45, 146, 205n3
Lizárraga, Féliz, 196n13
Llano, Eduardo del, 29, 205n3
Llorén, Washington, 30
Lloréns, Hilda, 22, 141, 196n9, 198n10
López Ayala, Gretchen, 32
López Dzur, Carlos, 60
López Nieves, Luis, 30
López-Nussa, Harold. See "El buey cansao"
López-Pellisa, Teresa, 11, 195n4
Lord, Karen, 195n12
Los Van Van (music group). See "El baile del buey cansao"
Lovecraft, H. P., 46, 145
Löwy, Michael, 128

Maduro, Nicolás, 63
Magical realism and fantastic literature, 7–8, 18, 194n8
Magic Island, The (Seabrook), 112
Maillo-Pozo, Sharina, 208n5
Malas hierbas. See under Cabiya, Pedro
Maldonado, Adál. See ADÁL
Mallarmé, Stéphane, 99
Mandinga (ethnic group and noun), 186
Man in the High Castle, The (Dick), 206n11
Martí, José, 59–60
Martin, George R. R., 185
Martínez, Rebeca, 38, 39–40, 42, 70
Masud-Piloto, Félix, 198n17
Más vampiros en la Habana (film), 203n11
Mateo, Oliverio ("Papá Liborio"), 47, 198n6
Matrix (film trilogy), 77, 85
McFarlane, Anna, 77
Memorias del subdesarrollo (film), 122, 203n18
Menéndez, Ronaldo, 85
Mentes Extremófilas (writer collective), 33, 193n3

Mesa, Alberto, 27
Métal Hurlant (French graphic novel), 199
Métraux, Alfred, 108
Miéville, China, 7–8, 41–42, 197n3
Mitchell, Tamara, 201n22
Molina, Jorge, 68, 198n19
Mond, F. (Félix Mondéjar), 25–26
"Monstro" (short story by Díaz). *See under* Díaz, Junot
Moore, Robin, 162
Morales, Ed, 201n21
Morales Cabrera, Pablo, 57–60
Morgan, Richard, 77
Morton, Timothy, 154
Mota, Erick, 13, 28, 34, 36, 78–79, 205n3; "Habana Cyberpunk" (photographic series), 74, 75, 199n5; *Habana Underguater* 14, 106, 107, 154–60, 206n3, 206n12, 207n16; "That Zombie Belongs to Fidel!" (short story), 111, 125–28, 146, 202n5
Movimiento San Isidro, 199n3
Moya Pons, Frank, 165, 175
"Muerte del tiempo" (poem by Lezama Lima), 99
MULA (electronic dance music trio), 33
"Mulâtresse" (short story by Arroyo Pizarro). *See under* Arroyo Pizarro, Yolanda
"Mundos Alternos: Art and Science Fiction in the Americas" (exhibit), 197n20
Muñoz, José Esteban, 8–9, 19
Munro, Martin, 149, 150, 180, 205n2
Murphy, Graham, 77, 199n6
"My Way" (song by Sid Vicious), 124

Nada + (film), 63, 123, 203n21
Nada que declarar (Enríquez Piñeiro), 205n3
Naimou, Angela, 190
Narrative, 40–41
Nazare, Joe, 78, 88
Nevins, Shaw, 195n12
NFTs (nonfungible tokens), 73, 199n2
Night of the Living Dead (film), 112–14
Niños de neón. *See under* Encinosa Fu, Michel
Nixon, Rob, 151, 206n7
Noroña, Juan Pablo, 27

Nostalgia, 38–39, 40
Novelistic form, 41
Noya, Elsa, 96
"Nuevarrativa cubana" (journal issue). *See Sampsonia Way* (journal)

Obama, Barack, 63
Obejas, Achy, 208n27
Oloff, Kerstin, 111, 139, 146–47, 171, 175
Omega 3 (film), 205n3
Ordas, Nuria, 205n3
Orion Project, 201n28
Orishas (Cuban music group), 72
Ortega, Gregorio, 25
Ortiz, Fernando, 203n23, 204n24
Osorbo, Maykel, 72
Otero Alcántar, Luis Manuel, 199n3

Padilla Cárdenas, Gilberto, 29
Padrón, Juan, 29, 203n11
Pagán Vélez, Alexandra, 32
Page, Joanna, 195n4
Papá Liborio. *See* Mateo, Oliverio
Para Bailar (Cuban TV show), 38
Pardo Lazo, Orlando, 20, 28, 84
"Patria y vida" (song), 72–73
Patterson, Orlando, 110
Paz, Senel, 203n20
Pérez, Julián, 196n13
Pérez, Matías, 67
Pérez Ortiz, Melanie, 98, 104, 137, 141, 193n3, 201n20
Periodo Especial en Tiempos de Paz. *See* Cuba: Special Period
Personal Belongings (film by Brugués), 63, 123, 203n21
Peter Pan (Barrie), 94
Picart, Georgina (Gina), 196n13
Pinochet, Augusto, 206n11
Pitaluga, Álvarez, 195n3
Poetics of Relation. *See under* Glissant, Édouard
Ponte, Antonio José, 200n18, 207n15
Porbén, Pedro Pablo, 11
Porcayo, Gerardo Horacio, 79–79
Portales Machado, Yasmín, 28
Portela, Ena Lucía, 85

Posmentier, Sonya, 150, 206n7
Postapocalypse. *See* Apocalypse and apocalyptic thought; Apocalyptic and postapocalyptic narrative in literature and film
Postmodernism, 75
Potter, Sara, 120, 203n14
Premio David, 83, 196n12
Premio Juventud Técnica, 196n12
Premio Luis Rogelio Nogueras, 196n12
Price, Rachel, 29, 157, 159, 162, 163, 207n16
Pride and Prejudice and Zombies (film), 202n1
Prietopunk: Antología de afrofuturismo caribeño (ed. Hernández Medina), 15, 34–36
Prietopunk 2.0 (exhibit), 34–35
Pruné, Miguel, 107
Puerto Rico: economic and debt crisis, 22–23, 96–97, 141, 151, 196n9, 201n21; emigration, 23, 97; environmental pollution, 56–57; family planning and female sterilization in, 55–56; history of, 21–23, 96–97; literary history of, 96; political context, 21–23; Puerto Rico Oversight, Management, and Economic Stability Act (PROMESA), 22; relations with the U.S. mainland, 21–23; and Section 936 of the U.S. tax code, 22, 96–97, 201n21; statehood issue, 21. *See also* Caribbean region; Cyberpunk: in Puerto Rico; Science Fiction in the Hispanic Caribbean: in Puerto Rico
Puerto Rico Oversight, Management, and Economic Stability Act (PROMESA), 22

Qubit (magazine), 28
Queerness, 8
Quijano, Aníbal, 205n6
Quinquenio Gris. *See under* Cuba
Quintero Herencia, Juan Carlos, 21–22, 50
Quintero Herencia, Noelia, 33, 186
Quiroga, José, 20, 84, 159

Ramé, Elena Palacios, 29, 197n17
Ramírez, Dixa, 21, 48, 166
Ramírez Mella, Edgar, 60
Rayuela (Cortázar), 130, 204n29
Regla de Ocha. *See* Santería
Renda, Mary, 202n7
Reuhel, Alejandra, 32

Revista Digital miNatura (magazine), 28
Revista i+Real (journal), 27
Rhys, Jean, 201n1
Ricoeur, Paul, 40–41
Rieder, John, 56, 203n10
Rivera, Alex, 164
Rivera, Ángel, 11, 30, 96, 97, 148, 207n18
Rivera Montes, Zorimar, 22–23
Rodríguez, Illeana Margarita, 65, 198n18
Rodríguez, Néstor, 21, 48, 166, 204n28, 207n21
Rojas, Agustín de, 25, 28
Rojo, Juan José "Pepe," 79–80
Román, Néstor, 11, 196n10
Romero, George, 112
Rosa, Luis Othoniel, 205n3
Rosado, José Ángel, 198n9
Roscoe, Theodore, 202n8
Ruido gris (Rojo), 80

Salazar Maciá, Malena, 28
Sampsonia Way (journal), 28–29
Sánchez, Luis Rafael, 97
San Juan de la Maguana, Dominican Republic, 47
Santana Castro, Moisés, 33
Santería (religious practice), as motif in fictional works, 161, 162–63, 170, 175, 176–77
Santos, Francis, 33
Santos Febres, Maya, 198n9
Satamar, Sofia, 190
Schmeink, Lars, 77, 199n6
Science fiction (genre): Afrofuturism, 35; and perceptions of cultural reality, 41–42; definitions of 4–7; history of in Latin America, 17–18; machines in, 9; and magical realism, 6–8; relation to colonialism and postcolonialism, 56; slipstream (science fiction mode), 201n23; uchronia (science fiction subgenre), 9–10, 156 (*see also* Mota, Erick: *Habana Underguater*). *See also* Science fiction in the Hispanic Caribbean
Science fiction in the Hispanic Caribbean: Afrofuturism in, 36, 190, 197n22; history of, 18, 25–34; in Cuba, 25–30, 83; in Cuban film, 29–30; in Puerto Rico, 30–32, 96; in Puerto Rican film, 32; in the Dominican Republic, 32–34; in Dominican Republic

film, 33–34; scholarship on, 11; shift toward transnational focus of, 34
Scott, Darieck, 183
Scott, David, 24, 151
Seabrook, William, 112
Se alquila un planeta (Yoss), 205n3
Selva Brasil (Causo), 206n11
Serret, Alberto, 25
Sharpe, Christina, 110, 190, 205n6
Shaun of the Dead (film), 114–16, 124, 203n13
Shiner, Lewis, 74
Shiralad (TV show), 27
Shirley, John, 74
Sierra Madero, Abel, 203n17
Silicone XXI (Sirkis), 200n12
Sirkis, Alfredo, 79, 200n12
Siskind, Mariano, 149
Sklodowska, Elzbieta, 84
slavery, 109–10, 149, 162, 206n6
slipstream. *See under* Science fiction (genre)
Snyder, Katherine, 171–72
Sobre los nerds y otras criaturas mitológicas (González Fernández), 1–2, 107
Soltero Sánchez, Evangelina, 25, 26, 27, 196n10, 196n13
Soviet Union, 19, 20, 26, 81, 83, 156, 200n16
Special Period (Período Especial en Tiempos de Paz). *See under* Cuba
Spielberg, Steven, 145
Spiritism (espiritismo). *See under* *El Informe Cabrera*
Sputnik (magazine), 26
Staff, Rialta, 197n19
Stanchich, Maritza, 22, 141, 196n9, 198n10
Sterling, Bruce, 76, 78, 106
Stevenson, Neil, 75
Stock, Ann Marie, 122, 195n3, 197n18, 203n11, 203n22
Strugatsky brothers (Arkady and Boris), 26
Suite Habana (documentary film), 63
Suvin, Darko, 45, 193n6
Synco (Bardit), 206n11

Taíno indigenous culture, 46–47, 117
Taller Espacio Abierto, 28, 83, 200n15
Taller Julio Verne, 26
Taller Oscar Hurtado, 26, 196n13

Tapia y Rivera, Alejandro, 30
Téjnika—Molodëzhi (magazine), 26
Tell My Horse (Hurston), 112
Tempest, The (Shakespeare), 170–71
Teoremas Turbios (Livmar). *See* Livmar, Pabsi: "Golpe de agua"
"That Zombie Belongs to Fidel!" (short story). *See under* Mota, Erick
Through the Looking Glass (Carroll), 98
Time Machine, The (Wells), 9
Timshel (Yoss), 83
Tira tu Pasillo (Cuban dance competition TV show), 37
Toledano Redondo, Juan Carlos, 11, 85, 86–87, 92, 107, 160, 197n21
Tolentino, Adriana, 34
Tolkien, J. R. R., 145, 198n8
Tomé, Patricia, 34
Torre Rodríguez, Javier de la, 156
Torres, John, 32
Totality and Infinity (Levinas), 101
Tourism and tourists, 193n2. *See also under* Cuba
Tourneur, Jacques, 112
Transculturation, 126, 204n24
Trujillo, Rafael Leónidas, 21, 166–69, 195n7, 207n19, 207n20, 207n21, 208n23; and "Parsley Massacre" (1967), 167
Trump, Donald, 63
Tsang, Martin, 176, 177
"Tupinipunk." *See under* Cyberpunk
Turits, Richard Lee, 208n22
2001: A Space Odyssey (film), 38

Uchronia (science fiction subgenre). *See under* Science fiction (genre)
Últimos días en la Habana (film), 63
Une Tempéte (Césaire), 208n25
United States: and Cuba, 19, 20, 63, 195n6; and the Dominican Republic, 21, 129; and Puerto Rico, 21–22, 55, 96–97
Utopia, 9, 81–82, 153, 156, 178, 194n10, 194n11

Valaida (Allen), 201n25
Valdés, Zoé, 85
Valdez, Diógenes, 32
¡Vampiros en la Habana! (film), 203n11

Vázquez, Alexandra, 20
Vega Serova, Ana Lydia, 85
Vera-Rojas, María, 30
Vicconius Zariah, Morgan, 33
Vicente, Ileana, 196n13
Vicious, Sid, 124
Vieques (island in Puerto Rico), 57, 196n8
Vilar Madruga, Elaine, 28, 43, 107, 198n8
Villares, Lía, 28
Vint, Sherryl, 11, 41–42, 76, 197n3
Viva Cuba (film), 123, 203n21
Vlak, Odilius, 32–33, 42, 43, 44, 198n8
Vodou, 112, 176
Vogel, Shane, 175

Warm Bodies (film), 202n9
Wells, H. G., 9
Wenders, Wym, 207n15
West, Benjamin, 199n9
White Zombie (film), 112
Whitfield, Esther, 160, 200n18
Wide Sargasso Sea (film), 201n1
Williams, Rosalind, 151
Womak, Ytasha, 35–36
Wright, Edgar, 115

Yiddish Policeman's Union, The (Chabon), 206n11
Yoss (José Miguel Sánchez Gómez), 11, 25, 27, 28, 77, 83, 119, 196n10, 200n14, 205n3
Yotuel (musician), 72

Zambrana, Rocío, 22–23
Zambrano, Benito, 123
Zamora, Lois Parkinson, 194n8
Zárate, José Luis, 79
Žižek, Slavoj, 149, 179
Zombi. *See* Zombie: in Haitian folklore
Zombi 2 (film), 202n2
Zombie, 108–46; as transnational figure, 112; narrative characteristics of, 109, 113; relation to colonialism, slavery, and exploitative labor, 109–11; in Dominican cultural production, 129; in Haitian folklore (*zombi*), 108–9, 112, 145, 110–11, 113 110; in Italian film, 202n2; redefinition of, as contagious cannibal, 113, 143–44, 203n10; relation to science fiction, 113–14; renewed global interest in, 108; "zom-com" film subgenre, 115, 203n13. *See also* Cabiya, Pedro: *Malas hierbas*; *Juan de los muertos* (film by Brugués); Mota, Erick: "That Zombie Belongs to Fidel"; Livmar, Pabsi: "Golpe de Agua"
Zombieland (film), 202n9

Emily A. Maguire is associate professor in the Department of Spanish and Portuguese at Northwestern University. She is the author of *Racial Experiments in Cuban Literature and Ethnography* and the coeditor, with Antonio Córdoba, of *Posthumanism in Latin(x) American Science Fiction*.

Reframing Media, Technology, and Culture in Latin/o America

Edited by Héctor Fernández L'Hoeste and Juan Carlos Rodríguez

Reframing Media, Technology, and Culture in Latin/o America explores how Latin American and Latino audiovisual (film, television, digital), musical (radio, recordings, live performances, dancing), and graphic (comics, photography, advertising) cultural practices reframe and reconfigure social, economic, and political discourses at a local, national, and global level. In addition, it looks at how information networks reshape public and private policies, and the enactment of new identities in civil society. The series also covers how different technologies have allowed and continue to allow for the construction of new ethnic spaces. It not only contemplates the interaction between new and old technologies but also how the development of brand-new technologies redefines cultural production.

Telling Migrant Stories: Latin American Diaspora in Documentary Film, edited by Esteban E. Loustaunau and Lauren E. Shaw (2018; paperback edition, 2021)

Mestizo Modernity: Race, Technology, and the Body in Postrevolutionary Mexico, by David S. Dalton (2018; first paperback edition, 2021)

The Insubordination of Photography: Documentary Practices under Chile's Dictatorship, by Ángeles Donoso Macaya (2020; first paperback edition, 2023)

Digital Humanities in Latin America, edited by Héctor Fernández L'Hoeste and Juan Carlos Rodríguez (2020; first paperback edition, 2023)

Pablo Escobar and Colombian Narcoculture, by Aldona Bialowas Pobutsky (2020)

The New Brazilian Mediascape: Television Production in the Digital Streaming Age, by Eli Lee Carter (2020; first paperback edition, 2024)

Univision, Telemundo, and the Rise of Spanish-Language Television in the United States, by Craig Allen (2020; first paperback edition, 2023)

Cuba's Digital Revolution: Citizen Innovation and State Policy, edited by Ted A. Henken and Sara Garcia Santamaria (2021; first paperback edition, 2022)

Afro-Latinx Digital Connections, edited by Eduard Arriaga and Andrés Villar (2021)

The Lost Cinema of Mexico: From Lucha Libre to Cine Familiar and Other Churros, edited by Olivia Cosentino and Brian Price (2022)

Neo-Authoritarian Masculinity in Brazilian Crime Film, by Jeremy Lehnen (2022)

The Rise of Central American Film in the Twenty-First Century, edited by Mauricio Espinoza and Jared List (2023)

Internet, Humor, and Nation in Latin America, edited by Héctor Fernández L'Hoeste and Juan Poblete (2024)

Tropical Time Machines: Science Fiction in the Contemporary Hispanic Caribbean, by Emily A. Maguire (2024)

Printed in the United States
by Baker & Taylor Publisher Services